FINANCIAL INNOVATION, EFFICIENCY, AND DISEQUILIBRIUM

FINANCIAL INNOVATION EFFICIENCY AND DISEQUILIBRIUM

Problems of Monetary Management
in the
United Kingdom
1971–1981

PETER D. SPENCER

CLARENDON PRESS · OXFORD
1986

Oxford University Press, Walton Street, Oxford OX2 6DP
Oxford New York Toronto
Delhi Bombay Calcutta Madras Karachi
Kuala Lumpur Singapore Hong Kong Tokyo
Nairobi Dar es Salaam Cape Town
Melbourne Auckland
and associated companies in
Beirut Berlin Ibadan Mexico City Nicosia

Oxford is a trade mark of Oxford University Press

Published in the United States
by Oxford University Press, New York

© Peter D. Spencer 1986

British Library Cataloguing in Publication Data

Spencer, Peter D.
Financial innovation, efficiency and
disequilibrium: problems of monetary management
in the United Kingdom 1971–1981.
1. Money supply—Great Britain—history—
20th century
I. Title
332.4'941   HG939.5
ISBN 0–19–828512–4

Library of Congress Cataloging in Publication Data

Spencer, Peter D.
Financial innovation, efficiency, and disequilibrium.
Bibliography: p.
Includes index.
1. Monetary policy—Great Britain.   2. Monetary
policy—Great Britain—Econometric models.   3. Great
Britain—Economic policy—1945–   .   4. Great Britain—
Economic policy—1945–   —Econometric models.
5. Banks and banking—Great Britain—Econometric models.
I. Title.
HG939.5.S65   1986   332.4'941   85–21671
ISBN 0–19–828512–4

Set by Spire Print Services Ltd., Salisbury
Printed in Great Britain by
The Alden Press, Oxford

To Jenifer, Emily, and Thomas

PREFACE

This book was written while I was a Gwillym Gibbon Research Fellow at Nuffield College, Oxford, during the academic year 1982/3, and was based on the research I had done since joining the Treasury in 1974. My main aim in writing it was to review the problems which had confronted the monetary authorities over the previous decade, using the results of my work at the Treasury to help throw light on some of the main issues.

The first part of the book deals with the determination of the money supply and interest rates in a modern economic system and is supported by the research which Colin Mowl and I did while developing a domestic financial sector for the Treasury model. Professor Marcus Miller was the academic consultant on this project. This work is set against the background of the monetary issues which confronted the authorities during the early 1970s. It reflects the move to a floating exchange rate, which led the major UK forecasting teams to develop models of the financial sector, initially as a way of determining interest and exchange rates. The second half of the book is concerned with the wider macroeconomic issues which arose in the late 1970s and is based on work which I did after the financial model became operational in 1978, when I was working on the exchange rate and the balance of payments.

Both parts start with a commentary on the main events and a review of the pertinent economic theory. The theoretical sections are designed to be selective, with the emphasis being given to the theories which were most relevant to the policy debate. I have tried to make these as accessible as possible, relegating the more technical analysis to appendices or endnotes. The commentaries are designed to bring out the main issues, as these were seen at the time. Subsequent chapters review the statistical evidence relating to these questions and attempt to resolve the ambiguities remaining from the theoretical treatment. Both parts conclude with chapters outlining the results of model simulation exercises, illustrating the general equilibrium properties of the system.

The scope and structure of this work can be assessed on a quick reading of the summaries contained at the beginning of each chapter. The final chapter offers a tentative review of developments since 1981, seen from the perspective of the earlier analysis, and draws together some of the dominant themes.

Much of the material which is presented in this book represents the result of a collective effort, and I am heavily indebted to Colin Mowl, Marcus Miller, and other collaborators for allowing me to use it here. I am also indebted to David Rampton for devising techniques for solving the various computer models which were employed. I would like to thank John Hunt, Eileen Howes, and Gary Roberts for providing such enthusiastic research assistance and Honor Stamler, Frank Cassell, Peter Middleton, Rachel Lomax, and Charles Goodhart for their encouragement and helpful advice.

This work has benefited from countless discussions with Treasury colleagues and academic associates and in particular Steven Bell, Adam Bennett, Charlie Bean, Anthony Courakis, and members of the Treasury's Academic Panel. I am also grateful to the Warden, fellows, and students of Nuffield College for providing such a stimulating and friendly working environment, and would particularly like to thank David Hendry, John Muellbauer, and Jim Poterba for their patient help and advice. I am of course responsible for the views expressed in this book, which do not necessarily represent those of the Treasury.

My thanks also go to Pat Spragg for doing an effective job on a difficult typescript, and to John Odling-Smee, Bill Martin, and Martin Weale for helpful comments on an early draft.

MARCH 1985   Peter D. Spencer

CONTENTS

PART TWO

Monetary Targets, the Exchange rate, and the role of
Expectations in an Open Economy

I

Introduction: The British Monetary Experience Since 1971

The last twenty years have witnessed fundamental changes in the British monetary system. The pace of innovation has quickened considerably and new money markets have sprung up alongside the old, coming to dominate them in both scale and economic significance. British financial institutions have also become much more exposed to international competition and developments in world financial markets.

These developments have gone hand in hand with a liberalization of the mechanism of monetary control. This has changed almost beyond recognition, from one based upon rationing of private-sector credit to one in which the demand for money is influenced entirely through interest rates and other market mechanisms. At the same time, doubts about the efficacy of counter-cyclical demand-management policies and worries about the costs of inflation have mounted and as a consequence monetary targets have become the central feature of macroeconomic policy. Fiscal policy has been largely subordinated to monetary policy as part of this process, dictated in the main by monetary constraints.

The purpose of this book is to review these developments and analyse some of the problems which they have posed for the monetary authorities. In order to assist in this, I will draw upon the available empirical evidence and in particular the econometric model developed by the Treasury for financial forecasting and policy analysis. The first half of the book examines the way in which the money supply is determined in a contemporary economy and the problems which bank competition and liability management pose for the monetary authorities. The second part goes on to look at open economy aspects of monetary control and some of the wider issues of macroeconomic policy. This chapter makes a start by taking a preliminary look at some of the main changes which have been taking place in recent years.

1 Financial innovation and the problem of structural change

During the early 1960s the British banking system was still dominated by the clearing banks with their branch network and cartelized interest-rate structure. But they were already coming under competitive pressure from secondary banking institutions which had introduced much better facilities for large (or wholesale) time deposits than were on offer from the clearers. The Competition and Credit Control reforms of 1971 opened the way to increased competition and innovation in the banking sector, particularly in the wholesale markets. By the mid-1970s competition was beginning to be felt in the markets for large demand-deposits and this developed rapidly following the abolition of the 'corset' in 1980 and the reforms of 1981. The range of chequing and transmission facilities offered by the banks also improved rapidly over this period as computer technology was applied.

At the same time the clearing banks' retail time-deposit business came under pressure from the building societies, who were offering convenient facilities through their extensive branch networks at very competitive interest rates. These institutions were handicapped by the problem they faced in providing chequing and other transmission facilities (which had to be provided through a clearing bank). They were also held back by the specialized nature of their business, which prevented them from offering a comprehensive financial service to their customers, and also the interest-rate cartel which they operated until mid-1983. Nevertheless, by the end of the 1970s the building societies were becoming effective competitors in the market for wholesale time deposits and had a larger share of the total sterling deposit market than the clearers. The developments envisaged in the Green Paper 'Building Societies: A New Framework' (Cmnd. 9316) will allow building societies to develop further the range of facilities they offer their customers, increasing the scope for competition with the banks.

These developments raise several fundamental issues and have presented the policy-maker with some formidable problems. They are the subject of the first half of this book (Chapters II–VI) and are discussed further in the concluding chapter.

The most fundamental of these questions relates to the appropriate definition of the money supply and the distinction between different types of financial intermediary, which we look at in the next chapter. There has been a long-standing debate between those who see banks as operators of the monetary transmission mechanism and in this sense quite different from other deposit taking institutions, and those who argue that this distinction is of little practical relevance. On the one hand it is argued that non-bank financial intermediaries can only lend funds which are deposited with them, so banks cannot loose deposits to such institutions once these are created. In this sense banks are immune from competition. The latter suggest that despite this apparent monopoly position, non-bank intermediaries provide close substitutes for bank deposits and effectively reduce the real demand for these by increasing the velocity of circulation. They are therefore in a very real sense in competition with the banks.

The logic of the second of these approaches was reflected in the extension of the monetary control arrangements during the 1960s and early 1970s to cover the secondary banks, and the inclusion of the liabilities of these institutions in the operational definition of the money supply—M3. It similarly underlies the attention being given to aggregates (such as M2 and PSL2) which include the liabilities of the building societies as these have become more directly competitive with the banks. However, this kind of structural change tends to occur gradually rather than abruptly and might in principle be handled by allowing appropriately for changes in velocity. Indeed, this can ultimately be used to justify a very narrow definition of the money supply (such as notes and coin, or perhaps the monetary base), an argument which is analysed in the concluding chapter.

2 The evolution of the monetary control mechanism

Although the underlying rate of technological change and innovation in the financial sector may be a gradual one, the authorities have naturally been cautious in adapting their monetary control arrangements to reflect these developments. Changes in the regulatory environment have therefore tended to occur in a discrete rather than in a continuous manner, making it difficult to interpret the behaviour of the aggregates in the subsequent period. In the case of the UK, the monetary control system underwent a radical change in 1971 and again in 1981. These reforms, discussed in Chapters III and XI respectively, leave the banking system entirely free of regulatory constraints designed to facilitate the operation of monetary policy. Banks are now subject only to prudential requirements. In view of the problems experienced in trying to manage a reserve-asset based system in the intervening years, the authorities had come to the conclusion that such controls were more trouble than they were worth.

This attitude represents a complete volte-face on that of the late 1960s, based as this was on direct controls over bank credit and interest rates. In order to put these developments into perspective it is interesting to take a brief look at the *Report* of the *Radcliffe Committee on the Working of the Monetary System*, (Cmnd. 827) published in 1959.

This was written at a time in which the financial system was in an exceptionally liquid situation following the war and the depression. The banks were considerably under-lent, making it difficult to contemplate a relaxation of controls over their portfolios. The *Report* expressed a great deal of scepticism about the effect of interest rates on economic activity—fiscal policy appeared to be much more useful in this respect—and these were viewed largely as a device for maintaining the exchange-rate parity. The availability of finance and the liquidity of the system was seen as a more obvious influence on spending decisions. In view of the ease of substitution between bank accounts and other instruments, Radcliffe played down the role of the money supply and suggested that the authorities should attempt to control the general liquidity of the system.

This control was to be exerted through the structure of interest rates, acting upon the demand for liquid assets and credit as well as their supply. It was accepted that it would be difficult to implement such market mechanisms during a crisis and that in such an event direct controls would be necessary. However, Radcliffe stressed the dangers of disintermediation which would follow from controls which were specific to bank portfolios and suggested that they should be applied more widely and, moreover, used only as a temporary expedient.

In the event, the balance of payments crises of the 1960s led the authorities into a progressive tightening of credit controls, with very little reliance upon market mechanisms. By the end of the decade these were biting hard across a wide range of lending institutions, raising serious questions about their allocative efficiency. At the same time evidence was emerging from econometric studies of the demand for money indicating that this could be explained simply in terms of the behaviour of nominal incomes and interest rates.

The direction of monetary policies towards the balance of payments following the IMF loan of 1969 served to reinforce interest in this subject. The IMF approach highlighted the money-supply identity (set out in Section II.4) which broke changes in the supply of money down into Domestic Credit Expansion (DCE) and external effects stemming from imbalances in international payments. With a fixed exchange rate and a reasonable degree of stability in the demand for money, it followed that changes in DCE would be matched in the external balance. The successful application of these policies, together with the growing body of empirical support for the monetary theory of the balance of payments therefore offered further evidence of a stable demand-for-money function. Moreover, the relationship between the M3 definition of the money supply, the fiscal deficit, bank lending, and the foreign-exchange reserves, helped to reassure those who were sceptical of the econometric evidence. It also lead to an instinctive preference for M3 over the narrow definition, M1.

The recession in activity and the turn-round in the balance of payments which followed the application of these policies left policy-makers in a situation in which they could afford to relax their quantitative controls and try a more market-oriented approach. However, in view of the large quantities of liquid assets still held by the banking system, it is not surprising that they decided to impose a minimum reserve-asset ratio upon the banks. The idea was (as shown in Section III.3) that this would act as a constraint on the banks and secure a firm base for open-market operations. Changes in the supply of reserves would, it was thought, induce banks to sell secondary reserve assets such as gilts, causing interest rates and the non-bank demand for money and credit to respond accordingly. In the event, however, the banks' new-found ability to bid reserve assets away from non-banks (or from other banks) by offering more attractive wholesale deposit facilities allowed them to side-step this constraint (at least at the individual level). Together with the unanticipated stickiness of banks' administered interest-rate structures, this made the control mechanism unstable. The authorities were eventually forced to abandon this and reintroduce a quantitative form of control in December 1973.

This experience was highly instructive and reveals a great deal about the behaviour of a system in which banks rely upon liability management. It also shows how difficult it is to manage a system which is still evolving and is in some respects highly competitive, yet in others still quite uncompetitive. In this situation reserve requirements and policies which are designed to induce a shortage of reserve assets may have quite untoward effects, forcing the authorities to rely upon more direct ways of influencing interest rates, through their rediscount rates perhaps, backed up by operations in the short-term money markets. Once the initial steps towards a more market-oriented control mechanism had been taken in 1971 there was little point in retaining the remaining controls on the banks.

3 Developments in macroeconomic theory and policy

The initial move towards a more liberal regulatory regime in 1971, and the perverse response of the system to the control mechanism, were followed by an explosive growth in the monetary aggregates. This was to some extent due to the expansionary fiscal policy adopted in the budget of 1972. However, M3 grew much faster than could be explained by movements in nominal incomes and interest rates, causing the simple econometric models of the demand for money to break down. At the time this breakdown was thought to be due largely to the structural changes which were taking place in the money and credit markets, and to this extent of little macroeconomic significance. Unfortunately such effects could not be readily quantified and these developments left policy-makers in a rather uncertain situation. In retrospect, it is quite apparent that these structural changes accounted for only a fraction of the growth in the money supply over this period (my own estimates are set out in Section IV.8). Indeed, it now appears that the growth in bank credit and hence the supply of money outstripped the growth in the demand for money, pushing the financial system into some sort of disequilibrium. This experience gave birth to the 'disequilibrium money' view (which is examined in Sections II.5 and 6).

Whether or not one takes this latter analysis at face value, it is difficult to escape the fact that the surge in monetary growth during 1972 and 1973 was associated with an unprecented upsurge in economic activity and followed by an inflationary explosion in 1974 and 1975. The timing of these events was exactly as predicted by basic Friedmanite monetary theory (which post-ulated a two-year lag between an increase in the money supply and the price level, with output rising temporarily during this interregnum). The ensuing inflation was somewhat greater than even monetarist commentators had predicted, due mainly to the effect of the increase in oil prices. This point was certainly not lost on the financial markets, which became extremely sensitive to movements in M3 following this experience.

Seen from a mainstream macroeconomic viewpoint, these events could be rationalized in terms of the effect of the expansionary fiscal policy. This had initially increased output as the incomes policy held, but was then spent in inflation as the restraint gave way under the strain. This experience seemed to suggest that prices and incomes policies could still be used to control inflation, providing that other macroeconomic policies were not set in too expansionary a way. So when incomes policies were reintroduced by the Labour administration in the autumn of 1975 policy-makers began to look for an indicator of the stance of macroeconomic policy which would be robust in the uncertain circumstances they found themselves in. Despite reservations about the structural changes which had affected the wider monetary aggregates, M3, with its strong fiscal and financial policy connections, had an obvious appeal. As the more obvious distortions unwound and they became more confident about their control methods, the authorities came increasingly to regard the growth rate of M3 as an effective constraint upon the overall stance of macroeconomic policy. An interesting account of these developments in official thinking, stressing the role of M3 as an indicator of the overall thrust of macroeconomic policy rather than just of monetary policy, is provided by Fford (1983a).

The Labour Government's incomes policy was a voluntary one and was prompted by the widespread fear that wage inflation was running out of control. It was initially accepted by the trade unions as a way of preventing a free-for-all occurring. However, as the damaging effects of the previous bout of wage inflation became more fully apparent—particularly the effect on employment—policy-makers became increasingly concerned about the dangers of inflation, and were naturally reluctant to abandon the incomes policy. The possibility of a return to the high levels of employment which had been seen during the 1950s and 1960s seemed increasingly less likely as this evidence accumulated.

During the 1960s and early 1970s the conventional wisdom had been that inflation tended to distort the economy due to the non-indexation of financial contracts and the tax system. The 'inflation tax' on money balances, the 'front-end loading' of nominal long-term loan arrangements, and 'fiscal drag' offered familiar examples of these effects. It was accepted that these distortions could cause unemployment, as could any failure of the authorities to adjust the exchange rate or the money supply as prices rose. Inflation could cause other social problems through its distributional effects, but generally speaking the costs of inflation were felt to be fairly well understood and worth risking in order to secure higher levels of output and employment.

The experience of the early 1970s served to show that the costs of inflation were rather more pervasive and subtle than had been thought. They were extremely difficult to catalogue comprehensively, let alone quantify. Yet it became fairly clear that high rates of inflation made it generally difficult to distinguish movements in the overall level of prices from those in relative prices, confusing the price signals upon which the efficiency of a market system depended. It was suggested for example that this effect might help explain the rise in the UK consumer saving ratio, since consumers would hestitate before buying goods which had increased in price, believing this to be a relative price increase. It was also suggested that firms would mistake increases in the general price level for increases in the relative price of their product and increase their output accordingly—the famous Lucas supply response.

Moreover, as Okun (1975) and others have pointed out, inflation imposes particularly severe costs upon imperfectly competitive markets in which customer or employee loyalties are important and, reflecting this, prices tend to be sticky. These markets are characterized by long-term contracts of either an explicit or an implicit nature, and inflation brings strong pressure to break or renegotiate these contracts and to switch to short-term arrangements. An obvious example of this phenomenon was the virtual disappearance of the UK debenture market during the 1970s, as companies switched to short-term bank finance.

At a more immediate level, the company sector had suffered badly from the rise in inflation. This was partly because wages had tended to rise faster than prices, reducing profitability and liquidity. The failure to index the tax system had also had an effect and the stock-relief scheme was introduced in November 1974 as an *ad hoc* way of alleviating these effects. Despite this, and despite the negative real rates of interest which prevailed, 1975 saw a severe cut-back in company expenditures, particularly on long-term investments and employment, causing a marked fall in the level of economic activity.

This general concern about the links between inflation and employment was reinforced by monetarist ideas which had originated in the US in the late 1960s but which had really only gained ground in the UK following the events of the 1970s. Until then the prevailing economic orthodoxy had been that macroeconomic policies could bring about higher levels of output and employment at the expense of a higher rate of inflation. (In diagramatic terms, the Phillips curve, relating unemployment and inflation, was negatively sloped.) However Friedman, Phelps, and other monetarists had argued that this relationship would only hold as long as the inflation was unanticipated. Once it became established and was taken into account by economic agents this would have the effect of shifting the Phillips curve and the rate of inflation in an upward direction.

The implication of this observation is that there exists only one unemployment rate—the 'natural' rate—which is consistent with a steady rate of inflation. If the economy is run at lower rate of unemployment this causes an ever-escalating rate of inflation. (The long run Phillips curve is a vertical line drawn through the natural rate of unemployment.) This natural rate is determined by structural labour-market factors and is usually assumed to be independent of the rate of inflation. However, if high rates of inflation damage the supply side of the economy this may result in a positively-sloped Phillips curve, helping to explain the association between high levels of inflation and unemployment—or stagflation as it became popularly known.

This model was originally based on the assumption of adaptive or backward-looking expectations, in which forecasts of inflation are based exclusively upon its own past behaviour and therefore adapt slowly in response to changes in policy. In this kind of framework expectational lags act as a kind of sheet-anchor and prices move in a smooth or continuous manner. The vertical Phillips-curve model was, however, taken much further by the 'new classical' macroeconomists Lucas, Sargent, Wallace, and others. These employed the rational-expectations framework in which agents are assumed to know the underlying structure of the economy and monitor the ultimate determinants of the price level, including the behaviour of the authorities. In this situation expectational lags no longer apply and prices begin to react as soon as changes in economic policy become known. Unless there are other frictions in the system, such as adjustment costs, prices will move immediately to their new equilibrium levels. The implications of this model are clearly very different from those of earlier monetarist models. (An enthusiastic presentation of this model is to be found in Minford and Peel (1984).)

Monetarist commentators also applied this kind of reasoning to such variables as exchange and interest rates, arguing that although the authorities might control the nominal values of these variables their real values were ultimately determined by structural factors. Real interest rates and international competitiveness were only within their grasp as long as the sheet-anchor of adaptive expectations continued to hold. Attempts to effect changes in these variables by manipulating their nominal magnitudes would ultimately fail, simply leading to an escalating rate of inflation.

These ideas proved very difficult to test empirically, due largely to the unobservable nature of the expectational variables upon which they depended. But although they remained the subject of controversy—especially those emerging from the new classical school—the inflationary potential of the economy at the time was such that they could not safely be ignored. Moreover, it became quite apparent to those using conventional econometric models of the economy that these had badly broken down. Their foundations had been disturbed by shifts in the rate of inflation and other hitherto-latent variables and needed to be rebuilt to take explicit account of these factors.

Perhaps the best example of this kind of breakdown was that of the consumption function—the centrepiece of the Keynesian model of the economy. This related real consumers' expenditure to a measure of their real disposable incomes and could not account for the rise in the saving ratio seen over these years. It was soon found, however, that this phenomenon could be explained by taking into account the effect of inflation on financial assets, redefining real disposable income as the level of expenditure which could be sustained whilst leaving the *real* value of wealth unchanged. These research efforts also indicated the importance of wealth and (in some cases) liquidity and real interest-rate effects. These findings had a dramatic effect on the properties of the mainstream macroeconomic models, radically altering their response to macroeconomic policies. In the case of a devaluation, for example, the short-run output effect of a gain in competitiveness was offset (and in the case of contemporary versions of the LBS model, more than offset) by the effect of higher prices on consumer expenditure, suggesting that as far as employment was concerned there was nothing to be gained from pursuing such a policy. These developments are reviewed in Chapter IX.

At about the same time the major forecasting teams began to develop models of the financial sector, initially as a way of determining interest and exchange rates. (These had previously been fixed exogenously, reflecting the macroeconomic policy stance.) They also determined the main monetary and liquidity measures, although at this stage such aggregates had no direct effects upon expenditure in any of the major forecasting models. The wider aggregates were in most cases built up using a counterparts analysis similar to that offered by the traditional M3 supply-side identity, since it proved difficult to re-establish simple demand relationships for such definitions. However, econometric work which ran inverse-demand relationships by regressing prices and output on alternative monetary aggregates in order to discover which had the most predictive or informational content then pointed strongly to the importance of M3. (See, for example, Mills (1982).) These results clearly reflected the timing of the events following the introduction of Competition and Credit Control.

As these monetarist ideas were gaining ground some important new developments were taking place in Keynesian macroeconomic theory, reflected in an important paper by Muellbauer and Portes (1978). This formalized the spillover effects between markets which were in disequilibrium due to price rigidities, and offered a much more general theory than the textbook Keynesian model. It showed that the Keynesian unemployment situation—in which real wages are too low and firms are constrained by a deficient demand for goods and consumers by a deficient demand for labour—was only one of four disequilibrium situations which could arise with imperfections in these two markets. Although conventional Keynesian macro-economic policies would be quite effective in this regime, they might not be in appropriate in these alternative situations. Indeed, in the case of 'classical unemployment', in which real wages are too high so that a deficient demand for labour persists alongside an excess demand for goods, such policies are counter-productive. This makes it crucially important for the policy-maker to know which of these situations prevails.

4   The evolution of a counter-inflationary macroeconomic strategy

In view of such arguments and evidence, policy-makers became increasingly concerned about the depreciation of the exchange rate, especially as this gained momentum in 1976. Although the improvement in competitiveness was of benefit to industrial companies this gain was offset by the clear threat to counter-inflation policy. So in order to restore confidence they arranged an IMF loan and published a formal target for M3. As part of this arrangement fiscal policy was tightened and limits on DCE were again agreed.

This had the desired effect on confidence in the financial markets, which rebounded strongly. The authorities initially used this as an opportunity to rebuild the reserves, effectively capping the rise in the exchange rate in order to preserve the gain in competitiveness. However, as the foreign-exchange inflows continued over the summer of 1977 these began to threaten the M3 target, forcing a difficult choice between this target and the competitiveness objective. Although their decision to uncap the exchange rate did not lead to any dramatic rise in sterling—the initial change was hardly noticeable—it was a significant step, underlining the new counter-inflationary policy commitment. Even so, the pressures on the incomes policy proved too great and this collapsed in the winter of 1978–9, leaving the monetary targets as the main expression of macroeconomic policy. A discussion of these events and of the role which monetary pressures may have played in undermining the incomes policy is to be found in Chapter VII.

The task of securing the monetary targets in the face of these inflationary pressures was taken up by the Conservative administration which succeeded the Labour Government in the spring of 1979. This administration was strongly influenced by monetarist ideas and adopted a much more radical policy, aimed at bringing inflation down steadily through a programme for reducing the growth in the money supply—the Medium Term Financial Strategy (MTFS). The announcement of the MTFS was designed to secure the maximum favourable effect upon inflationary expectations in order to minimize the short-run employment effect of reducing the prevailing rate of inflation. Assumptions about prices and output were published alongside projections of the money supply (now expressed in terms of *sterling* M3) as part of the MTFS. However, it was made clear that although prices and output remained the ultimate objectives of policy, the assumptions about these variables could at the most be indicative. By contrast, the assumed sterling M3 target range for the year ahead constituted a definite policy objective and the target ranges for later years provided a firm indication of the direction of policy. This fitted in very closely with the monetarist notion that the authorities could only attempt to meet intermediate targets for nominal variables such as the money supply or nominal incomes, leaving the ultimate output–price combination to be determined by the private sector. The experience with the sterling M3 target is the focus of the analysis reported in the second half of this book, Chapters VII–XI.

Although the successful targeting of sterling M3 became the centrepiece of counter-inflation strategy, this aggregate became seriously distorted and it proved impossible to achieve the target range while keeping interest rates within acceptable limits. The abolition of exchange controls in October 1979 rendered direct controls such as the corset futile, and this was abolished in June 1980, opening the way to large-scale reintermediation and to a further phase of innovation in financial behaviour. As was the case in the early 1970s, it proved impossible to evaluate the scale of these distortions. In addition to this, the shift in real incomes from companies to persons caused by the wage increases of 1979–80 increased bank intermediation between these sectors.

This reopened the debate about the appropriate definition of the money supply and the associated control procedures, issues which are taken up again in the concluding chapter. The authorities initially argued that their fiscal and funding instruments, together with short-term interest rates, offered the necessary degree of control over the year-to-year growth of sterling M3. The reforms of 1981 were nevertheless aimed at making these controls more effective. And as the scale of the distortions to sterling M3 became apparent this led to a more formal use of multiple indicators, announced in the 1982 budget. Narrow measures of the money supply came to be used together with the wider measures and other indicators, including the exchange rate, in assessing monetary conditions and deciding upon the appropriate range for short-term interest rates.

PART ONE

Competition, Credit Control, and the Role of Banks in the Money-supply Process

II

Portfolio Disequilibrium and the Role of Banks in the Money-supply Process

Introduction and summary

As the old saying goes, money doesn't grow on trees. Nor is it simply printed by the Bank of England. It is the result of a complex interaction of the decisions of the monetary authorities, the banks, and the general public. This chapter takes a preliminary look at the way the money supply is determined in a modern economy and some of the economic models which have been used to represent this process.

The 'orthodox' view of the money-supply process offers an obvious starting point. This model describes a system in which banks are unable to compete for deposits since the interest yield on these is fixed at an uncompetitive level by convention—or perhaps by the monetary authorities. This assumption results in the familiar money-multiplier model in which the money supply depends upon the supply of cash (or other bank reserves) by the authorities and the scope for leakages of reserves from the system. In contrast, the 'new view' shows how the money supply is determined when the banks can offset such leakages by offering competitive rates on their deposits and thus bidding reserves away from the non-banks.

This is followed by a discussion of the demand-for-money approach, most relevant under a fixed exchange-rate system, and the 'disequilibrium money' view which combines features of both the orthodox supply and demand for money approaches. I will argue that these disequilibrium models cannot explain the short-run determination of the money supply and interest rates in a contemporary banking system since they do not tell us how the banks react when they experience a leakage of reserves. They also offer a very restrictive view of the interaction between real and financial decisions since they assume that disequilibrium in non-bank portfolios is confined to holdings of money balances.

It is arguably more realistic to draw a distinction between switches in financial asset portfolios (which are relatively costless) and adjustments in the overall size of the financial portfolio brought about through savings and real investment decisions (which are costly and optimally spread out over time). These real adjustments are particularly difficult to effect at an aggregate level where one agent's attempt to achieve equilibrium can cause another to move into disequilibrium. Such disequilibrium will be reflected in the financial wealth of the non-bank sector and this will tend to affect all its asset holdings in a way which may be indicated by the data (via a portfolio allocation model). In this framework, which is the one adopted in this book, changes in bank credit will affect the demand for bank deposits through its effect on the overall size of the portfolio. In this sense credit affects the short-run demand for money as in the disequilibrium money model. However, in this model demands for other assets may also increase, causing a net loss of reserves from the banks, which they must counter by issuing wholesale deposits and increasing administered interest rates. The money supply is therefore determined along with interest rates as part of a general equilibrium process. The last two sections of the chapter give a brief account of the way these variables are determined in the version of the Treasury model used in the simulation work reported in later chapters.

1 The orthodox view of the money-supply process

The orthodox model needs little introduction, having dominated economists' thinking about the money-supply process until at least the post-war era and still furnishing the model of the basic textbooks.[1] This views a bank deposit as a kind of hot potato which is put into circulation by a bank as part of the process of credit creation. The salient features of this type of model can be seen by imagining for a moment a cashless system in which bank deposit accounts are the only means of settling transactions between non-banks and must be kept in credit. Banks would of course need to maintain accounts with a central clearing house or perhaps a central bank in order to settle inter-bank transactions.

When a bank makes a loan to a non-bank in such a system this is matched automatically by a deposit credited to it. As this is spent it will be passed to another non-bank who will probably transfer it to a second bank. In this case, the second bank acquires a deposit with the first, or some other form of inter-bank settlement takes place, but the simple balance-sheet identities of this system ensure that money, once created through the process of credit creation, continues to circulate. Imbalances between the banks prevent an excessive expansion by an individual bank, but there is nothing in this model to prevent a balanced expansion of the system. The extra deposits are held on a temporary basis since non-banks will usually only accept them in order to pass them on to someone else as part of the process of exchange. But in this sense the short-run demand for money increases in line with the supply of credit, and banks collectively enjoy a 'widow's cruse'. Since there is no way the deposits can be extinguished, it is the economy which has to adjust, bringing the equilibrium demand for deposits into line with the increased supply through increases in prices and activity.

Banks cannot loose deposits to non-bank financial intermediaries (NBFIs) in this kind of system, since the latter maintain balances with the banks (rather than at the central clearing house) in order to settle their accounts.

When someone transfers a deposit by cheque from a bank to an NBFI account, this transfers ownership of the bank account to the NBFI in exactly the same way as if ownership were transferred to another bank. Unlike a bank, however, the NBFI cannot present this cheque for settlement at the clearing house. It must either hold the bank deposit on its own account or onlend it in the credit market.

Of course, in practice no banking system has ever been able to operate as a closed system, primarily because deposits are not the only means of payment. The public also hold cash, and in order to maintain the convertibility of their deposits banks also have to hold some of their assets in this form. This tendency has usually been reinforced by the monetary authorities who have made bank holdings of cash or other liquid assets mandatory in order to facilitate monetary and credit control. In the standard textbook version of the model, banks are assumed to hold some fraction (k) of their deposit liabilities (D) in the form of cash. Non-banks are assumed to use both cash (C) and deposits (D), holding these in a fixed proportion $(c = C/D)$. They may hold other assets as well, but leakage into these items is offset since it is assumed that the authorities control the total supply of cash (H) to the system.[2] These assumptions allow the money supply to be determined in the cash and deposit markets, independently of what is happening in the rest of the system.

In this situation an increase in the supply of credit by the banks will only be partially financed by an increase in the supply of deposits by non-banks. The banks will lose reserves to the non-banks at the same time as their own requirement for reserves increases. So deposits and credit can only be increased if the authorities supply cash to the system, allowing both banks and non-banks to keep their portfolios to the desired ratios. In this system notes and coin act as the hot potato, being passed between banks and non-banks until their credit and deposit portfolios are back in balance. Given its definition $(M_s = C + D = (1 + c)D)$ the money supply and the supply of credit are fixed multiples of the cash or high-powered money base $(H = C + kD = (c + k)D)$ so it is irrelevant which of these aggregates is monitored by the authorities. In the case of the money supply we have:

$$M_s = \frac{(1 + c)}{(c + k)} H = mH \tag{1}$$

2 The 'new view'

The orthodox model emphasizes clearly the potential for bank-credit expansion and shows the way in which leakages into non-monetary assets act as a restraint upon such expansion. But as Tobin (1963) has pointed out, this model is only realistic as a description of a regulated banking system in which banks are prevented from competing for deposits, for example by interest-rate ceilings of the 'regulation Q' type variety seen until quite recently in the USA.[3] He argues that in other respects banks are like NBFIs and, if unregulated, will compete for business until the marginal return on loans equals the marginal cost of deposits. This is the natural equilibrium point for any competitive system, giving a determinate solution for the money supply (as in the model set out in Chapter IV Section 1). Interest-rate ceilings prevent this point from being reached, so that if these are applied banks always find it profitable to expand their portfolios when they find themselves with excess cash reserves, and injections of reserves always lead to a multiple expansion. Such constraints also rule out the possibility that banks can bid reserve assets away from the non-banks, expanding the money supply without an injection of reserves through a change in the non-bank cash/deposit ratio. This constitutes the 'new view' of the money-supply process, which originated in the work of Gurley and Shaw (1960). A critical analysis of the 'old' and 'new' views is to be found in Chick (1973) and Peirce and Shaw (1979).

The orthodox model is therefore of very little relevance to a modern banking system in which regulations take other forms, and are designed to allow deposit-rate competition. Once this point is recognized and both banks and non-banks are seen as choosing their portfolios in the light of relative interest rates, the base-money multiplier becomes endogenous and will vary as the supply of cash to the system changes. (This multiplier is represented by the coefficient (m) in equation (1).) The analysis of money multipliers loses its simple appeal once this happens. An interesting analysis of the US money-supply process based on variable multipliers is however available in Burger (1971).

Relatively simple models of the determination of the money supply and interest rates in a competitive system have been developed by Tobin and Brainard (1963) and Brainard (1964). These assume that banks face constant costs of intermediation so that competition links deposit rates to lending rates in a rigid way. Banks freely accept deposits at this rate so the money market is always in equilibrium in this sense. The loan rate is assumed to bring the demand and supply of loans into equilibrium without any rationing effects. This kind of model can be used to answer a variety of important questions about the effects of open-market operations, changes in reserve requirements, and the like in a straightforward way. It also shows how an increase in activity by NBFIs which supply deposits and loans that are close substitutes for those of the banks will affect the velocity of circulation, prices, and hence the real demand for bank deposits. In this sense NBFIs may be viewed as being in competition with the banks, as was noted in the introduction.

Unfortunately this model still does not offer a very accurate description of the way contemporary financial systems work. In the real world banks face variable costs and may not be perfectly competitive, so there are unlikely to be simple links between rates on their assets and liabilities. They want to hold diversified asset portfolios in order to spread risk and this further complicates the equilibrium interest-rate relationships.

Moreover, contemporary systems typically feature competitive markets in wholesale but not retail bank deposits. Reflecting this, banks do not automatically accept wholesale deposits in the same way as they do retail deposits and so in an *ex ante* sense the wholesale market may be in disequilibrium, requiring an adjustment of money-market interest rates to bring it back into equilibrium *ex post*. On the other hand, rates on retail items may well be 'sticky', complicating the dynamics of adjustment. The effects of credit rationing and an active market in reserve assets may also have to be taken into account (Spencer (1982)). In such circumstances the monetary aggregates and interest rates can only be determined jointly, as part of the general equilibrium of the system. This is essentially the approach which is pursued here. Recent work at NIESR (Cutherbertson (1983)) and the LBS (Keating (1984)) has also adopted this kind of approach.

3 The disequilibrium-money approach

Of course, if interest rates are held fixed, either by the authorities, or perhaps by international capital movements under a fixed exchange-rate regime, then this simplifies the problem enormously since the monetary aggregates are then purely demand determined. The money supply and the banks' reserve base simply accommodate changes in the demand for these items, either through the operations of the authorities in domestic financial markets or, in the latter case, through the exchange reserves. Reflecting this, econometric studies of the demand for money during the 1960s using a relatively simple specification featuring income and interest-rate variables were initially very successful. They seemed to reveal a simple but stable demand function which could be used by the authorities to forecast and control the monetary aggregates. (For a review of both the US and the UK literature see Morgan (1978).) Monetary studies of the balance of payments also seemed to imply a stable underlying demand for money function.

This state of affairs did not last for very long. The move to the more liberal Competition and Credit Control (CCC) regime in September 1971 was followed by a dramatic increase both in bank lending to the private sector and the monetary aggregates, coinciding with a move to a floating exchange rate. These developments are described in the next chapter. The aggregates increased well beyond the values predicted by the simple demand functions estimated during the 1960s and early 1970s and this spelt the end of the simple demand for money approach. The growth of the aggregates moderated during 1974 and 1975, at a time when prices were increasing rapidly, bringing the real values of money balances and credit back to the kind of levels seen in earlier years. This behaviour is shown in Figure II.A. So, in

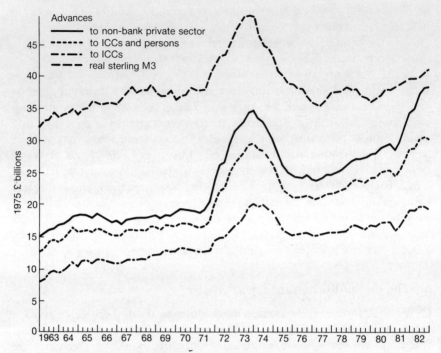

Fig. II.A. Real sterling M3 and bank lending

retrospect the early CCC years appear to have involved a marked and simultaneous deviation from trend in the behaviour of both bank credit and the wider monetary aggregates.

This coincidence naturally lead to a re-examination of the UK money-supply process and in particular the links between money and bank credit. The rapid growth of credit was most obviously explained as a supply-side effect associated with the lifting of the previous controls, although as we shall see it is difficult to explain the surge in company borrowing in this way. The coincidental explosion in the money supply was evidently a consequence of the financing constraint facing the banks and the simultaneous move to a floating exchange rate. It was argued, notably by Artis and Lewis (1976, 1981) and Coghlan (1981) that this caused a disequilibrium situation in which the extra deposits created by the banks were originally held either involuntarily or perhaps temporarily as in the orthodox model outlined above. Their analysis marks a return to a supply-side view of the monetary aggregates, but with the crucial difference that in this kind of analysis the behaviour of both banks and non-banks is responsive to interest rates and therefore affects the outcome of the money-supply process.

The money multiplier is therefore not assumed to be fixed. Rather, this analysis is based upon the 'money-supply identity', relating the change in a broad monetary aggregate to supply factors such as gilt sales, bank lending, and the PSBR. For example, in the case of (sterling) M3 which has been the basic target variable in the UK, this is defined in stock terms as:

£M3 = (a) Non-bank residents' holdings of notes and coin, plus
(b) Non-bank residents' holdings of sterling bank deposits, and
(c) Public Sector holdings of bank deposits.

The first two of these items are supplied by the public and banking sectors and so the budget identities of these two sectors (together with that of the overseas sector) may be substituted into this definition to give the required representation in terms of supply factors. (This is demonstrated by Artis and Lewis (1981), Chapter 4 for example). In flow terms we have:

The sum of
(i) PSBR (financial deficit plus net acquisitions of bank deposits, equities, etc.)
(ii) sterling bank lending to UK private residents
(iii) Sterling bank lending to non-residents
less
(iv) sales of public-sector debt (excluding notes and coin) to UK non-bank residents
equals Domestic Credit Expansion (DCE)
less
(v) increase in banks' non-deposit liabilities (NDLs, financial surplus plus equity issues)
less
(vi) external and foreign-currency (*fc*) adjustments, comprising:
—balance for official financing (intervention)
—overseas inflows into public sector debt
—public sector borrowing in *fc* from UK banks
—banks' net *fc* deposits
equals Change in sterling M3.

This breakdown is identical to the one used in the presentation of official monetary statistics (see Table 7.3 *Financial Statistics* and Table 11 *BEQB*, December 1983 issues for example). But it is important to note that these counterparts are ambiguous since items such as (ii) and (iv) might well be determined by non-bank demand rather than public or banking-sector supply. They are the counterparts to money in the balance sheet of the non-bank private sector as well as the balance sheet of the public and banking sectors.[4] In equilibrium the demands and supplies of these items (and hence, money itself) will be equal, so there is no ambiguity *ex post*. However, the disequilibrium school asserts that equilibrium may not attain, in which case these items are determined on the supply side, that is by the banks and the authorities, pushing the non-bank sector off its equilibrium demand for money schedule.

The original work by Artis and Lewis (1976) arose out of an attempt to investigate the factors which various commentators had used to rationalize the behaviour of the aggregates and the breakdown of the simple demand for money functions—company arbitrage between overdrafts and wholesale deposits being the one most often cited. Artis and Lewis showed that even if an allowance was made for these influences, the equations still broke down. However, with the benefit of hindsight it is now clear that they seriously underestimated the degree of financial innovation which took place during the early 1970s, only allowing for this by taking Certificates of Deposit out of the money supply statistics. In fact the CD issue was just the tip of an iceberg. As the next chapter makes clear, the London Clearing Banks became very competitive at a branch level as well as in the money markets. Their wholesale branch deposits—those linked to market rather than 7-day rates—increased from nothing in 1971 to £4.0 billion (or 21 per cent of their net deposits) by 1974. The increase in these liabilities was much larger than that of their CD issue (£1.4 billion).

Artis and Lewis also found that the monetary aggregates were influenced by supply-side influences such as the PSBR, the stock of high-powered money and credit-restraint dummies, as well as the usual demand-side factors. They took this as prima facie evidence that the market was in disequilibrium. (A similar result has been obtained for the US by Judd and Scadding (1982) using bank loans as an explanatory supply-side variable. This kind of evidence is of course entirely consistent with the view that expected interest rates, competition in the provision of new deposit facilities, or some other omitted variable cleared the market—as indeed is shown by the Artis model of the bank-credit market discussed in Chapter IV.) They went on to estimate 'inverse' or indirect demand for money functions in which they regressed interest rates upon other demand for money variables such as income, together with the money stock, taken to be an exogenous supply of money. Artis and Lewis noted that if interest rates cleared the market and their effect on the demand for money was partly lagged, then they would have to overshoot in response to exogenous supply shocks. In fact they found that lagged interest terms were significant in this specification, suggesting that interest rates were undershooting, failing to clear the market. Moreover, the resulting regression equations seemed to be stable, suggesting that this was the appropriate specification to use over this period.

This stability result is potentially very interesting—although even Artis and Lewis express concern about the exogenity assumptions upon which it is based. It has been reproduced by several other researchers who have been lead to the same conclusion. Yet this is exactly what we would expect if the rate of return on money were subject to measurement error.[5] If the demand for money function is estimated directly then this induces measurement error in an explanatory variable, resulting in bias and instability—a standard econometric result. If the equation is estimated indirectly, as in the Artis and Lewis specification, then the measurement error occurs in the dependent variable and there is no resulting bias or instability. If, as we would expect, this error is auto-correlated this would also account for the interest-rate undershooting effect apparent in the Artis and Lewis work.

The Artis and Lewis specification cannot distinguish between a situation in which some unobservable variable clears the market and one in which a genuine disequilibrium occurs. My own results, reported in Chapter VIII, suggest that expected capital gains on gilts are important market-clearing variables and that it is inappropriate to use a simple gilt-money yield differential as in the Artis and Lewis work on M3. Moreover, by restricting their attention to this differential Artis and Lewis rule out any non-bank substitution between wholesale deposits and overdrafts. The results reported in Chapter IV suggest that this was very important, especially in the case of companies. Although expected returns and arbitrage differentials are difficult to handle in econometric work, and the equations which are employed to do this often permit differing interpretations, these results point clearly towards a market-clearing model.

4 Portfolio disequilibrium and the interaction of real and financial variables

The more recent research of Coghlan (1981) represents an important development of the disequilibrium-money model. This follows work on the Australian system by Johnson *et al.* (1976) in allowing the quantity of money in circulation to be determined endogenously as the sum of the decisions of the monetary authorities and banks, together with the short-run expenditure and portfolio decisions of the non-banks.[6] Coghlan makes it clear that in his view the quantity of money is always held willingly by non-banks, so this would appear to rule out the possibility of market disequilibrium of the classical type. He argues that this follows from the general acceptance of money as a means of payment, as in the orthodox model of the money-supply process. But despite the very significant degree of control which non-banks have over their money holdings in this version of the model—both through real and financial transactions—the stock of money which results from this process in the short run is described as the 'money supply'. The demand for money label is reserved for the amount of money which non-banks plan to hold in long-run equilibrium. The difference between the demand and supply of money in this specification is in fact just the difference between the non-banks short-run and long-run demand. Disequilibrium therefore occurs in portfolios and not in markets, due to adjustment and other lags rather than spillover effects. This rather misleading terminology now seems to have been adopted by Artis and Lewis (1981).

Since there can never be any difference between the short-run demand and supply of money in this kind of model, the rate of return on monetary assets and thus the money stock is formally indeterminate. Coghlan assumes that bank interest rates are exogenous to his model in order to resolve this indeterminancy. Reflecting this, it is never clear whether bank lending is automatically self-financing or whether the banks have to go out and actively bid for funds to cover this. Coghlan himself seems to favour the first of these views, although this clearly ignores the scope for leakages of cash and reserves from the system and the ability of the banks to counter this by raising their interest rates. As we have seen this indeterminancy is resolved in the old- or new-view models through the respective payment of either a regulated or a perfectly competitive rate on deposits. A simple formula for the money supply may be obtained in either case, in terms of the potential for leakage from the system in the first case or marginal profitability conditions in the second.

Putting the problem of indeterminacy to one side, the distinction between the short- and long-run demand for money made in Coghlan's work is a useful one and has important implications for medium-term macroeconomic analysis. Seen from this perspective, the empirical version of the model represents an attempt to describe non-bank real and financial decisions in an integrated way, allowing for adjustment and perhaps expectational lags. As such it is of considerable potential interest.

The feature which distinguishes this model from others of this type (for example the 'Liverpool model' of Minford *et al.* (1984)) is its narrow focus upon the money supply. In his theoretical treatment Coghlan emphasizes the role of bank deposits as a means of payment, which points to the use of a narrow definition of money: cash and current accounts. But he then notes (as do Artis and Lewis (1976)) that the costs of switching between these and other broad money assets is negligible, so that any portfolio disequilibrium in the former will immediately be spread amongst the latter, and argues that this makes M3 the most suitable measure for use in empirical work. However it is not clear why the logical flow of this argument should be arrested at this precise point. Judging by interest-rate differentials (as indicators of marginal savings in transactions costs) it applies *a fortiori* to switches between components of M3 (such as CDs) and other liquid assets (local authority (LA) deposits), an argument which I develop in Chapter V. Indeed my results suggest that CD–LA distinction is a rather weak one upon which to depend.

The only possible justification for drawing the line at this point is that a non-bank switch between bank deposits and other assets will disturb bank portfolios and may cause an offsetting movement in interest rates. But given the high substitution elasticities observed in both bank and non-bank portfolios this cannot be an important consideration. Furthermore, on the 'efficient financial markets' view (discussed in Chapter VIII) there would seem to be little reason to distinguish capital-certain and uncertain assets, an argument which suggests that some measure of financial or total wealth is a more suitable measure of expenditure and portfolio disequilibrium in a competitive system. This would certainly appear to be more reasonable a priori. Although there may be a separate role for both liquid and financial assets to play, the evidence suggests that the overall finacial-asset position provides a better explanation of the behaviour of both consumers expenditure (Bean (1978)) and total private expenditure (Bennett (1986)) than does the liquid-asset position.

Although Keynesians tend to regard real and financial assets as close substitutes, this distinction between real and financial markets is a rather Keynesian one. Imperfections in the goods and labour markets leading to sticky prices and wages are fundamental to the Keynesian disequilibrium view of the economy, resulting in spillover effects such as the familiar demand multiplier. These disequilibrium effects will tend to spill over into financial markets since they frustrate savings and investment plans, causing financial positions to deviate from their long-run desired or notional values, just as money does in the disequilibrium-money model. Neo-Keynesian models of the financial sector such as those based on the work of Tobin (1969) typically employ some measure of financial wealth together with income in order to capture such disequilibrium effects. In other words, the demand for financial assets, including money, is represented conditional upon wealth and income, being specified in effective demand terms in the same way as expenditure. (Equations (7)–(9) of Appendix III offer an example of such a specification.)

In this 'Yale-school' kind of specification, financial markets are, as we have seen, assumed to be competitive and prices adjust to bring these effective demands into line with supply, even though portfolios and perhaps markets may be in disequilibrium in notional terms. Yet imperfections in the credit and retail-deposit markets could frustrate this process (indeed they could spill over into real markets) and it is important to allow for this possibility by representing asset demands conditional upon credit as well as net financial wealth.

Keynesian models naturally emphasize the relationships between expenditure and income flows and often leave the stock demand for financial assets (particularly non-monetary assets) undefined.[7] This misspecification can be a serious one if portfolio-disequilibrium effects are as important as they seem to have been in recent years. In order to ensure that the long-run demand for financial assets is well specified it is important to allow for financial wealth or portfolio disequilibrium effects on expenditure flows. The relationship between long-run asset demand and expenditure relationships is discussed in Appendix III.

Recent econometric models of the UK economy such as the Treasury's have incorporated both flow- and stock-adjustment effects. They therefore tend to exhibit both Keynesian and Monetarist features. For example, an increase in government expenditure, financed by borrowing or monetary expansion, tends to increase output in the short run through conventional multiplier effects. The private sector accumulates financial assets as part of this process, pushing portfolios into disequilibrium. But over the longer term it attempts to increase its expenditure in order to reattain portfolio equilibrium. The price level and, depending upon the stance of monetary policy, interest rates, will increase as part of this process. The nature of these portfolio equilibrium effects on prices and interest rates is explored in Appendix III.

5   A model of portfolio disequilibrium and the monetary aggregates

The expenditure equations of the version of the Treasury model used in the work reported in this book are based on the view that in the long run the financial-asset stocks of the private sector will be kept in line with income. For example, the expenditure of the personal sector depends upon its disposable incomes in the short run, but in a way which ensures that its net financial-asset position is increased in line with nominal incomes in equilibrium (Bean (1978), Grice (1981)). Similarly, company holdings of both real and financial assets are in equilibrium related to the level of output. (A more recent description of these relationships is to be found in Barber (1984).)

In the short run, however, the financial-asset positions of the non-bank sectors can diverge widely from these equilibrium values, particularly in the face of unanticipated changes in the rate of inflation. It is reasonable to suppose that it takes a significant period of time for such shocks to be offset through savings and other accumulation processes. This is especially true at an aggregate level where one individual's attempt to achieve financial equilibrium can throw another into disequilibrium. Treasury estimates suggest that in the case of consumers' expenditure these lags are extremely long. Moreover, disequilibrium effects may also arise in this model because of credit rationing.

If the overall financial position is in disequilibrium for this kind of reason this affects the demand for all financial assets, not only those of monetary nature. In the Treasury model these are modelled in terms of the net financial wealth and bank-credit position of the individual or sector concerned, as well as conventional demand-side variables such as incomes and interest rates. The use of this portfolio-wide approach at the estimation stage allows the data to dictate the way in which disequilibrium in the overall position affects holdings of specific assets. To the extent that it affects the demand for money, a disequilibrium in savings or bank credit will then cause the short-run demand for money to diverge from its equilibrium value as in the Coghlan model, the only difference being that such effects are not confined to money balances.

The non-bank asset-demand functions which emerge from this approach show the effective short-run demand at any given financial and credit position, income, and structure of interest rates. A set of decision relationships is similarly defined for the banking sector, showing its effective supply of money-market deposits and effective demands for reserve and other assets, in terms of the non-bank supply of retail deposits and the size of its loan portfolio, together with interest rates. In this specification changes in the amount of credit extended to non-banks are in part returned to the banks as retail deposits, leaving the banks to go out into the wholesale markets or perhaps sell secondary reserve assets to cover the rest. So an effective *ex ante* excess supply of money-market deposits—matched by an excess demand for other assets—will occur at the original set of interest rates. These interest rates must therefore adjust (together with retail deposit and credit flows) in order to bring effective short-run demands and supplies for these items back into effective balance *ex post*. The theory of short-run price determination in this kind of conditional demand system has been studied by Veendorp (1975).

6 Relationships between the demand for credit, money, and other assets

If non-banks can borrow from the banks, disequilibrium in their overall financial situation may be reflected in bank borrowing rather than holdings of money or other assets. This has been used as a criticism of the disequilibrium-money model by Kaldor (1980). Many non-banks do not hold financial assets on any significant scale, but instead rely on overdraft borrowing as a way of financing changes in their overall financial position. Indeed, traditional descriptions of the money-supply process have tended to categorize non-banks either as 'deficit units' which borrow but do not deposit, or 'surplus units' which deposit but do not borrow. This allows a clear-cut separation of the demand for money on the one hand and the demand for credit or the money-supply on the other.

Yet, as the Miller and Sprenkle (1981) model makes clear, this dichotomy is unrealistic in a world of high interest rates, where it is expensive to hold sight deposits with the banks. In this situation, surplus units economize their sight deposits and rely upon overdraft or other forms of liability-side liquidity in order to meet unforeseen transactions. Financial surpluses are invested in time deposits or other interest-earning assets instead. In this situation non-banks will typically find themselves holding time deposits with the banks and borrowing on overdraft—even when interest rates on the latter are higher than on the former. This blurs the distinction between the demand for money and credit. The Miller–Sprenkle model suggests that given the kind of interest rates seen in recent years interactions between the demand for time deposits and credit will be very important, a point which we take up in Chapter IV and analyse further in Appendix I. Of course, if relative interest rates positively encourage overdraft arbitrage, as in the UK during 1973, the demands for money and credit will be highly interrelated.

In principle these unrationed borrowers will decide how much they plan to borrow and invest in the various different financial markets simultaneously. Such a decision process is difficult to model mathematically, involving both the precautionary aspects stemming from uncertain transactions require- ments and the speculative aspects resulting from uncertain asset returns. However Appendix I shows that if these risks are independent and the overall financial-wealth position (and the level of interest rates) are high enough to make it optimal to hold some time deposits (or similar assets), then the portfolio-selection problem breaks down into two relatively simple sub-problems. The first involves the choice of an initial bank balance, which may of course either be left in credit or in overdraft. This is chosen in the light of precautionary considerations and independently of speculative and expectational factors. It will also be independent of the overall financial position under these assumptions. The second problem involves the choice of speculative assets such as gilts, independently of precautionary considera- tions.

This separability property allows the researcher to investigate the behaviour of bank lending and the associated monetary effects without con- cerning himself unduly with speculative and expectational effects spilling over from the gilts and foreign-exchange markets. This is essentially the focus of the next four chapters, which examine the behaviour of bank lending and the money markets and look at the problems which these posed for the authorities in the first half of the 1970s.

It is important to note at this stage, however, that although this kind of separability assumption may be used to simplify the demands for the pre- cautionary and speculative items in the portfolio, it still implies a complex specification of the demand for broad monetary aggregates such as M3. This is because time deposits act as a slack variable in the non-bank portfolio in this situation, accommodating fluctuations in the precautionary and specula- tive items and financial wealth. Since time deposits are included in the wider aggregates the demand function will thus reflect all of these factors. But the demand for the narrower aggregates will be much simpler given the separa- bility assumption, involving just transactional and precautionary considera- tions.

Notes

1. The basic version of this model was developed by Phillips (1924), although the elements of this kind of model can be found in the writings of earlier monetary theorists.
2. For example, a public-sector financial surplus, financed by a rundown of bank deposits by the general public would cause the banks to lose cash (or, in a modern system, bankers' balances with the central bank), but this would be offset

by an open-market purchase of domestic securities by the authorities, designed to keep the monetary base unchanged.

3. Bank Rate cartel maintained by the London Clearing Banks until 1971 had similar effects. A useful analysis of the effect of changes in interest-rate ceilings, required reserve ratios, and the like in a perfectly competitive system is to be found in Tobin and Brainard (1963).

4. Reflecting this ambiguity, the official breakdown refers to these as components of the change in the money *stock* and to (iv) as *purchases* of public-sector debt. In order to reinforce this point it may be helpful to derive the money-stock identity relationship from the demand side, by first substituting items (*a*) and (*b*) using the non-bank budget identity, represented as:

Change in (*a*) + (*b*)

> = (ii)   sterling bank borrowing
> − (iv)   purchases of public-sector debt
> + (vii) non-bank financial surplus
> − (viii) purchases of equities from other residents
> + (ix)   non-bank capital-account transactions
> − (x)   net non-bank foreign-currency deposits with UK banks.

Adding the change in item (*c*), the definition of the PSBR and banks NDLs then allows us to substitute the relationship:

$$(\text{vii}) - (\text{viii}) + \text{change in } (c) = (\text{i}) - (\text{v}) + (\text{xi})$$

where: (xi) = the current account surplus (or overseas sector financial deficit). So we may derive the money stock identity as:

$$\text{change in £M3} = (\text{i}) + (\text{ii}) + (\text{iii}) - (\text{iv}) - (\text{v}) - (\text{vi})'$$

where (vi)′ = (iii) − (ix) + (x) − (xi). In this representation, (vi)′ represents an alternative definition of the external adjustments, defined from the perspective of the non-bank balance sheet. It equals the conventional definition (vi), given the overseas-sector balance-sheet indentity. This representation shows quite clearly that *ceteris paribus*, item (iii), sterling lending to the overseas sector, does not affect the money supply, only the split between DCE and the externals. It also shows that, putting this technical adjustment to one side, the externals are simply the sum of:

> (xi) the balance of payments on current account
> (ix) non-bank capital account
> (x) (less) non-bank foreign-currency deposits (net) with UK banks.

A breakdown of the externals along these lines is available in Table 7.4 of *Financial Statistics*. This representation is somewhat easier to understand than the conventional one, and clearly shows the way in which the externals have been affected in recent years by the abolition of exchange controls, North Sea oil, and other current-account effects. A more detailed analysis of the external adjustments is available in Lomax and Mowl (1978) and of the various money stock identities in Spencer and Mowl (1978, Annex 4).

5. Suppose, following Artis and Lewis (Section 4) that the demand for money (M_d) depends upon income (Y) and expected interest rates (r^b) together with an error

term (u). Also, suppose that M_s represents the money supply and the market clears:

$$M_s = M_d = a + br^p + cY + u \qquad c \geq 0; b \leq 0$$

Also suppose that the expectation (r^p) equals the observed yield (r) plus a measurement-error (or expected capital-gain) term (v) and substitute this into the above equation to give:

$$M_s = a + br + cY + w$$

where:

$$r = r^p - v$$
$$w = u + bv$$

The simultaneity and measurement-error biases which can arise in this kind of situation are discussed in general terms in Section VIII.2. But for the purpose of the present discussion I will simply follow Artis and Lewis in assuming an exogenous money supply. I will also assume that the measurement-error term (v) is independent of the market-clearing variable (r^p) and its determinants, so that it is negatively correlated with the observed interest rate (r). In this case, one way to proceed, as Artis and Lewis point out, is to estimate an indirect demand for money function of the form:

$$r = b^{-1}M_s - ab^{-1} - cb^{-1}Y + e$$

where:

$$e = -v - b^{-1}u$$

If the underlying structural parameters are stable, this model will exhibit parameter stability even if, as we would expect, the nature of the expectations-formation or measurement-error process changes over time. (We might observe instability in the equation standard error, but this is not reported by Artis and Lewis). If measurement errors are auto-correlated, this will result in low Durbin Watson statistics as observed in the static version of the Artis and Lewis M3—based interest-rate equation. In this case, a lagged interest-rate term will attract a significant positive coefficient, giving the impression that interest rates 'undershoot' their equilibrium value. Of course, if the demand for money equation is estimated directly, biased coefficient estimates will emerge. Furthermore, as the nature of the measurement-error process changes, this will give the impression of parameter instability.

6. The stock of money is defined as the non-banks holding of M3, in order to focus on the behaviour of this sector. It is determined by a stock identity similar, *mutatis mutandis*, to the conventional one, interpreted of course as a bank-supply rather than a non-bank-demand relationship.

7. Such models usually incorporate an explicit demand for money function but ignore wealth effects, thus leaving the demand for bonds indeterminate. For example in the standard IS–LM model of the textbooks, a one-shot fiscal expansion will increase activity and interest rates temporarily given a fixed money supply. But once this policy is discontinued, interest rates and activity return to their original levels and the stock demand for bonds remains permanently higher. The supply of bonds by the authorities is automatically met by demand at prices which are unchanged in the long run. Similar criticisms can be levelled at many monetarist models, which tend to emphasize the demand for money at the expense of the demand for non-monetary assets.

III

The Experience of Competition and Credit Control

Introduction and summary

The Competition and Credit Control (CCC) reforms of 1971 represent a clear turning-point in the monetary history of the UK, ushering in a regime which was much more liberal and competitive than that of the 1960s. As noted in the introductory chapter, monetary policy during these years had been marked by an increasing reliance upon direct controls on lending to the private sector. These years had also seen the traditional deposit business of the clearing banks come under increasing competitive pressure from the growth of the secondary banks and the new markets in wholesale deposits. This chapter begins with a more detailed review of these developments and a look at the reforms themselves against this background. It then goes on to discuss the operational problems which were experienced with the new system.

These problems led directly to the imposition of the Supplementary Special Deposit (SSD) scheme in December 1974, designed to prevent excessive liability management by the banks. This chapter takes a preliminary look at the way in which this worked, the circumstances in which it was employed between 1974 and its abandonment in 1980, and the *modus operandi* the authorities adopted during phases in which it was not in place. This involved an administered MLR and the use of special deposit calls and short-term market operations, both as a way of backing this up and also of avoiding undue pressure on bank reserve-asset positions and the money markets. The pre- and post-1974 versions of the CCC regimes are then compared.

The chapter concludes with an analysis of the way in which the 1971 reforms and the ensuing developments affected the deposit-side business of the clearing banks. This is based on detailed information on their deposit structure given to the Wilson Committee. This evidence shows the extent to which they took advantage of their new freedom to compete, both in the wholesale markets and—a point which is not generally appreciated—at a branch level. By 1976 over 45 per cent of clearing-bank deposits were of a wholesale variety, taken in at market rates rather than the 7-day deposit rate.

1 The development of the banking sector and money markets during the 1960s

The 1960s saw the beginning of a radical change in the UK money markets and the way the banks went about their business. At the beginning of the decade the UK monetary scene was dominated by the clearing banks which operated exclusively through their branch networks in a way which had changed little since the beginning of the century. They supplied 95 per cent of the sterling bank deposits held by UK residents, as Table III.1 shows. Most of these deposits were still on current account, interest rates on other deposits being linked via the famous 'Bank Rate cartel' arrangement to the Bank of England's rediscount rate. So banks could only compete for deposits though non-price means; by expanding the size of their branch networks for example. In this respect they were very much the kind of institution envisaged by the authors of the orthodox model of the money-supply process. These deposits were supported by bank holdings of cash and liquid assets, Treasury and commercial bills, and call money with the discount market, which the clearing banks held to ratios set by the Bank of England. There were well-developed secondary markets in Treasury and commercial bills, bank liquidity being ultimately supported by the Bank of England's operations in these markets and the rediscount facility open to the discount houses. Imbalances between the different banks were reflected largely in their position with the discount market rather than through inter-bank transactions, and accounts were settled through the Bank of England. Markets in other short-term instruments were still relatively thin.

This had changed dramatically by the end of the decade. As Table III.1 makes clear, the clearing banks had lost out significantly to the non-clearers, especially to the subsidiaries of American and other overseas banks in London. I will refer to these banks collectively as secondary banks, following Revell (1969). These institutions had initially developed alongside the London markets in dollar deposits—the Eurodollar market—but had then found it profitable to take on business in sterling. These banks acted on a wholesale basis in the euromarkets, taking in large-domination deposits for a fixed period of time and lending them on in a similarly structured way. If these funds were not needed to accommodate the bank's customers they would be lent on to another bank. Conversely, if a bank found itself with more lending opportunities than deposits it would obtain the necessary funds through the inter-bank market. Transactions between these banks were settled through dollar accounts held with commercial banks in the appropriate national centre rather than through a central bank. In contrast to retail banks, these institutions maintained the viability of their balance sheets by matching the maturity of their liabilities to that of their assets rather than by holding balances of liquid assets. A useful analysis of eurobanking business is provided by Johnston (1983a).

The overseas banks brought these techniques with them when they moved into their new sterling habitat. They proved quite suited to this environment. Together with indigenous secondary banks such as the accepting houses they helped establish the sterling inter-bank market during the 1960s and in 1967 and were amongst the first institutions to issue sterling certificates of deposit

Table III.1. Changes in the distribution of UK residents' sterling bank deposits during the 1960s. (£ millions, end December. Figures in parentheses show percentage of total deposits)

	1962	1963	1964	1965	1966	1967	1968	1969	1970	1971
(a) London clearing banks	7,168	7,609	8,065	8,477	8,533	9,261	9,766	9,711	10,297	12,201
	(84.5)	(82.8)	(82.0)	(80.5)	(79.6)	(77.4)	(75.1)	(74.5)	(73.6)	(74.9)
(b) Other clearing banks	886	921	949	1,006	1,030	1,136	1,208	1,215	1,313	1,438
	(10.4)	(10.0)	(9.6)	(9.5)	(9.6)	(9.5)	(9.3)	(9.3)	(9.4)	(8.8)
(c) Other UK banks	431	656	815	1,047	1,159	1,571	1,939	2,103	2,375	2,648
	(5.1)	(7.2)	(8.4)	(10.0)	(10.8)	(13.1)	(15.0)	(16.2)	(17.0)	(16.3)
(d) Total	8,485	9,186	9,829	10,530	10,722	11,968	12,907	13,029	13,985	16,287

Source: Wilson (1978) V, Table 1, p. 112

Banks and the Money Supply Process

Table III.2. The London sterling money markets, 1957–1979 (end-year, £ million)

	1957	1962	1967	1972	1977	1978[b]	1979
Money at call with discount market	903	1,186	1,662	2,530	3,513	4,004	4,435
Treasury bills	3,388	3,042	3,156	1,719	3,950	2,813	2,480
Commercial bills[a]	250	400	725	1,188	2,169	3,393	5,588
Local authority bills	—	—	—	240	443	499	599
Other local authority temporary debt	450	1,071	1,750	2,145	2,896	3,788	5,135
Deposits with finance houses	99	337	591	437	921	967	1,117
Inter-bank deposits	..	508	1,309	5,068	11,407	13,205	16,433
Sterling certificates deposit	—	—	—	4,934	4,546	3,678	3,692
Other market loans by the banking sector	..	..	..	..	4,296	4,581	5,314
Total	5,090	6,544	9,193	18,261	34,141	36,928	44,793

[a]This excludes acceptances held outside the banking sector:
[b]A sectoral breakdown of these holdings at end 1978 is shown in Table III.4.
Source: Wilson (1978) Appendix 3, p. 510

(CDs). Together with the discount houses they developed an active secondary market in sterling CDs. This innovation allowed the issuing bank to take in money at a fixed interest rate and maturity (typically three months) whilst giving the holder the option of liquidating his deposit at any time by selling it on to a third party.

In the meantime an active wholesale market in Local Authority deposits had grown up. These were held by banks initially, but non-bank holdings grew rapidly, avoiding the need for bank intermediation. These markets grew up alongside the established markets in Treasury and commercial bills and call money with the discount market and for this reason were dubbed the 'parallel money markets' in a widely-read article reviewing their development, published in the *Midland Bank Review* in August 1966. Table III.2 clearly shows the growth of the parallel markets during the pre-CCC years as well as their size relative to existing markets. Reid (1982) gives a very readable account of the rise of the secondary banks and useful descriptions of the main institutions and instruments involved are to be found in Wilson (1978), Appendix III.

The loss of market share experienced by the clearing banks over this period reflected the Radcliffe proposition that the main effect of controlling any set of financial institutions such as the clearing banks would be to cause their business to be lost to competitors. The clearing banks were clearly handicapped by the special-deposit and liquid-asset conventions which they obeyed. Yet the major handicap seems to have been the bank-rate cartel arrangements which ruled out the issue of wholesale deposits. Under these arrangements they could only take in 7-day deposits, at interest rates linked to the Bank of England rediscount or 'Bank Rate'. They were, however, able to set up subsidiaries which operated outside these arrangements, and by the early 1970s most of the major London Clearers had done this. They were thus well placed to take advantage of these new developments when the Competition and Credit Control reforms were introduced.

2   The initial Competition and Credit Control arrangements

The Bank of England's initial proposals for Competition and Credit Control were published as a consultative document in May 1971. The underlying principle was that the Bank of England would act upon the banks' sterling-deposit base rather than by directly guiding their lending to the private sector. In order to provide a 'firm base' for this policy the banks were to observe a minimum reserve–asset ratio. In addition they would place special deposits with the Bank of England when these were called for. This policy implied a greater reliance upon changes in interest rates as a way of controlling private lending and in order to facilitate such changes the Bank's tactical support of the gilt-edged market was to be limited. The idea was that this policy would be more flexible than the previous one, putting all banks on a common basis and allowing them to compete freely. In order to make way for this, the clearing banks agreed to abandon the bank-rate cartel agreement.

The operational arrangements were agreed with the banks over the summer months, coming into effect in September. The precise details were published in the December 1971 *Bulletin*, (Bank of England (1971c)). Basically, the banks were to maintain a minimum of $12\frac{1}{2}$ per cent of their 'eligible liabilities' in the form of 'eligible reserve assets'. The definition of eligible liabilities encompassed all of the banks sterling deposit liabilities with an original maturity of less than two years, (less any of these deposits on lent to other UK banks including unsecured lending to the discount market). It included, in addition, any net resources obtained by switching foreign-currency deposits into sterling (if this was positive). Eligible reserve assets included balances with the Bank of England, Treasury and eligible local-authority bills, British government stocks of one year maturity or less, and call money with the discount market. In addition, commercial bills eligible for discount at the Bank of England could count up to a maximum of 2 per cent of eligible liabilities. Clearing-bank holdings of notes and coin were not eligible as reserve assets under these arrangements.

Call money with the discount market qualified without limit as a bank-reserve asset. Together with their rediscount facility at the Bank of England, this gave the discount houses a privileged position in the new system. As part of the quid pro quo they agreed that they would continue to cover the weekly Treasury bill tender. They also agreed to invest at least half of their borrowed funds in public-sector debt. (Bank of England (1971c).) In the event this arrangement proved disruptive and had to be replaced. (see page 42 below). Although these arrangements left the discount market with a potential for creating reserve assets when the banks were under pressure, this did not in fact prove a problem for the authorities (Zawadski (1981), Chapter 1).

3   The control mechanism envisaged by the authorities

An invaluable insight into the way the authorities expected these arrangements to work in practice is provided by the address by the Governor of the Bank of England to a conference of international bankers in Munich on 28 May 1971 (Bank of England (1971a).) Two of the more relevant passages are reproduced below:

It is not expected that the mechanism of the minimum asset ratio and special deposits can be used to achieve some precise multiple contraction or expansion of bank assets. Rather the intention is to use our control over liquidity, which these instruments will reinforce, to influence the structure of interest rates. The resulting changes in relative rates of return will then induce shifts in the asset portfolios of both the public and the banks. Of course, we do not envisage that there can be a nicely calculated relationship between the size of calls for special deposits and the achievement of a desired objective. We expect rather to achieve our objectives through market mechanisms. Special deposits can be used not only to mop up any abnormal excess liquidity, but also to oblige the banking system to seek to dispose of assets not eligible for the liquidity ratio, for example gilt-edged stocks of over one year's maturity. By using special deposits in this way we shall be able to exert, when appropriate, upward pressure on interest rates—not only rates in the inter-bank market but also rates in the local authority market and yields on short-term gilt-edged stock.

Of course, the extent of the pressure we shall be able to bring to bear on interest rates by our open-market policies, backed up if necessary by calls for special deposits, will be affected by many factors: for example, the financial position of the central government or the current sensitivity of foreign exchange flows to short-term rates in London. However, no limitation is envisaged on the authorities' ability to neutralise excess liquidity or to bring about sufficiently strong upward pressure on bank lending rates.

These extracts spell out the intended control mechanism quite clearly. The Governor saw bank liquidity as being influenced both directly by the supply of reserve assets (via public sector borrowing from the banks) and indirectly by calls for special deposits. The latter was referred to elsewhere in the speech as the 'second leg' of the policy. The banks would then respond to this reserve-asset pressure by selling secondary reserve assets such as short-term gilts and local authority deposits, increasing yields in the associated market as well as in the inter-bank market. This in turn would put upward pressure on bank lending rates and presumably lead to a reduction in private borrowing.

There are several facets of this analysis which are striking, especially in the light of what followed. The first is the emphasis given to the control of private-sector credit. There is no mention of the possibility of controlling public-sector borrowing in order to help contain monetary growth. Fiscal and monetary policy are regarded as being quite distinct. Nor is there any suggestion that operations in the gilt-edged market could be used actively in this respect, although support for the market had to be curtailed in order to prevent the banks escaping from reserve-asset pressures by selling gilts at unchanged prices (as they had been able to do under the previous system). Instead the banks would have to sell a range of assets at reduced prices until the authorities interest objectives were achieved. The Bank presumably felt that this arms-length approach was less arbitrary than one in which the government broker was instructed to sell directly to the market. Given their attitude to gilt sales and the PSBR, the authorities had little scope for influencing bank liquidity when interest rates were rising and were in the event forced to rely heavily on the second leg of their policy—the special deposit call.

As Gowland (1978) has commented, in relying upon the control of bank lending to the private sector, the new policy represented a continuation of the old. The innovation was that this was to be controlled by price and not by fiat. Given the previous reliance on quantitative controls, no one knew how price sensitive this was, or indeed how large was the demand which had been frustrated by the controls. This interest sensitivity had to be taken as an act of faith.

It is interesting to note the Governor's dismissal of the simple reserve-multiplier model of the money-supply process, which featured so prominently in the textbooks of the time. His speech reflects the 'new view' of the money-supply process discussed in the second chapter. The authorities saw the banks facing an interest-elastic demand for credit but were clearly loath to let the market find the natural equilibrium appropriate to an unregulated competitive system. The reserve ratios agreed with the banks (together with an arrangement made with the clearers to convert into gilts some of the liquid assets held by them under the previous system) left the banks with only moderate excess reserves as the new arrangements came into force. Moreover, the authorities continued to monitor this excess-reserve position, presumably regarding it as an indicator of future credit expansion.

Finally, one is struck by the emphasis the Governor's speech puts on asset as against liability management. Although the effect of a reserve-asset squeeze on inter-bank rate is noted, the authorities underestimated the extent to which the clearing banks came to depend upon the new wholesale deposit markets. This was only natural given the uncertainty surrounding the new arrangements, and had the system developed in other directions as they intended it might have had few serious consequences. After all, it matters little whether banks sell gilts and other assets out of their portfolios or issue CDs in response to a reserve-asset squeeze. Both reactions have the effect of pushing up market interest rates, the only difference being that in the latter case the banks may need to bid for reserve assets to preserve their reserve ratios. In the kind of competitive environment the Governor envisaged this would have lead to an increase in bank lending rates. Yet in an imperfectly competitive system the effect could be quite different.

4   The early operational experience

The Competition and Credit Control system began its existence facing pressures of a large and unknown magnitude in the shape of the frustrated demand for credit hanging over from the previous regime. The scale of these pressures quickly revealed itself as bank lending to the previously restricted sectors accelerated. The stock of bank lending to property companies increased from £450 millions (or $4\frac{1}{2}$ per cent of total lending to UK residents) in August 1971 to £1,150 millons (or 7 per cent) by November 1972. Lending to the personal sector (other than for house purchase) increased from £770 millions (or 8 per cent of the total) to £1,820 millions ($11\frac{1}{2}$ per cent) over this period.

Although bank lending was generally growing rapidly over this period, the observation that it was growing most rapidly in the sectors which had hitherto been restricted suggested that it was in large part a once-and-for-all adjustment to the reforms. This, together with the fact that the economy was recovering from a recession, suggested that there was little cause for concern. The Chancellor made it clear in his budget speech of March 1972 that monetary growth would accommodate the recovery. It was quite clear that bank lending to the private sector was by far and away the most important component of monetary growth during 1972. This is also reflected in Figure II.A which shows bank lending and sterling M3, both deflated by the Total Final Expenditure deflator.

The exchange rate came under strong downward pressure during 1972. This came to a head in June, forcing the government to let sterling float. By the end of the year the effective rate had fallen by nearly 10 per cent against its rate at the end of May. Given the significance which has come to be attached to the exchange rate as an indicator of the monetary-policy stance this would now be regarded as ominous. Yet at the time the exchange rate was regarded as an unwarranted constraint on economic policy, which should not be allowed to stand in the way of economic growth. Indeed, in announcing the famous 'dash for growth' in the March 1973 budget speech the Chancellor had also anticipated this problem and already determined to side-step it by adopting a more flexible exchange-rate policy.

Nevertheless the capital outflow which preceeded the float had been large enough to put bank balance-sheets under pressure. The official reserves fell by about £1 billion, almost half of this representing an outflow of overseas deposits. The banks had responded to these outflows by drawing in funds from the parallel money markets, pushing up the associated interest rates. (The behaviour of 3-month CD and prime lending rates is shown in Figure III.A.) The authorities initially aquiesed in this movement, increasing Bank Rate from 5 to 6 per cent on 22 June, and were followed after a few days by the clearing banks. In the normal course of events interest rates would have risen further, but the Bank headed off this movement, engaging in a sale and repurchase agreement (for £356 millions of gilts) with the banks. So on this occasion the control mechanism was largely overridden in the pursuit of economic recovery.

In October Bank Rate was renamed Minimum Lending Rate (MLR) and linked to Treasury bill (T-bill) rate by 'the formula'.[1] At about the same time sterling weakened and the authorities had become concerned about the banks' liquidity position which, despite the high level of lending, looked excessive. So the first call for special deposits was announced on 9 November. A further call was made on 31 December, increasing the rate effective from 17 January of the following year to 3 per cent. (The call is shown on an effective basis in Figure III.B together with CD and T-bill rates). The banks responded by running down both their reserve and parallel money-market positions,[2] tending to push up rates in both markets. The authorities re-inforced the rise in T-bill rate with an increase in the T-bill tender and various

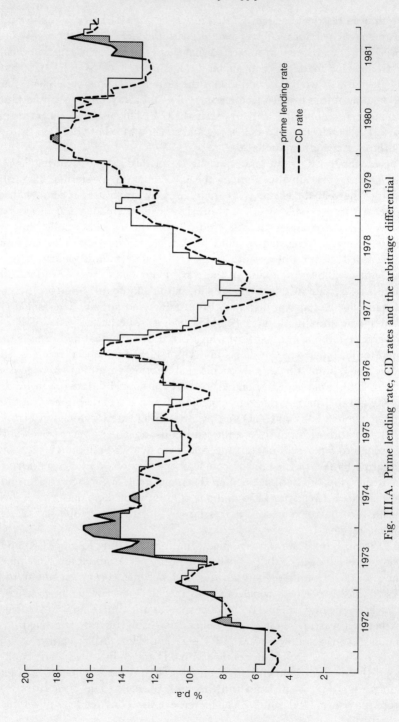

Fig. III.A. Prime lending rate, CD rates and the arbitrage differential

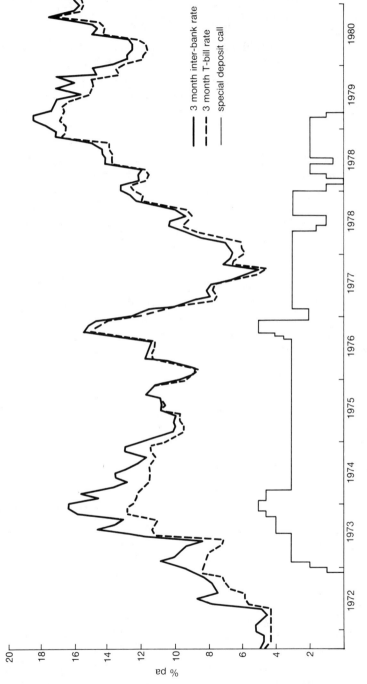

Fig. III.B. Short-term Interest Rate Differentials and the Special Deposit Call

signals to the discount market, triggering a rise in MLR under the formula to 9 per cent on 22 December. The banks were slow to adjust their base rates, confused perhaps by the new system.

In the meantime short-term money-market rates (on both a 7-day and the three-month basis shown in Figure III.A) had increased from 9 to almost 11 per cent, allowing profitable opportunities for 'round tripping'—borrowing from the banks on overdraft in order to invest in money-market instruments, notably CDs. Reflecting this, bank lending to the private sector (together with holdings of CD and other wholesale deposits) rose particularly sharply in the January and February 1973 banking months. The banks put a temporary break on these developments by increasing base rates to $9\frac{1}{2}$ per cent on 25 February. The statistics then indicated a marked fall in the rate of growth of bank lending and the money supply during March, April, and May.[3] The banks' CD issue also fell back, partly in response to the plugging of the CD tax loophole in the 1973 budget. (The effect of this loophole is explained by Gowland (1978) p. 122). Together with a marked strengthening of sterling against the dollar (largely reflecting the weakness of the latter) this encouraged a fall in interest rates. Money market and base rates had fallen back to 8 per cent by the end of June.

The 50 per cent public-sector debt ratio agreed with the discount houses had by this stage proved to have rather disruptive implications for short-term interest-rate differentials. The premium rate of interest on Treasury bills had encouraged the discount houses to keep close to the minimum, so that when the Bank bought these in support of the market, so increasing the premium, they were forced to sell other assets, such as CDs, reinforcing the premium. Given the 'formula' this had the potential to push MLR and T-bill rates in the opposite direction to other rates, and on occasion had forced the Bank into buying assets other than T-bills when supporting the market. So on 19 July (1973) a new agreement was reached with the discount houses. (Bank of England (1973).) They were to limit their holdings of certain 'undefined assets' (essentially bank and other private sector liabilities) to a maximum of twenty times their capital and reserve base (calculated on a three-year moving average basis). This rule was known as the 'undefined assets multiple' and in practice worked much more smoothly than its predecessor.

The fall in interest rates seen during the first half of 1973 proved temporary. Interest rates moved up in international markets during July and the slide in sterling resumed. Moreover, domestic financial conditions were also looking worse, the public-sector deficit was increasing strongly, gilt sales had virtually dried up, and it looked as if this would come through into bank liquidity. In order to tighten the banks position the authorities made a further 1 per cent call for special deposits on 19 July, effective by the end of August. They also tightened up their operations in the reserve-asset market, forcing MLR up to $11\frac{1}{2}$ per cent by 27 July. As they had done in late 1972, bank base rates fell well behind MLR, being raised to only 10 per cent on 2

August and 11 per cent on 22 August. Interest rates in the money markets rose sharply as the banks met the call, reaching $14\frac{1}{2}$ per cent on a three-month basis by the end of August. On this occasion there was little scope for a reduction in their holdings of reserve assets, so the pressure was concentrated in the parallel money markets. Indeed, in contrast to the episode of the previous year, banks continued to expand their portfolios and their demand for reserves—particularly T-bills—rose strongly. Partly because of this, T-bill rates failed to keep up with parallel market rates and the formula triggered a slight fall in MLR (to $11\frac{1}{4}$ per cent) during October. The banks were asked to keep the rates they offered on deposits of less than £10,000 at (or below) $9\frac{1}{2}$ per cent in September, as the authorities became concerned about the pressure on building societies.

The failure of the banks to keep their prime lending rates in line with the market reopened the margins in favour of round tripping, which recommenced on a large scale. This configuration of interest rates is shown quite clearly in Figure III.A. The effect of these differentials more than offset any effect which the rise in lending rates may have had, and private-sector borrowing continued strongly. (This growth was spectacular even when seen in real terms as in Figure II.A.) So on 13 November the authorities tried some more of the same medicine. A further 2 per cent call for special deposits was made bringing the total required by 2 January to 6 per cent. This was a large call in view of the seasonal pressures which would have been anticipated. They did vary their prescription slightly, however, suspending the formula and increasing MLR from $11\frac{1}{2}$ per cent to 13 per cent by administrative decision. Base rates were raised to the same level over the next couple of days. They also attempted to relieve pressure in the parallel money markets by placing funds in the LA deposit and bond markets. Nevertheless, parallel money-market rates continued to rise well beyond posted rates, three-month CD rate reaching 16 per cent early in December, re-establishing the perverse arbitrage differential (again shown in Figure III.A). It became clear that a rather different form of treatment was required, and on 17 December the remaining 1 per cent of the November call was withdrawn and the Supplementary Special Deposit (SSD) scheme announced. This was designed to burst the arbitrage bubble by imposing a steeply increasing marginal cost of deposits upon the banks. The marginal interest-rate cost was effectively doubled if their interest-bearing eligible liabilities exceed the ceiling by more than 3 per cent. Given the prohibitive scale of these costs the scheme effectively acted as a ceiling, giving it its popular name—the 'corset'. The Bank simultaneously restored terms control on hire purchase.

The authorities had evidently reworked their original plan for Competition and Credit Control. However, it is possible to exaggerate the difference between the old design and the new (see, for example, Hall (1983) p. 17). Although this marked the return of quantitiative controls, these were placed on the liability side of bank-balance sheets and not the asset side. This partly reflects the shift in emphasis from credit to monetary control. But the design of the scheme shows that it was aimed at preventing excessive liability management and not necessarily credit expansion. This is a crucial difference and suggests that the authorities still believed that it was possible to control private credit by variations in interest rates, providing that perverse differentials could be avoided. Their new *modus operandi* also points strongly in this direction.

5   The use of short-term market instruments in the later CCC period

Both the banks and the monetary authorities learnt a great deal from the initial CCC experience. Reflecting this hard learning process, the system worked relatively well between the introduction of the SSD scheme in 1974 and the new arrangements of August 1981. Although perverse interest-rate differentials emerged from time to time, both the banks and the authorities were keen to keep their rates in line with money-market rates. This is quite apparent from Figure III.B which shows a convergence of short-term market interest rates after 1973.

Although this was in part due to the authorities frequent reliance upon the SSD scheme the system also seems to have behaved tolerably well over the periods when this device was not in place. This reflects the mounting concern about the effect of the PSBR on monetary growth and the reliance upon gilt sales as a way of countering this. The authorities also became increasingly willing to intervene directly to set MLR instead of relying on the indirect effect of the Treasury-bill rate. This culminated in the announcement of an administered rate from April 1978.

Short-term money-market operations and the special deposit call were largely used as a way of bolstering the desired level of interest rates, and smoothing the effect of the exchequer accounts and other influences on bank liquidity. The pressures on the system were also eased by the considerable reduction in the growth of bank lending between early 1974 and mid-1976. Lending in sterling to the private sector actually fell (by £370 millions) during 1975. Seen in real terms (Figure II.A), against the background of historically very high rates of inflation, the fall in bank lending was every bit as dramatic as the previous rise had been. There were several reasons for this. The first was the unwinding of the money-market arbitrage which had boosted borrowing during the previous two years. This was initially due to the effect of the SSD scheme which compressed market differentials, and within a few months pushed money-market rates well below base rates. Then, as the general level of interest rates came down during 1975 the base-rate lags tended to leave these rates higher than market rates. At the same time the banks, anticipating a recurrence of the merry go round, began to link their wholesale lending rates to money-market rates.

Disintermediation probably also occurred as a result of the secondary banking collapse of 1974, though the main impact of this seems to have been to switch deposits from the secondary institutions to the clearing banks. This shift was largely accommodated by the Bank of England's 'lifeboat' recycling operation. The problem was in large part due to the banks' involvement in the collapse of the property market and lending to property companies was also unwound to some extent during this period as the banks tried to reduce their commitment to this sector. A vivid blow-by-blow account of the crisis is also available in Reid (1982).

Bank lending was also depressed by the recession which began during 1974 and emerged more strongly during 1975. This followed the world-wide recession, triggered by the oil price rises of 1973–4. But it was also the consequence of the large switch of disposable income from companies to persons resulting from the wage explosion of 1974. This depressed company expenditures, leading to a large reduction in the work-force, particularly in manufacturing industry. On the one hand consumers tended to save rather than spend the increase in their disposable incomes, in order to offset the effect of inflation on their savings. Reflecting this, persons tended to reduce their bank borrowing. On the other hand companies, presumably reflecting movements in interest-rate differentials, ran down the liquid assets which they had built up during the previous two years. Both of these effects reduced the rate of monetary growth.

As this winding-down process took place, the authorities felt able to reduce the call for special deposits. They were concerned about the effect of this on bank liquidity, however, and initially did this under the cover of the SSD scheme, and only when money-market conditions were unduly tight. The unwinding of special deposits began on 4 February 1974 as banks' reserve ratios came under seasonal pressure from the exchequer accounts. The call was reduced by $\frac{1}{2}$ per cent. A further reduction of 1 per cent was announced at the end of March, aimed it seems at a reduction in market interest rates. This fall was consolidated by a further reduction of $\frac{1}{2}$ per cent in late April. Then throughout the remainder of 1974 and 1975 the call remained at 3 per cent. The moderation in the rate of monetary growth, helped by the recovery of the gilts and other long-term markets early in 1975, allowed the authorities to suspend the SSD scheme in February of that year. The Special Deposit call was left unchanged until 6 January 1976. With heavy sales of gilts and a large seasonal exchequer surplus anticipated, the Bank announced a reduction of 1 per cent, to be repaid on 10 February when the situation was expected to have eased. This was the first reduction made without the safety net of the SSD scheme and the first time the call was used as a temporary smoothing service.

Later in the year special deposits were used in earnest, as the exchange rate continued to fall and as worries about the PSBR, lending to the private sector, and bank reserve ratios re-emerged. By mid-August, the latter reached 15.2 per cent and looked likely to go higher. MLR was pushed up by market pressures to 13 per cent on 10 September and was soon followed by bank lending rates. This was reinforced by a 1 per cent call for special deposits on the 16th. Although this rekindled sales of gilts, the exchange rate weakened further. So on 7 October MLR was raised to 15 per cent by administrative decision and another 2 per cent call for special deposits was announced. Market interest rates rose across the board (as is clear from Figure III.B) and the rise in MLR triggered a rise in banks' base rates to 14 per cent almost immediately. This implied a prime lending rate of 15 per cent, in line with or only just below most money-market rates. Opportunities for round tripping were very limited on this occasion (Figure III.A).

The authorities reintroduced the SSD scheme on 18 November. Interbank rates remained at high levels, however, as the banks' reserve assets came under the usual seasonal pressure, reinforced by heavy sales of gilts. Half of the payments of special deposits called in October had been postponed on 5 November. This was further postponed during December, and as the pressures on bank reserves intensified the Bank announced, on 13 January 1977, a reduction in the call from 6 per cent to 3 per cent. Both market and administered rates fell back in response. On 27th a further 1 per cent reduction was made but this was announced as temporary.

Interest rates continued to fall as confidence rebounded during 1977 following the agreement with the IMF and the associated public-expenditure cuts. Private borrowing from the banks also fell back as the effects of the high level of interest rates worked through. The monetary figures and banks' reserve ratios were pulled strongly in different directions by this recovery in confidence. The authorities initially tried to moderate the fall in long-term interest rates, resulting in very large sales of gilts. However, they simultaneously pegged the exchange rate, capping it first against the dollar and then, as this weakened against other currencies over the summer, on an effective basis. This provoked large overseas inflows, mainly into bank deposits and other short-term market instruments, offsetting the monetary effects of gilt sales almost exactly and neutralizing the effect on bank reserve ratios. There was therefore no need to vary the special deposit call over this period.

Although monetary growth during the first half of 1977 was not an immediate concern to the authorities, the capping of the exchange rate was achieved at the expense of a drastic reduction in short-term interest rates. MLR was reduced to 5 per cent in October. This faced the authorities with a choice between the exchange-rate peg and the newly announced monetary targets. In the event they opted for the latter, lifting the cap on sterling in October. The discussion of this episode is taken up in Chapter VII.

6   The effect of the CCC reforms on the structure of clearing-bank deposit liabilities

It is interesting, by way of conclusion, to note the effects of these developments upon the liability structure of clearing banks' balance sheets. Unfor-

Table III.3. Changes in the structure of LBC deposits during the 1970s (end-November, £ million)

	1971	1972	1973	1974	1975	1976
A. *Branch retail deposits*						
(i) current accounts	6,312	6,932	7,179	7,498	8,806	9,499
(ii) 7-day deposits	4,612	4,874	6,060	8,038	8,337	8,238
(Total)	(10,924)	(11,806)	(13,239)	(15,536)	(17,143)	(17,737)
B. *Wholesale deposits*						
(i) branch wholesale deposits	—	901	2,790	4,041	3,976	4,890
(ii) inter-bank deposits (gross)	287	541	1,357	1,115	716	817
(iii) CD issues	156	1,230	2,112	1,523	581	862
(Total)	(434)	(2,672)	(6,259)	(6,679)	(5,273)	(6,569)
C. Gross deposits (A + B)	11,358	14,532	19,498	22,215	22,419	24,303
D. CD holdings and inter-bank claims	284	1,406	2,486	3,213	2,800	2,757
E. Net deposits (C − D)	11,074	13,126	17,012	19,002	19,619	21,549

Source: Table 4, p. 119, Vol. V, *Evidence on the Financing of Industry and Trade* (Wilson (1978)); and Table 8/2 B of E *Bulletin*, various issues.

Table III.4. Sectoral holdings of sterling money-market instruments (end 1978)

	Banks in UK	Discount market	Public sector	Other financial institutions	Other domestic sectors	Overseas sector	Total
Money at call with discount market	3,452	10	18	493		31	4,004
Treasury bills	892	1,006	209	135	75	436	2,813
Commercial bills[a]	1,202	1,925	..	..	..	..	3,393
Local-authority bills	155	62	..	46	836	—	499
Other local-authority tempory debt	537		870	1,701			44
Deposits with finance houses	377	—		117		402	71
Inter-bank deposits	13,104	65	—	—	—		13,205
Sterling certificates of deposit	2,167	368	—	612	438	93	3,678
Other market loans by the banking sector	4,581			—	—	—	4,581

[a]No details are available of sector holding of acceptances outside the banking sector.
Source: Wilson (1978) Appendix III, p. 511.

tunately the regular banking statistics collected at the time did not offer the kind of detailed information required for such an analysis, distinguishing only between sigh deposits (essentially current accounts), CDs, and other time deposits. However, a useful breakdown on an annual basis for the years 1971–6 was provided by the London Clearing Banks (LCBs) as part of their evidence to the Wilson Committee (Wilson (1978)). This has been summarized in Table III.3. Since June 1982 these kind of data have been collected as part of the regular banking statistics, and is used in the construction of the new M2 series.[4]

Table III.3 shows the strong contrast between the growth of the retail and wholesale elements of the LCB's deposits during 1972 and 1973. Retail deposits increased by only £2.3 billion (20 per cent) during these two years whilst wholesale deposits, including those taken in through the branch networks, grew by £5.8 billion. These figures were no doubt swollen artificially by arbitrage transactions, though it is interesting to note that branch wholesale deposits continued to grow strongly during 1974—after the arbitrage bubble had been pricked—reaching 21 per cent of total net deposits by November of that year. Taking the LCBs together with their subsidiaries, their total wholesale deposits reached 45 per cent of total sterling deposits by the end of 1976 and have apparently remained at about this level since (Wilson (1978)V, paragraph 15). The LCBs clearly used the opportunities opened up by the abandonment of the cartel to become more competetive in both the money markets and at a branch level. They were no longer the kind of passive creatures envisaged by the orthodox model. Even so, they faced continued pressure from the secondary banks, and reflecting this, their share of total sterling deposits continued to fall during 1971–4. The markets in other short-term instruments continued to develop over this period, as is evident from Table III.2. A sectoral breakdown of money-market holdings is shown in Table III.4.

Notes

1. MLR was to equal T-bill rate rounded up to the nearest $\frac{1}{4}$ per cent, plus $\frac{1}{2}$ per cent.
2. The effect of the former on their reported reserve-asset position was however offset as £500 million of their short gilt holdings matured into reserve assets.
3. Lending grew by 4 per cent over three months, as against 9 per cent over the previous three.
4. The introduction of this new definition was primarily motivated by concern about the appropriateness of M1 as a measure of balances held for transactions purposes It may prove a more reliable indicator than sterling M3 in some circumstances since it excludes wholesale deposit items. The new aggregate includes:
    (*a*) notes and coin in circulation
    (*b*) all non-interest-bearing sight deposits
    (*c*) all other deposits (regardless of size and maturity) on which cheques can be drawn and

(*d*)   other 'retail' deposits (i.e. deposits of less than £100,000 having a residual
maturity of less than one month).

The new aggregate covers deposits with the monetary sector, building societies,
and National Savings Bank ordinary accounts but excludes public-sector deposits.
The aim is to include in one definition all deposits which can be readily used for
transactions purposes. A detailed description of this statistic is to be found in the
June 1982 *Bank of England Bulletin*.

IV

The Behaviour of Bank Rates and Lending to the Private Sector

Introduction and summary

The next two chapters review some of the statistical evidence relating to the Competition and Credit Control period, in order to follow up some of the points emerging from the review of the operational experience and help clear up some of the ambiguities emerging from the theoretical treatment set out in Appendix II. As far as possible this evidence is presented in the form of econometric relationships which offer a very convenient way of organizing and summarizing such information. A major objective of the analysis is to show up some of the differences between the original control process and that which finally emerged and to throw empirical light on the stability of the system. This work is taken further by the model simulation exercises of Chapter VI.

This chapter begins with a quick look at the way bank lending rates would be determined in a perfectly competitive system and goes on to a simple monthly regression analysis of the behaviour of MLR and base rates; first under the MLR 'formula', Oct. 1972–April 1978; and then under the 'administered MLR', May 1978–Aug. 1981. Since reserve assets act as an imput to the banking process, a fall in reserve-asset rates would increase base lending rates in a competitive system. However, the regression results for the first of these periods show that base rates are positively related to both money-market rates and MLR, with significant lags. MLR of course follows the Treasury-bill rate, so a fall in the latter due to a reserve-asset squeeze tends to reduce base rates and encourage overdraft-arbitrage effects. Over the second period, MLR gives a clear-cut signal of the authorities intentions and is immediately followed by the banks' base rates. Since the authorities keep Treasury-bill rates in line with other market rates no perverse results occur.

These results are discussed in the light of the London Clearing Banks' submission to the Wilson Committee. This evidence shows quite clearly that the banks do not act as short-run profit maximizers and that they like to have a clear lead from the authorities. This could either be because it solves the problem of changing prices in an oligopolistic situation—acting as a signal to the market—or because it makes a change in base rates easier to sell to the general public. In either case this strongly indicates market imperfection.

No evidence was found to suggest that base-rate changes reflected an excess demand for bank credit. Prima facie, this suggests that the loan market is usually in some kind of disequilibrium. Two empirical models of the credit market which allow for this are then discussed. The first is the Artis (1978) model in which some unobservable variable, such as repayment structure, collateral, or other terms effectively clears the market, even though loan rates do not. This results in a linear reduced form explaining the quantity of lending in terms of factors influencing demand and supply, including the loan rate. Empirical research has generally found that this approach (or in some cases a pure demand-side approach) best explains company borrowing. The second is the classical model in which the quantity is set by the short side of the market, and equals the minimum of demand and supply. This is the basis of my model of lending to the personal sector.

The empirical work suggests that most of the increase in lending to persons and financial companies which followed the 1971 reforms was due to the frustrated demand left over from the previous regime, reflected in official restraint and CCC shift dummies. The demand-dominated nature of the specification, and the insignificance of restraint dummies, suggests that this was of little relevance to company borrowing. And yet a CCC shift dummy is significant in this context, perhaps reflecting the dramatic improvement in branch wholesale deposit facilities remarked upon in the previous chapter, which companies were well placed to take up. Overdraft-arbitrage indicators also have a very significant effect on company borrowing.

1   A theoretical perspective

A paper by Stiglitz and Weiss (1981) offers a very useful theoretical background to any discussion of bank rates and credit rationing. This considers a competitive system in which banks raise deposits in a perfect market and mark up the rate charged to borrowers (r_B) in order to cover default risk, so that the expected return (p) equals the deposit rate. They note that the rate a bank charges is likely to affect the riskiness of its loan portfolio $[p = p(r_B)]$. They show that an increase in this rate will tend to discourage borrowers undertaking safer types of investment (the adverse selection effect) and cause those who are still prepared to borrow to undertake riskier investments (the adverse incentive effect). These effects are likely to remain even after banks have discriminated between loan applications on the basis of observable criteria, since they derive from the imperfection of the banks information set.[1]

Stiglitz and Weiss give examples of cases in which these effects are significant enough to make the expected return a decreasing function of the bank lending rate after a certain critical value (r_B^*) is reached. An example is shown in Figure IV.A(i). This phenomenon imposes an effective upper limit to bank lending (and deposit) rates. Banks will not charge higher rates than

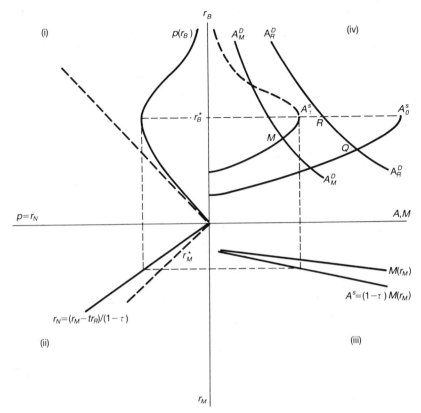

Fig. IV.A. A model of a competitive banking system with credit rationing

this since they know that on average the returns on such lending will be lower than if they charged r_B^*. If loan demand at this rate exceeds the supply of deposits they will simply ration credit.

A relatively simple model which takes account of this point, whilst allowing for the role of reserve assets, may be developed by assuming that the banks only hold advances (A) and reserve assets (R) and supposing that the latter are held as a fixed proportion (τ) of deposits. It will be assumed here that deposits are all of a competitive money-market variety (M) bearing a rate of interest (r_M). In order to raise a pound's worth of finance for lending a bank must then raise $£(1 - \tau)^{-1}$ in the money markets. If reserve assets bear an interest rate of r_R, then the marginal cost of these deposits will be $r_M(1 - \tau)^{-1}$, offset by returns of $r_R\tau(1 - \tau)^{-1}$ on the associated reserves. The net unit cost is therefore:

$$r_N = (r_M - \tau r_R)/(1 - \tau). \tag{1}$$

A relationship of this form is shown in Figure IV.A (ii) assuming a fixed reserve-asset rate. In a competitive system the net cost of deposits will be equated with the expected rate of return on loans ($p = r_N$).[2] Figures (i) and (ii) show how the maximum economic loan rate r_B^* dictates the maximum money market rate r_M^*. The general relationship between these rates is given by:

$$p(r_B) = r_N = (r_M - \tau r_R)/(1 - \tau) \qquad \text{if} \qquad r_M \leq r_M^* \qquad (2)$$

which, assuming $p(r_B)$ to be an increasing function of r_B over this range, may be inverted to give a bank-lending rate equation:

$$\begin{aligned} r_B &= p^{-1}(r_N) \\ &= f(r_M, r_R, \tau) \end{aligned} \qquad (3)$$

where $f_{rM} \geq 1$, $f_{rR} \leq 0$, $(f_{rM} + f_{rR}) \geq 1$

and $f_\tau \geq 0$ \qquad if \qquad $r_M \geq r_R$

The links between the loan, deposit, and reserve-asset markets are given by relationships determining the bank demand for reserves ($R = \tau M$) and the supply of advances ($A^s = (1 - \tau)M$) in terms of the non-bank demand for deposits ($M(r_M)$). These relationships are shown in Figure IV.A (iii). Taken together, these various equations define the loan supply curve shown in Figure IV.A (iv).

This simple system is completed by specifying the non-bank demand for bank loans as a function of the lending rate ($A^D(r_B)$). Provided that there is an excess supply of loans at r_B^*, then a non-rationing equilibrium will occur (as at M, for example, given A_M^D). However, if there is an excess demand at this rate (as at R, given A_R^D) a rationing equilibrium will occur.

The effect of changes in monetary-policy instruments in this model depends critically upon which of these solutions obtains. Consider for example the effect of a reduction in reserve asset requirements (τ). This has the effect of rotating the r_N and A^s lines in Figure IV.A (ii) and (iii) in an anticlockwise direction. Since the relationship between lending rates and expected returns [(i)] is unaffected, this causes the loan supply curve in (iv) to move rightwards, without changing r_B^*. The limiting case is reached at A_0^s when there are no reserve requirements.

If a non-rationing equilibrium occurs in the initial situation, as at M for example, then a reduction in reserve requirements causes the system to move down along the loan-demand curve so that bank lending rates fall, deposit rates rise, and the level of intermediation increases. Yet if the initial situation is one in which rationing occurs, such reductions simply increase the supply of credit at unchanged lending rates. Lending rates are only affected if and when the supply of credit rises to meet the demand prevailing at r_B^*, at which point the non-rationing solution obtains. For example, if the initial position is described by A_τ^s and A_R^D in (iv), then the system initially moves from A_τ^s to R and then down the demand curve to Q. Although this analysis is a partial one, in that it assumes a fixed cost of reserve assets and abstracts from other assets, these assumptions are readily relaxed as Appendix II shows.

The phenomenon of credit rationing is important from the policy perspective since it opens up an avenue through which monetary policy might affect the economy even when the interest elasticity of expenditure is low. This point was well appreciated during the 1950s and 1960s and underpinned the 'availability doctrine' of the time. The recent theoretical interest in availability effects and credit rationing stems from the realization that such effects may not only be the result of official interference or monopolistic tendencies but may be a natural feature of competitive credit markets.

The Stiglitz–Weiss explanation of credit rationing is a very subtle one, and it would be difficult to test for such effects in empirical work. In the case of the UK such phenomena would in any case have been hidden by effects stemming from the imperfectly competitive nature of the system and the actions of the authorities. The competitive model is nevertheless an essential reference point for an examination of such markets. In particular, it provides (via equation (3)) an interesting specification of the behaviour of lending rates against which empirical relationships can be compared in order to gauge the degree of market imperfection.

2 The empirical relationship between administered and market rates

Some simple monthly regression equations relating the banks' prime lending rate to market interest rates and MLR are shown in Table IV.1. These are estimated over the period October 1972–August 1981 during which the Bank announced an MLR, under the formula until April 1978 and by administrative decision thereafter. Figure III.A displays the basic data used in this study and shows clearly the large differentials which occurred during the early part of the period. The significance of the coefficient on the lagged base-rate term in the first equation, estimated over the full period, reflects the tendency for bank rates to lag behind other rates. This may reflect the stickiness of administered prices often seen in an oligopolistic market due to the uncertain outcome facing the firm which moves first. As a check on the effect of such stickiness, the second regression shows the result of running the same specification over the months during which base rates actually changed. Although this reduces this inertial coefficient by a factor of two, it remains significant, suggesting that some additional kind of lag was at work, or perhaps that the equation is in some way misspecified. I initially tried checking this by introducing other explanatory variables, indicating the excess demand for bank advances and the like, but without finding any of these to be significant.

The significant weight attached to the Treasury-bill rate in this equation clearly reflects the role played by MLR in the banks' decision process. This effect is shown directly in the third equation, which is in other respects very little different. The next two regressions re-estimate this equation over the

Table IV.1. Some simple monthly regression results for base rate and MLR (t-statistics in parentheses)

Dependent variable	Estimation period	Number of obs	Regression statistics			Constant	Coefficients on			
			R²	DW	ESE	Constant	LDV[b]	Interest rates		
								CDs[c]	T-bills[c]	MLR
1. Base rate	Oct. 1972–Aug. 1981	106	0.9704	—	0.4889	−0.1281 (1.09)	0.4235 (10.47)	0.1663 (2.97)	0.3872 (5.93)	—
2. Base rate	Oct. 1972–Aug. 1981[a]	42	0.9603	—	0.5103	0.5026 (1.02)	0.2516 (4.96)	0.1476 (1.58)	0.5513 (5.27)	—
3. Base rate	Oct. 1972–Aug. 1981[a]	42	0.9503	—	0.4499	0.1278 (0.52)	0.2368 (5.31)	0.1432 (1.92)	—	0.5838 (6.83)
4. Base rate	Oct. 1972–Apr. 1978[a]	31	0.9769	—	0.3313	0.0874 (0.20)	0.3474 (8.30)	0.3205 (4.87)	—	0.2726 (3.31)
5. Base rate	May 1978–Oct. 1981[a]	11	0.9963	—	0.1698	0.0962 (0.15)	0.0040 (0.10)	0.0524 (0.69)	—	0.9332 (12.78)
6. Base rate	May 1978–Oct. 1981[a]	11	0.9963	—	0.1590	0.1034 (0.45)	—	0.0565 (0.91)	—	0.9325 (13.70)
7. Base rate	May 1978–Oct. 1981	38	0.9890	2.081	0.0792	0.0064 (0.01)	—	0.0380 (1.69)	—	0.9666 (48.39)
8. MLR	Oct. 1972–Apr. 1978	67	0.9963	2.276	0.1370	0.8273 (11.38)	—	−0.0105 (0.60)	0.9615 (48.14)	—
9. MLR	May 1978–Aug. 1981	39	0.9435	0.963	0.5931	0.5936 (1.05)	—	0.3157 (1.56)	0.6475 (2.28)	—
10. MLR	May 1978–Aug. 1981[a]	11	0.9174	—	0.6754	0.7178 (0.58)	—	0.1278 (0.33)	0.8515 (1.99)	—
11. MLR	May 1978–Aug. 1981[a]	11	0.9360	—	0.7104 (0.41)	0.5596 (0.01)	0.0707 (0.48)	−0.0085 (1.94)	0.9336	—

[a] Excluding months in which there was no change in the dependent variable.
[b] Lagged dependent variable.
[c] 3-month maturity.

sub-periods during which the two different MLR-setting procedures were in operation, as a check on the structural stability of the bank response. The result (4) for the 'formula' period is very similar to the full-period result. This situation was clearly a complex one and it is doubtful whether a simple equation of this type can capture it adequately. On the other hand, although they are based on relatively few observations, the results (5–7) for the administered-rate period suggest that banks simply followed changes in MLR. There is no evidence at all of inertia in these results. The figure gives the same impression and this may be confirmed by a more detailed inspection of the data for this period. This shows that with one or two minor exceptions, banks followed changes in MLR point for point, within a few days of the change being announced. In this situation the Bank of England seems to have acted as a market leader, resolving the problem of the first move. In order to explain the behaviour of base rates over this period it is therefore necessary to explain the behaviour of MLR.

Some simple regression results using MLR as the dependent variable are reported in the table. Equation 8 is run over the first sub-period and repro-duces 'the formula' quite closely. The second runs the same specification over the administered rate period. The low Durbin–Watson statistic in this equation is worrying since it indicates a possible dynamic or other mis-specification. However, a more detailed analysis of this period shows that the authorities have been quick to respond to changes in market rates where these have been significant, and have indeed led the market on several occa-sions. This is reflected in the last two equations which are estimated over periods in which MLR changed—periods in which large changes in market rates occurred.

None of the coefficients in these administered-rate equations are very well determined. This reflects the high degree of collinearity between the bill and money-market rates, a result of the attempts by the authorities to keep these rates in line. However, the stability analysis of Appendix II tells us that in such a situation the overall weight given to market interest rates is all we need to know. Although there must be some doubt about the simple nature of the specification, the coefficients in these equations are close to unity in sum. This tends to confirm the impression given by the commentary of the pre-vious chapter that the administered MLR version of the CCC system was a robust one. On these results it would certainly appear to have been a lot more robust than the MLR-formula based version.

It would be a little premature to comment on the behaviour of base rates under the August 1981 arrangements. Under this system the authorities do not in the normal course of events post an MLR—though they are prepared to rediscount bills for the discount market at discretionary rates. Figure III.A reveals that banks were slow off the mark when market interest rates rose in the autumn of 1981, allowing an arbitrage differential to develop for any customers who could still borrow on overdraft at prime rates. However, this does not appear to have had any dramatic effect on borrowing and since then the banks have kept their rates in line with the market.[3]

Despite extensive checks, none of these results suggested that base rates responded to the degree of excess demand pressure in the loan market. The implication is that this market will usually be in a state of dynamic dis-equilibrium. It is therefore important to allow for this when attempting to model the loan market.

3 A possible rationalization

These econometric results simply describe the behaviour of bank rates and do not in themselves offer much by way of explanation. This response is difficult to rationalize. I have already remarked upon the lags observed over the period in which the formula applied and suggested that these were due to the imperfect nature of the market. However, there are aspects of these results which are rather more difficult to explain on economic grounds.

The first is the strong positive correlation observed between MLR and base rates. This would perhaps have been reasonable had the MLR actually represented a penal rate at which the banks could (indirectly) have borrowed in a crisis. The old 'Bank Rate' had originally fulfilled this role when banks relied upon their call money with the discount market (and similar items) as a source of liquidity. But as these arrangements became formalized into a system of requirements banks tended to keep to these fairly closely, relying first upon holdings of secondary reserves and then issues of wholesale deposits as the prime source of liquidity. Indeed, as we have seen, the authorities relied upon this kind of effect when designing their control mechanism and then tried to keep bank liquidity tight in order to retain control. As long as Bank of England assistance was confined to switches between reserve assets and cash and the scope for discount-market arbitrage between reserve and parallel markets was limited, there was little reason for the banks to keep their weather eye on MLR. Inter-bank rates were probably more important in this respect.

It is well known that firms in an olipopolistic market often use some exogenous variable as a signal to a change in prices, even though it may be of little direct relevance. This is a form of implicit collusion. The banks' reaction to MLR under the administered rate system—when it offered a clear signal of the authorities' intentions—can perhaps be rationalized in this way. This does not, however, offer a very good explanation of behaviour under the formula which was designed to de-politicize MLR and make the banks look more towards market rates. Indeed, the analysis of Section 2 would suggest a negative relationship between base rates and MLR given the link between MLR and reserve-asset rates implied by the formula.

Very few of these economic considerations feature in the banks own expla-nations of their base-rate setting procedure, such as that given in the evidence of the LCBs to the Wilson Committee (Wilson (1978), paragraphs 211–16). Although they note the discriminatory effect on margins of their $1\frac{1}{2}$ per cent requirement for bankers' balances (which did not apply to the non-clearers), there is no mention of any similar reserve-asset effect. Indeed, the clearing banks have always stressed the importance of average rather than marginal costs. In this particular submission they do nevertheless accept the importance of avoiding disruptive arbitrage differentials:

> In determining the level of its base rate each of the banks has to take into account not only the average cost of its total funds, and the net operating costs of collecting deposits, but also the cost of funds on the wholesale money markets. For if its base rate is seriously out of line with market rates, disruptive shifts in deposits and borrowing can result. Indeed if the gap is too wide, it can pay a company to borrow from the bank and deposits the funds on the money markets. These so-called 'arbitrage' operations occurred on a significant scale in 1972–1973.

> Thus when short-term interest rates as a whole rise sharply—as they did for instance at the direct instigation of the Authorities in November 1973 and September 1976—the banks must raise their base rates by similar amounts. Indeed the banks would effectively be defying official policy if they failed to do so. The banks have, however, usually managed to hold their base rates a little below market rates when the latter have been high. In this way the banks have been able to pass on some of the so-called 'endowment' effect to their borrowing customers.

The second of these paragraphs makes it quite clear that the banks to not set base rates in order to maximize profits, at least in the short run. When interest rates are high they pass on some of their endowment profits to borrowers. This presumably helps maintain the goodwill of their customers, a characteristic of the Okun (1975)—Hicks (1982) analysis of pricing behaviour in imperfect markets. It also reduces the adverse publicity that the banks tend to get when their profits increase at a time when those in other industries are being squeezed. This was almost certainly a major factor in 1972 and 1973. This behaviour is of course consistent with the maximization of long-term profit subject to the constraints imposed by the customer relationship and the threat of nationalization or excess-profit taxes.

In this respect it is interesting to note the attention drawn in this submission to the actions of the authorities in the autumn months of 1973 and 1976. During these crises MLR was raised with a maximum of publicity, usually by administrative decision. The banks evidently felt it easier to raise their base rates in response to this kind of move, rather than in response to market pressures. This might just reflect a signalling effect. But it seems more plausible to view this as a public-relations effect: by following a rise in MLR the banks were able to say that they were just implementing the interest-rate policies desired by the monetary authorities.

Of course, it is sometimes said that the authorities wanted to see a low level of interest rates during the early years of CCC and kept Treasury-bill rates and MLR down in order to achieve this. As the commentary showed, they certainly seemed reluctant to see a large rise in building-society interest rates. However, such a strategy would only have worked if bank rates followed MLR rather than money-market rates. So even if one accepts this explanation, the instability of the original CCC system still indicates a high degree of market imperfection.

4 Empirical models of the loan market

The dramatic behaviour of the money and bank-credit aggregates during the early 1970s has been discussed in previous chapters. These developments were obviously due to in some way to the removal of the restrictions on base rates and lending. However, there are at least four different effects which could have been at work:

(i) the frustrated demand left over from the previous regime;

(ii) competition in the loan market;

(iii) competition in the deposit market;

(iv) the development of perverse interest-rate differentials.

I have already argued—so far on an informal basis—that the first of these effects was significant in the case of borrowing by persons and financial companies, but not in the case of borrowing by industrial companies. In order to check this kind of proposition it is necessary to develop empirical models of bank lending to these sectors, allowing for the likelihood of credit rationing, particularly 'disequilibrium rationing' stemming from sticky lending rates. In an attempt to model such disequilibrium effects it is assumed that each sector's demand for bank credit can be represented by a linear function of interest rates, investment opportunities, and other variables. It is also assumed that the amount of such lending banks want to accommodate at any given interest-rate structure can be represented by a linear supply function.[4] If the interest rate were to move such demands and supplies into line then we could solve for the equilibrium price and quantity, and attempt to explain these in a conventional way. But as we have seen, bank base rates are in practice sticky—strongly influenced by the monetary authorities.

There are two possible ways of proceeding in such circumstances. A relatively simple model results if it is assumed that there exist unobservable variables which will adjust sufficiently quickly to clear the market if prices do not. Several such variables can be found in the bank-credit market. For example, published credit aggregates cover overdrafts, commercial bills, fixed-term loans, and in more recent years mortgage, factoring, and leasing arrangements. So if there were an excess demand for one type of loan the banks might be able to pursuade their clients to accept a less convenient form of finance, this having the effect of increasing supply and decreasing demand at unchanged interest rates. Similarly, the maturity or repayment structure of a loan might be changed to suit either party or banks might be prepared

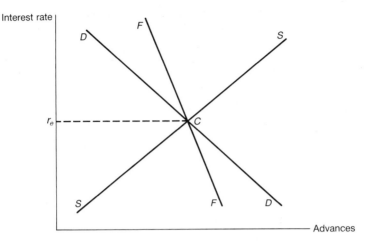

Fig. IV.B. Empirical models of the loan market

to increase their lending to customers offering collateral. Alternatively, the terms of the project to be financed might be variable—bank accountants are often involved at an early stage in commercial ventures and besides offering advice can often persuade firms to reconsider features which they find objectionable. Such factors might be flexible enough to shift demand and supply into line at the existing rate structure. In terms of Figure IV.B, changes in lending rates induce shifts in the demand and supply schedules ensuring that they always intersect no matter what the rate, generating a locus of pseudo-equilibrium points such as FF'.

If the underlying model is linear it is possible to solve for the quantity of credit as a linear function (or pseudo-reduced form) of observable demand and supply factors, including the bank rate. For example, if demand and supply both depend upon some unobservable market clearing variable Z and a vector of observable factors X we have the simple model:

$$A^D = a_1 Z + b_1'X + e_1 \qquad\qquad 4(a)$$
$$A^S = a_2 Z + b_2'X + e_2 \qquad\qquad 4(b)$$
$$A = A^S = A^D \qquad\qquad 4(c)$$

Model 1: Pseudo market equilibrium

and we can solve for A as:

$$A = \frac{(a_1 b_1 - a_2 b_2)'X + a_1 e_2 - a_2 e_1}{a_1 - a_2}$$

Unfortunately there are several problems with this simple solution.[5] The most apparent is that even if this kind of system is identified in the usual econometric sense (Goldberger (1964) p. 306) by exclusion or other restrictions on the structural parameters (a, b) we cannot solve for these in the usual way since we cannot estimate a twin reduced-form equation for the market-clearing variable. It is also difficult to think of a priori restrictions to apply in such a situation; we just have to accept what the data tell us. Nevertheless, this simple model has been applied to several financial markets, notably by Norton (1969) and Artis (1978) to clearing-bank advances and Riley (1976) to building-society mortgages. Linear bank-credit models incorporating both demand and supply influences, presumably based on this kind of rationale, have also been estimated by Savage (1978). Work by Bank of England researchers on company borrowing (Moore and Threadgold (1985)) has, however, emphasized demand factors, and has found that supply factors are insignificant in some specifications. This is consistent with their view that given the prevailing level of interest rates banks automatically meet demands which are related to the cost of financing production.

In the absence of a non-price market-clearing variable it is reasonable to suppose that in such circumstances the observed quantity of lending will be dictated by the short side of the market, and will equal the minimum of demand and supply. So we have:

$$A^D = b_1'X + e_1 \qquad\qquad 5(a)$$
$$A^S = b_2'X + e_2 \qquad\qquad 5(b)$$
$$A = \text{Min}\ (A^D, A^S) \qquad\qquad 5(c)$$

Model 2: Market Disequilibrum

The locus of price and quantity points traced out by movements in the interest rate under this assumption is shown by the locus DCS in Figure IV.B If interest rates are initially low and we have an excess-demand situation, rises in lending rates will induce an increase in supply and hence observed lending until the situation becomes one of excess supply (at r_0). Further increases in rates impinge upon demand and hence reduce observed lending. This kind of switch is difficult to handle econometrically, but the likelihood function for this problem has been derived by Maddala and Nelson (1974), allowing maximum-likelihood estimation methods to be employed. These techniques have been used to investigate the US loan market by Laffont and Garcia (1977).

5   An empirical model of bank lending to industrial and commercial companies

My preliminary work on bank lending to industrial and commercial companies (ICCs) showed that this was dominated by demand-side influences. Official credit-restraint variables developed by Norton (1969) and Artis (1978) were not significant. Indeed, the only significant variables which could have been rationalized as supply factors were shift dummies reflecting the introduction of CCC. Once this effect was allowed for, variables showing the lending resources of the banks (the capital and retail-deposit base) became insignificant.

This work was strongly influenced by the precautionary-demand analysis of Miller and Sprenkle (1981) discussed in Section II.6 and Appendix I. This views overdraft or liability-side liquidity as an alternative to the more traditional asset-side liquidity offered by cash balances. Miller and Sprenkle show that when transactions needs are uncertain, companies will strike a balance between these two forms of liquidity—trying to avoid both surplus cash balances and excessive overdrafts. Because the opportunity cost of the former is related to the overall level of market interest rates whilst that of the latter is related to the much smaller differential between market rates and overdraft rates, companies will usually find it profitable to keep their bank accounts in overdraft, placing any surplus funds in the money markets. This model suggests that it will be optimal to behave in such a way even if overdraft rates exceed money-market rates. Moreover, in this model a rise in the overall level of interest rates— increasing the cost of asset-side liquidity but leaving the cost of liability-side liquidity unchanged—will tend to *increase* the level of borrowing.

In Appendix I, I introduce speculative assets and risk aversion into this model in order to develop a more comprehensive specification of the demand for money. This analysis shows that the basic Miller and Sprenkle results still stand, although the introduction of risk aversion naturally tends to diminish the tendency towards liability management. It also shows that given certain assumptions about the distribution of cash flows, the model can be solved analytically to show the level of overdraft borrowing as a non-linear function of various bank charges and interest rates, the overdraft limit and the variance of transactions—independently of the overall financial position and the returns on speculative assets (equation (28) of Appendix I). The company arbitrage indicator (RMS) employed in the company-bank borrowing equation employs formula (28) of Appendix I, and is based on the theory developed by Miller and Sprenkle. In order to use this formula it is necessary to make some assumption about the rate of return paid on holdings of sight deposits (c), which I assumed to be 3 per cent over this period. Assuming that the aggregate overdraft limit (Q) is constant and that the unauthorized overdraft rate (p) is a constant mark-up (k) over prime lending rate, gives the formula:

$$\text{RMS} = \log\left[(r_P - r_L + ((r_P - r_L)^2 + K(r_P - 3))^{1/2}\right] - \log(r_P - 3) \quad (6)$$

where $K = k \exp(-\alpha Q)$ and K is assumed to be constant.[6] This formula is general enough to represent both hard arbitrage effects (those movements of funds which take place when r_L exceeds r_P) and soft arbitrage (or substitution) effects.

Of course, this specification only describes the behaviour of companies that are well placed to take advantages of favourable arbitrage opportunities. To be more specific, these companies must be able to borrow from the banks at prime rates and have a net financial position and overdraft limit which

allows them to hold time deposits and similar instruments. It is also important to allow for the behaviour of companies that are not in such a good
position, and need to use their borrowing resources to finance the basic needs
of their business. These companies will tend to borrow more from the banks
when their overall financial position deteriorates. They will also tend to cut
back on their expenditure and borrowing when there is a rise in the general
level of interest rates. In order to allow for these effects the empirical
specification employed here uses terms reflecting inflationary expectations (PE), the level of output (Y), and the level of bank-lending rates (RP) in
addition to the arbitrage indicator designed to represent the behaviour of
cash-rich companies. A typical result obtained using this specification is
presented in Table IV.2.

Table IV.2 tells us quite a lot about the role which company borrowing
played in the drama of the early 1970s. The CCC shift dummy suggests that
the reforms caused a permanent upward shift of about (1975) £2½ billions (or
20 per cent) in bank lending to ICCs. This may have been due to deposit-
market competition, reflected in a general improvement in the terms and
facilities offered to companies, influences which are difficult to capture
econometrically. It may also have been the effect of increased competition in
the loan market or the removal of official restraint, although attempts to
model the latter over the 1960s period would suggest that this was not an
important influence. The shift may in addition have reflected factors unrelated to CCC, such as the breakdown of the debenture market which occurred over the same period.

The company-arbitrage indicator explains almost all of the temporary rise
in borrowing which occurred during the early years of CCC, pushing up
borrowing by 20 per cent during 1973–4 and reducing it by the same amount
during 1975. The above equation suggests that the effects of this kind of
anomaly are quite persistent. For example, a hard arbitrage differential of
one per cent lasting for just one quarter increases the stock of lending
immediately by £1 billion, but this is not run off until fifteen months later.
This lag may, however, be the result of measurement error and other biases
and should be taken with a large pinch of salt. The output variable plays a
very significant role in this specification and the overall effect of a rise in
interest rates is negative—suggesting that there is quite a strong connection
between bank borrowing and expenditure, at least for some companies.

Although this does not play a prime role in the early CCC episode, there is
one other feature of this specification which is worth pointing out at this
stage—it exhibits short-run homogeneity in the price level, represented by
the TFE deflator. (The lending and other counterpart series used in the
initial work were all deflated by the same economy-wide deflator in order to
preserve additivity and facilitate various cross-portfolio coefficient tests.)
This feature of the equation has been checked at several times during its
career. The rapid response to inflationary pressures presumably occurs

Table IV.2. Bank lending to industrial companies 1965(3)–1979(2) (t-statistics in parentheses)

Long run form:

$$\text{LENDIC} = 3616 + 2322 \text{ CCCDUM} - 2270 \text{ RMS} + 0.33\,Y - 419\,r_p + 90\text{PE}$$
$$\quad\;\; (4.0) \quad\; (8.4) \qquad\qquad\;\; (15.0) \qquad (6.1) \qquad (4.5) \quad\; (2.2)$$

$$R^2 = 0.994 \qquad\qquad \text{ESE} = 217\ (1.6\%) \qquad\qquad \text{DW} = 2.08$$

Almon lag distributions[a]:

	CCCDUM		RMS		Y		r_P		PE	
Lag/Var.	A(8,2,10,0)		A(6,4,1,1)		A(5,2,1,0)		A(6,4,1,1)		A(3,2,0.0)	
0	202	(1.0)	−450	(10.1)	0.00	(0.0)	−84	(3.3)	120	(3.0)
1	287	(2.7)	−370	(10.2)	0.08	(4.6)	−62	(3.2)	20	(0.4)
2	339	(7.0)	−370	(9.8)	0.10	(2.8)	−37	(1.6)	−25	(0.6)
3	360	(6.6)	−400	(9.7)	0.10	(1.9)	−54	(2.2)	−25	(0.6)
4	350	(4.4)	−380	(6.5)	0.09	(1.7)	−94	(3.9)		
5	309	(3.5)	−320	(5.9)			−87	(2.9)		
6	286	(3.1)								
7	183	(2.7)								
	2322	(9.4)	−2270	(15.0)	0.33	(6.1)	−419	(4.8)	90	(2.0)

Explanatory variables:

CCCDUM—CCC dummy = 0 before 1971(3), 1 afterwards
RMS—company arbitrage indicator
r_P—prime lending rate
PE—price-expectation indicator
Y—Gross Domestic Product

[a] A(l,o,e,b) where l = lag length, o = polynominal order, and e, b show the number of beginning and end-period restrictions

because these appear first in the costs which companies have to finance. It appears that the TFE deflator works better than other economy-wide measures such as the GDP deflator because of the weight which it gives to import costs. It might be possible to construct a more appropriate price index for this item, but as it stands the TFE deflator works surprisingly well.

This empirical result—which is more apparent from model-simulation results than the regression equation—reveals an important channel through which the exchange rate affects the money supply and prices. Its importance can best be seen from the point of view of the monetary theory of the balance of payments. This empirical result reminds us that domestic credit must be restrained following a devaluation if this is to improve the reserves. Otherwise the increase in the demand for money caused by the rise in the price level will be met from domestic rather than external sources. This result suggests that the domestic components of the money supply will be automatically boosted by a devaluation, rapidly in the case of company borrowing, making them difficult to contain. Although there may be some improvement in the balance of payments if net wealth effects result, the implication is that action on interest rates, public expenditure, and the like will be necessary if a devaluation is to work.

It is difficult to compare this equation with those used by the NIESR and Bank of England since these explain the flow rather than the stock of borrowing (the latter in nominal terms) relating this to the level rather than the change in interest rates (and some of the other explanatory variables). Consequently a rise in lending rates implies a cumulative effect on the long-run stock in these specifications. Nevertheless, the NIESR equation does underline the importance of interest-rate differentials and the CCC shift. The Bank of England's research suggests that the CCC shift is insignificant, but since the round-tripping variable has a permanent effect on the stock of borrowing in their specification it is probably acting in the role of a shift variable. These various specifications are compared in Cuthbertson and Foster (1982).

6 Bank lending to Other Financial Institutions

As was noted in the commentary, bank lending to other financial institutions (OFIs) exhibited a rapid rate of growth during the early 1970s, associated with the ending of controls and developments in the property market. However, very little work has been done on this series and the work which I have

Table IV.3. Bank lending to other financial institutions, 1963(2)–1975(2)

Long-run form:

$$\text{LENDFI} = 650 + 0.339 \, \text{LENDFI}_{-1} + 61.1 \, r_L - 72.6 \, r_P + 192.2 \, \text{CCCDUM}$$

$\quad\quad\quad$ (2.3)$\quad$(3.9)$\quad\quad\quad\quad\quad\quad$(2.1)$\quad\quad$(2.8)$\quad\quad$(3.1)

$$\quad\quad\quad\quad - 30.5 \, \text{REST} - 122.8 \, \text{SSDUM} + 0.082 \, \text{BASE}$$

$\quad\quad\quad$ (2.5)$\quad\quad\quad\quad$(3.1)$\quad\quad\quad\quad\quad$(1.9)

$\quad\quad R^2 = 0.986 \quad\quad\quad \text{ESE} = 93.0 \quad\quad \text{DW} = 2.16$

Almon lag distribution:

lag/var.	r_P A(5,3,1,0)		r_L A(2,2)	
0	−13.6	(0.8)	32.2	(1.8)
1	−26.6	(1.9)	28.9	(1.5)
2	−13.2	(0.9)		
3	−1.1	(0.0)		
4	−18.1	(1.5)		
S	−72.6	(2.8)	61.1	(2.1)

Specific explanatory variables:[7]

REST—Norton/Artis official credit restraint indicator.
SSDUM—dummy variable for SSD Scheme (0, 1)
BASE = BB + WB + $(1 - t)D$ – banks' capital and deposit base.

done has been little more than an attempt to estimate its sensitivity to interest rates and official credit restraint. In view of the difficulty of representing expected rates of return on long-term assets such as property investments no explicit allowance was made for this kind of effect. The original model equation is reported in Table IV.3.

The result of Table IV.3 suggests that lending to OFIs is quite sensitive to supply-side factors, reflected in the three dummy variables and the banks' capital and retail-deposit base. The latter increases the series by £400 millions between the end of 1971 and 1974. Together with the effect of the CCC dummy, this accounts for two-thirds of the real increase in the series over this period.

7 A disequilibrium model of bank lending to persons

Initial work in this area also used a linear model but revealed a great deal of structural instability, suggesting that the market might be switching between demand- and supply-determined regimes. In order to handle this effect the classical disequilibrium model discussed in Section 4 was adopted. It was found that a high degree of explanation could be obtained using relatively few explanatory variables within this framework. Indeed, several variables which are significant in linear models of this series are not significant when introduced into this model. The estimation technique and early experiments are described in Spencer (1976). A typical result is reported in Table IV.4.[8]

Lagged adjustment effects are handled in this specification by introducing the lagged quantity of lending into the separate regime equations. The results suggest that these effects are most relevant in an excess-supply situation when the demand regime is dominant. Interest-rate effects are also important in this case. The low t-values on the interest-rate coefficients in the demand equation reflect the collinearity between market and lending rates

Table IV.4. Bank lending to persons 1963(3)–1977(3)

$\text{LENDPE} = \min(D, S)$

where

$$D = 2824 + 0.847 \, \text{LENDPE}_{-1} - 73.2 \, r_P + 26.1 \, r_M + 0.037 \, \text{YPDI} + 412 \, \text{TREL}$$
$$\quad (2.6) \quad (11.2) \qquad\qquad (1.9) \qquad (1.3) \qquad (4.1) \qquad\qquad (3.8)$$

$$S = 3166 + 0.358 \, \text{LENDPE}_{-1} - 132 \, \text{REST} + 1670 \, \text{CCCDUM} + 27.0 \, (r_P - r_L)$$
$$\quad (4.0) \quad (2.4) \qquad\qquad (2.7) \qquad\qquad (4.3) \qquad\qquad (1.8)$$

$$\text{SE} = 135.1 \qquad\qquad R^2 = 0.9900 \qquad\qquad \text{DW} = 1.92$$

Specific explanatory variables:[7]

TREL—rate of interest at which tax relief is available on personal loans other than for house purchase.
YPDI—real personal disposable income.
REST—Norton–Artis indicator of official restraint.

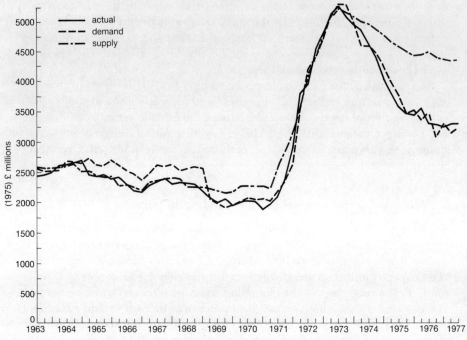

Fig. IV.C. A disequilibrium model of bank lending to persons

which means that the effect of a differential change in interest rates is not
very well determined, even though that of a general increase is. Changes in
interest-rate relief allowed on non-mortgage borrowing were initially allowed
for by introducing both intercept and interest-cost slope dummies but the
collinearity between these variables meant that their separate effect was
indeterminate. Introducing them separately, a better fit is obtained using the
former, as in the reported result. Little evidence was found of interest-rate
effects in the supply regime.

Estimated demand, supply, and observed quantity are shown in Figure
IV.C. The historical picture painted by this graph is a relatively simple one.
The period to the end of 1968 is dominated by the supply regime, restrained
throughout most of this period by official lending requests. Lending is quite
flat in real terms, explaining the insignificance of interest rates and other
variables in the supply equation. Then in 1969 both demand and supply are
depressed, the former by a combination of rising interest rates and the ending
of interest relief on non-mortgage borrowing and the latter by a tightening of
official restraint. They were apparently evenly matched at this low level until
mid-1971 when they both rose dramatically as the restraints were removed
and primary interest-rate relief was reintroduced. The latter obscures the
effect of high interest rates until it is again removed in 1975, pushing demand
below supply. This situation continues until the end of the estimation period,

with demand-side variables such as interest rates and disposable incomes explaining the minor fluctuations in the real stock which occur.

It should be admitted that this specification failed to predict the surge in personal borrowing in recent years. (This is shown in Figure II.A, exaggerated somewhat by the inclusion of bank lending for house purchase.) The reason for this remains something of a mystery. Recent work at the Treasury has attempted to check this using a linear model in order to keep the econometrics simple, but with very little success. Nevertheless, the reported result offers a plausible explanation of the experience of the early 1970s, suggesting that the removal of controls pushed up the equilibrium supply by £2.5 billions. This was mirrored almost exactly by the net effect of tax relief and rising interest rates on demand, so that the estimated quantity rises by a similar amount.

8   The pressures on bank lending in the initial CCC period

These empirical results give a good indication of the pressures which bank lending and liability management imposed upon the early CCC system which are conveniently reviewed under the headings listed in Section 4. The most obvious of these strains was the hangover of frustrated demand from the previous regime. This is in principle captured by the Norton–Artis dummy coefficients. But in view of the large increase in lending which took place when the restraints were lifted—reflected in the CCC shift dummies—it is likely that this variable only shows the effect of variations in the degree of restraint under the old regime, and not the overall effect. The large CCC shift dummies featured in the personal and OFI borrowing equations almost certainly show the effect of removing the controls. Taking these two dummy variables together and interpreting them as the result of item (i), £1½ billion (in 1975 prices) of the increase in lending to OFIs was apparently due to their effect. They also boost bank lending to persons in this specification by £1½ billion between the end of 1970 and 1973. The effect of the reintroduction of primary interest relief on personal borrowing could be considered as an additional exogenous pressure on the system. On my calculations this is worth another £2¼ billion over this period.

It is doubtful whether credit restraint had any significant impact on bank lending to ICCs. The effect of the CCC shift dummy in this equation can reasonably be attributed to increased bank competition in the provision of both deposit and loan facilities to companies. This competition was an integral part of the Bank of England's initial proposal and should be considered as another exogenous factor, worth another £2¼ billion. It is difficult to say to what extent this reflects (ii) rather than (iii). In addition, a hard arbitrage effect worth £2¼ billion has been identified, which should be considered as endogenous since it reflected the dynamics of the system.

Table IV.5. Identified bank-lending pressures in the early 1970s (1975 £ billion)

A.		Exogenous	
	1.	Frustrated demand	
		—OFIs	$1\frac{1}{2}$
		—Persons	1
	2.	Personal interest relief	$2\frac{1}{2}$
	3.	Competition in corporate-banking facilities	$2\frac{1}{2}$
		Total exogenous effect	$7\frac{1}{2}$
B.		Endogenous	
	1.	Corporate arbitrage	$2\frac{1}{2}$
		Total identified effect	10

In order to conclude this chapter it is now interesting to return to return to the question posed in Chapter II and ask in what sense this increase in bank credit affected the demand for money by non-banks. This obviously has important implications for the impact this had upon activity and prices. In the case of companies, the fact that both time deposits and bank loans were observed in individual balance sheets constitutes strong prima facie evidence in favour of some degree of substitution between these items in their port-folios. Changes in their relative rates of return are thus likely to alter the demands for both simultaneously. The Miller–Sprenkle model would suggest that this kind of effect would be significant given the kind of interest levels and differentials seen over the CCC years, and our empirical results tend to confirm this.

Of course, the hard arbitrage effects seen during 1972–3 were reversed during 1974–5, so these have affected the demand for money only temporar-ily. However, this leaves a large question mark hanging over the effects of bank competition in the provision of deposit facilities, and the effect of the very high level of nominal interest rates seen throughout the 1970s. Both of these will have tended to increase companies demands for wholesale money on a more permanent basis and are probably reflected in the shift which appears to have taken place in their borrowing behaviour. These various demand for money effects will have partially neutralized the effect of com-pany borrowing on activity and prices during the early CCC years. Interest-ingly, this kind of argument seems to be accepted by both Artis and Lewis (1976), p. 176, and Coghlan (1981), p. 35–6, who note that an increase in the supply of credit which the banks finance by bidding for funds in the wholesale markets will have very different effects from one which is financed automatically through retail deposits at unchanged interest rates.

It is more difficult to evaluate the effect of the surge in bank credit to persons and OFIs. This was evidently a supply rather than a demand-side effect. These funds were presumably taken out to finance real expenditures or investment in real assets, although it is conceivable that the relaxation of the lending constraint (or perhaps bank competition in deposit markets) caused these sectors to increase their equilibrium demand for money as well. Of course, it was difficult to adjust such expenditures quickly—especially at a sectoral level—and so these funds will have swollen the short-run demand for money.

Notes

1. It is important to note that borrowers are assumed to be honest in this model and do not deliberately intend to default. The effects which dishonest borrowing can have in this kind of situation are analysed by Jaffee and Russell (1976). In their model, risk increases with the size of the loan, as well as the rate, and banks may find it optimal to restrict both.
2. This specification is based on the assumption that banks are expected profit maximizers and therefore neglects risk premiums associated with the uncertainty of returns. This assumption is relaxed in the next chapter in order to motivate the holding of diversified portfolios. However, it is unlikely that such premiums would affect the lending-rate specification significantly.
3. Barclays Bank, for example, has now adopted an explicit formula which sets its base rate in line with money-market rates.
4. This obviously rules out 'equilibrium rationing' of the Stiglitz–Weiss type.
5. Stiglitz and Weiss show that if rationing is optimal due to the presence of adverse selection or incentive effects, it will not pay the bank to vary collateral or other terms in order to remove this. These terms will only be varied if the market fails to clear due to interest-rate inertia or official interference.
6. Experiments with a trend term suggested that the constant specification was quite reasonable. The value of K was estimated by grid search, the best fit being obtained with a value of 0.0005. Although no formal significance tests were conducted, this seemed well determined and extreme values certainly produced a dramatic deterioration in fit. Since (α) is the inverse of the regression coefficient, it is in principle possible to use equation (6) to deduce the subjective penalty costs (k) attached by the average company to infringement of the overdraft constraint, given a plausible value for Q. For example, if $Q = 1975$ £20 billions, just above the maximum value of company borrowing over this period, then $k = 33$ per cent p.a. It is also worth noting that arbitrage formulae such as (6) are highly nonlinear and that my more recent researches have shown that it is better to evaluate them using weekly interest-rate data and then take quarterly averages, rather than to evaluate them using quarterly averages of interest rates as in the present example.
7. Full definitions of these variables are to be found in Spencer and Mowl (1978).
8. These techniques performed little better than linear reduced forms in the case of company borrowing, suggesting that demand side influences were dominant and that credit rationing had not been very extensive in this sector.

V

Bank Portfolio Behaviour and the Wholesale Money Markets

Introduction and summary

The general picture of the pre-1981 system which emerges from the previous chapter is one in which banks follow any lead given by the Bank of England on lending rates and then attempt to accommodate any reasonable requests for loans put to them by their customers, subject to official restraint. There is strong evidence of credit rationing of persons and OFIs during the 1960s but this may not have been important during the 1970s. There is hardly any suggestion that the banks' retail deposit and capital base has constrained their lending or that demand pressures affect lending rates. Lending will to some extent be automatically self-financing through retail deposits, but banks must finance the residual difference between their advances and retail deposits in the wholesale money or other short-term markets. This is essentially the way bankers themselves describe their decision process (Barge and Wise (1977)).

There are various markets in which such a discrepancy can be financed and this chapter examines the way banks go about this. The various balance-sheet items and influences involved are discussed, distinguishing the precautionary factors (which essentially motivate the holding of cash and excess reserves which yield less than other money-capital-safe assets) from the speculative factors (influencing the composition of the rest of the portfolio). The mathematical model used in this work incorporates both of these effects and is set out in Spencer (1984). Here I simply discuss the resulting demand and supply functions and the control requirements which constrain them. I then consider these requirements as a 'tax' on bank intermediation and extend the analogy by asking what the incidence of this 'tax' has been. Empirically it turns out that the elasticity of substitution between wholesale bank deposits and other items in non-bank portfolios such as LA deposits is extremely high, linking their rates of returns together on a 'pre-tax' basis. The tax therefore falls upon banks and not their wholesale customers. This finding means that the parallel money markets can be modelled as a single unified market.

The empirical model of bank portfolio behaviour is discussed in the remaining sections. This is estimated conditional upon the demand for retail deposits and advances and shows that any discrepancy which emerges between these two items (through reserve requirements and leakage into other assets) is almost entirely matched in the parallel money market (by selling

CDs or LA deposits). Given the unified market result it matters little which of these occurs—similar effects on money market rates will emerge in either case. The effect does, however, depend upon the initial configuration of interest rates and the banks' excess-reserve position. If this is initially large the banks run it off as parallel money-market rates increase, reducing the pressure on the parallel money market at the same time. This behaviour will tend to keep Treasury-bill rates and hence base rates in line with other short-term rates, avoiding perverse overdraft-arbitrage effects. If reserves are initially close to the minimum, however, the banks need to acquire reserves as they expand their CD issue, tending to depress their relative rate of return. When the MLR 'formula' is in operation this will also tend to depress base rates relative to other rates, encouraging arbitrage effects. The response of bank portfolios and interest rates to an increase in bank lending or a special deposit call is thus likely to be non-linear and this effect is identified clearly in the empirical results. These non-linearities can be seen most clearly through model simulations, such as those set out in the next chapter.

1 The banks' balance sheet

There are in practice many marketable instruments which the banks can use in order to finance an outflow of funds. In the first instance this will be automatically met out of balances at the Bank of England or till cash, depending upon how their customers run down their accounts. Then there are the traditional call-money, Treasury-bill, and short-term gilt-edged instruments (those with a maturity of less than one year) which constituted the reserve assets of the CCC system. Banks also hold gilts in the 1–5-year maturity range as a secondary reserve, and as I have shown they have been very active in the parallel money markets and to a more limited extent the covered foreign-currency (*fc*) markets. Together with retail deposits and advances, both of which we will regard as exogenous at this stage of the analysis, this gives the balance-sheet representation shown in Table V.1 below. This balance sheet obeys the following budget constraint:

$$WB = AB + LB + GB + FB + MB + RB + CB - DB - BB \quad (1)$$

During the 1970s banks held significant amounts of cash and *excess* reserves in their portfolios, despite the fact that interest yields on these items were usually significantly below those on other items with similar speculative-risk characteristics, such as CDs and LA deposits. It is difficult to rationalize this observation using the kind of mean-variance model employed by Parkin *et al.* (1970) to explain bank behaviour during the 1950s and 1960s. This behaviour can really only be rationalized on precautionary grounds, similar to those used by Grey and Parkin (1973) and Miller and Sprenkle (1981) to explain non-bank behaviour. The model of bank portfolio behaviour which is employed here therefore allows for both the precautionary motive, as a way

Table V.1. A simple representation of a typical bank balance sheet

Liabilities	Assets
DB —retail sterling deposits	AB —advances
BB —net miscellaneous liabilities	CB —cash balances
WB—non-deposit liabilities	RB —reserve assets and special deposits[1]
(net worth and share capital)	LB —local authority securities
	GB —gilt-edged securities
	FB —foreign-currency assets[2] net of liabilities
	MB—money-market position[2] (net claims on inter-bank market less CD issues)

[1,2]See notes at end of chapter.

of rationalizing such balances, and the speculative motive as a way of explaining holdings of other items such as gilts.

2   The original CCC conventions

Under the CCC conventions banks had to hold at least $12\frac{1}{2}$ per cent of certain 'eligible liabilities' as reserve assets and in addition keep a variable fraction in the form of special deposits with the Bank of England (Bank of England (1971b)). In terms of our balance-sheet variables, we may define these eligible liabilities[3] as retail sterling deposits (D) plus net money-market deposits $(-M)$. Now let τ represent the reserve-asset ratio plus the special deposit call (both expressed as fractions), so that these two rules may be written as a single condition:

$$RB \geq \tau(DB - MB) \qquad (2)$$

In order to satisfy this condition in the face of random changes in deposit and overdrafts banks need to maintain a certain amount of slack in the equality. It is therefore convenient to rewrite this in terms of holdings of excess reserves (X):

$$X = RB - \tau\,(DB - MB) \geq 0 \qquad (3)$$

Since there was no cash-ratio rule under CCC banks had simply to satisfy their customers in this respect, maintaining precautionary balances in order to do this. It is not clear what penalties, if any, the banks faced for failing to observe these rules. But in order to motivate the holding of precautionary balances it is assumed that if initial holdings of cash or reserves are deficient the bank has to make an unplanned sale of some other instrument, or perhaps face embarrassment costs.

3   Excess reserves and the net money-market position

In view of these conventions it is important to distinguish between excess and required reserves. The distinction between retail and money market deposits also makes it important to differentiate between reserves required against the former, which we shall consider to be exogenous to the bank's decision procedure (and represented by $T = \tau DB$), and those held against the latter (τMB) which are clearly endogenous to the problem. In order to deal with the latter it is useful to consider the money-market position net of such requirements, where this is defined as:

$$N = (1 - \tau)MB \tag{4}$$

The transformed variables X and N are the natural working variables in this problem given these conventions and so the bank's budget constraint will thus be rewritten as:

$$WB = LB + GB + FB + N + CB + X + T + AB - DB - BB \tag{5}$$

The risk and return characteristics of the composite items X and N depend in a fairly obvious way upon those of their component items. For example, a bank must issue $£(1 - \tau)^{-1}$ worth of money-market deposits in order to obtain a pound's worth of net finance to increase non-reserve assets or excess reserves. Following the discussion of Section IV.2 the return on the net money-market position given the original CCC conventions may be written as:

$$
\begin{aligned}
r_N &= (r_M - \tau r_R)/(1 - \tau) \\
&= r_M + t
\end{aligned} \tag{6}
$$

where $\qquad t = (r_M - r_R)/(1 - \tau)$

Such requirements are often interpreted as a tax on bank intermediation, and expression (8) is typical of those which emerge from this kind of approach (compare Equation (1) in Wills (1981) for example). The net money-market rate may in this sense be viewed as a 'post-tax' rate. The formula shows quite clearly that the post-tax rate (r_N) will exceed the pre-tax rate (r_M) as long as this exceeds the reserve-asset rate (r_R). The wider implications of this kind of effect have been studied by Wills (1981) and Spencer (1982). Figure V.A shows the 3-month inter-bank rate on a 'pre-tax' basis together with the implied reserve asset and special-deposit tax. The effect of the large gap which opened up between T-bill and inter-bank rates during 1973 is quite apparent. It is worth pointing out here that a change in the special deposit call will have two effects in this model, working through the parameter (τ). The first is a simple 'freezing' of retail-deposits effect reflected in a change in T. The second is the tax effect, reflected in r_N (given r_M and r_R).

4 Supplementary Special Deposits

Under the original CCC arrangements the basic tax parameter (t) was independent of the scale of a bank's business. However, the Supplementary Special Deposit (SSD) Scheme introduced in November 1973 (Bank of England (1982)) was specifically designed to work on the margin, by obliging a

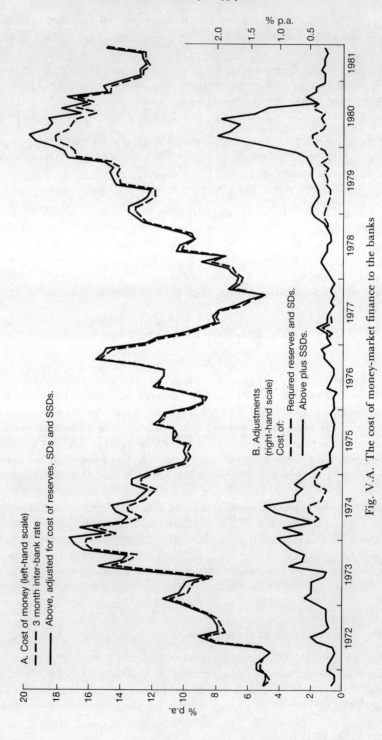

Fig. V.A. The cost of money-market finance to the banks

bank to deposit with the Bank of England an additional fraction of any excess of interest-bearing eligible liabilities (IBELs) above a pre-specified ceiling. This fraction rose from 5 per cent for an excess of up to 3 per cent to 50 per cent for an excess of over 5 per cent. Since these supplementary deposits did not yield any interest this could have a dramatic effect on the marginal cost of deposits. If we represent this fraction by σ, then following through the argument of Section IV.2 the marginal net cost becomes:

$$r_N = (r_M - \tau r_R)/(1 - \tau - \sigma)$$
$$= r_M + t + s \qquad (7)$$

where

$$s = (r_M + t)\sigma/(1 - \tau - \sigma)$$

The average cost to the banks of the SSD scheme will of course depend upon the fraction of the total in each of the three penalty zones, which we will represent by f_1, f_2, and f_3, together with the corresponding deposit rates σ_1, σ_2, and σ_3:

$$s = (r_M + \tau) \sum_{i=1}^{3} f_i \sigma_i/(1 - \tau - \sigma_i) \qquad (8)$$

This cost can be calculated using the figures for the number of banks in each zone published in the Appendix to the Bank of England (1982) article on the SSD scheme, together with a figure (of 230) for the number of banks affected by the scheme, supplied by the Bank. A monthly series based on the inter-bank rate is shown in Figure V.A. Because the SSD scheme only works on the margin, the 'freezing' effect is in this case negligible.

5 The incidence of the control requirements in the wholesale markets

It is interesting to digress slightly at this stage in order to take the tax analogy further and ask what the incidence of this tax was: did it fall on bank profits, depositors, or borrowers?[4] This has important ramifications for the way in which bank behaviour and the parallel money markets are modelled empirically. As with a tax proper, the outcome depends upon the various price elasticities involved. The extent to which the cost can be passed back to wholesale depositors, for example, depends upon the degree of substitution between bank deposits or CDs and LA or other wholesale items. We would expect this to be very high, ruling out any such incidence effect.

The obvious way to check this is to investigate the behaviour of interest rates in these markets. For example, using monthly data for the period October 1971–July 1981 I found the mean differential between 3-month inter-bank (r_M) and local authority (r_L) rates to be 0.002 (per cent p.a.) before adjustment. This rose to 0.225 after adjusting for reserve requirements and SDs and 0.305 after also adjusting for SSDs. I have also checked this by regressing CD and inter-bank rates on LA rates and the various tax parameters. A typical result using inter-bank rate as the dependent variable is reported in Table V.2.

Table V.2. The incidence of the CCC requirements on wholesale bank-deposit rates (monthly, 1971(10)–1981(7))

$r_M = 0.278 + 0.978r_L - 0.022\tau - 0.015\,(r_R - r_L) - 0.246f\sigma$
$\quad\;\;(2.0)\quad\;(91.1)\quad\;\;(1.1)\quad\;\;(0.4)\qquad\qquad\quad(0.2)$

$R^2 = 0.9930 \qquad\qquad ESE = 0.289 \qquad\qquad DW = 1.728$

---

where: $f\sigma = \sum_{i=1}^{3} f_i\sigma_i$

The appropriate F-tests on the equation presented in Table V.2 show quite conclusively that the tax parameters do not have any significant effect on inter-bank rate, either jointly or separately. This kind of regression shows that wholesale bank rates equal LA rates plus a small white-noise error term and suggests that the rate of substitution between these wholesale deposit terms in *non-bank* portfolios is extremely high. Indeed, the variance of the unadjusted differentials probably only reflects measurement error, making it impossible to estimate these elasticities directly. In this situation it is, however, reasonable to adopt the simplifying assumption that non-banks regard these deposits as perfect substitutes, switching between them in order to equate the unadjusted rates of return. Given this, separate non-bank demand functions for these items are not well defined—only a total demand for parallel money-market deposits can be identified. The parallel money markets may then be regarded as a single unified market, with equilibrium given by a unified market-clearing condition:

$$0 = M + L + MB + LB + MF + LF + MD + LD - LG \qquad (9)$$

Given equilibrium in this market, the non-bank demand for parallel money can then be split into wholesale bank and LA deposits using the two individual market identities and the demands and supplies of the other sectors. This is in fact the way the Treasury model is specified:

$$L = LG - LB - LD \qquad (10)$$

$$M = -(MB + MF + MF) \qquad (11)$$

This observation suggests a word of caution about the way in which the behaviour of monetary aggregates such as £M3, which include wholesale bank deposits but exclude items such as LA deposits which are close substitutes, are interpreted. As will be shown in the next chapter, there are circumstances such as an application of the SSD scheme in which £M3 falls because non-banks switch out of the former into the latter. The present analysis suggests that such a reduction should be regarded as being largely cosmetic.

The corollary to these money-market rate results is that the differential between the LA deposit rate and the inter-bank rate adjusted for the effect of the requirements does vary significantly, thus allowing us to estimate the elasticity of response of bank portfolios to changes in both these rates and the requirements. They also establish a prima facie case for believing that inter-bank rates may be viewed as exogenous in econometric work of this kind.[5] However, even under this assumption the net marginal cost of wholesale deposits was not exogenous when the SSD scheme was in operation, since it depended upon where the banks IBELs (denoted by IBL) were in relation to the ceiling (LIBL). This relationship is non-linear, depending upon the distribution of IBELs across the different banks, but a satisfactory degree of explanation can be obtained using a simple exponential relationship of the form:

$$s = \delta(r_M + \tau) \exp\left[\eta(\text{IBL} - \text{LIBL})\right] + e \qquad (12)$$

where δ and η are parameters to be estimated, e is an error term, and IBL is generated by an identity relating it to the money-market position and other IBELs (OBL):

$$\text{IBL} = \text{OBL} - M = \text{OBL} - N/(1 - \tau) \qquad (13)$$

6   An empirical model of bank-portfolio behaviour

The optimization problem facing the typical bank in this situation is quite similar to that facing the typical non-bank analysed in Appendix I, in that it involves both precautionary and speculative risks. The problem facing such a bank is analysed mathematically in Spencer (1984) and (1985b): we will not go into it in any great depth here. The bank portfolio equations suggested by this analysis are of the following algebraic form:

(*a*)   **precautionary asset demands (cash and excess reserves)**

$$\text{CB} = \mu_1 + \phi_{11}\text{DB} - \phi_{12}\text{AB} + \theta_1 \log r_0 + \delta_{11}\Delta\text{AB} + \delta_{12}\Delta\text{DB} \qquad (14)$$

$$X = \mu_2 + \phi_{21}\text{DB} - \phi_{22}\text{AB} + \theta_2 \log (r_0 - r_R) + \delta_{21}\Delta\text{AB} + \delta_{22}\Delta\text{DB} \qquad (15)$$

(*b*)   **speculative asset demands (gilts, foreign currency, money market and LA deposits)**

$$\begin{aligned}
\text{GB} = {} & \phi_{33}\theta_1 \log r_0 + \phi_{33}\theta_2 \log(r_0 - r_R) + \theta_{33}r_G + \theta_{34}r_F + \theta_{35}r_N + \theta_{36}r_L \\
& + \phi_{31}\text{DB} + \phi_{32}\text{AB} - \phi_{33}T + \phi_{34}\text{BB} + \phi_{35}\text{WB} + \delta_{31}\Delta\text{AB} \\
& + \delta_{32}\Delta\text{DB} + \phi_{33}(\mu_1 + \mu_2)
\end{aligned} \qquad (16)$$

$$\begin{aligned}
\text{FB} = {} & \phi_{43}\theta_1 \log r_0 + \phi_{43}\theta_2 \log(r_0 - r_R) + \theta_{34}r_G + \theta_{44}r_F + \theta_{45}r_N + \theta_{46}r_L \\
& + \phi_{41}\text{DB} + \phi_{42}\text{AB} - \phi_{43}T + \phi_{44}\text{BB} + \phi_{45}\text{WB} + \delta_{41}\Delta\text{AB} \\
& + \delta_{42}\Delta\text{DB} + \phi_{43}(\mu_1 + \mu_2)
\end{aligned} \qquad (17)$$

$$\begin{aligned}
N = {} & \phi_{53}\theta_1 \log r_0 + \phi_{53}\theta_2 \log(r_0 - r_R) + \theta_{35}r_G + \theta_{45}r_F + \theta_{55}r_N + \theta_{56}r_L \\
& + \phi_{51}\text{DB} + \phi_{52}\text{AB} - \phi_{53}T + \phi_{54}\text{BB} + \phi_{55}\text{WB} + \delta_{51}\Delta\text{AB} \\
& + \delta_{52}\Delta\text{DB} + \phi_{53}(\mu_1 + \mu_2)
\end{aligned} \qquad (18)$$

$$\text{LB} = \phi_{63}\theta_1 \log r_0 + \phi_{63}\theta_2 \log(r_0 - r_R) + \theta_{36}r_G + \theta_{46}r_L + \theta_{56}r_N + \theta_{66}r_L$$
$$+ \phi_{61}\text{DB} + \phi_{62}\text{AB} - \phi_{63}T + \phi_{64}\text{BB} + \phi_{65}\text{WB} + \delta_{61}\Delta\text{AB}$$
$$+ \delta_{62}\Delta\text{DB} + \phi_{63}(\mu_1 + \mu_2) \tag{19}$$

where

$$r_0 = \phi_{33}r_G + \phi_{43}r_F + \phi_{55}r_N + \phi_{63}r_L \tag{20}$$

and where the μs, ϕs, θs, and δs represent parameters, estimated subject to the restrictions:

$$\sum_{i=1}^{6} \phi_{ij} = 1 \quad j = 1,\dots,5; \qquad \sum_{i=1}^{6} \delta_{ij} = 0 \quad j = 1, 2$$

$$\sum_{i=3}^{6} \theta_{ij} = 0 \quad j = 3,\dots,6; \qquad \theta_{ij} = \theta_{ji} \quad i,j = 1,\dots,6$$

This model distinguishes cash and excess reserves from the other items. The demand for each of these precautionary assets is related to the logarithm of its interest-rate opportunity cost (14) and (15). In the case of cash balances this is simply the rate of return on interest-earning assets which have similar speculative-risk characteristics but yield no precautionary benefits. This opportunity cost is represented by r_0 (defined in (20)) and is a weighted average of the rates of return on non-precautionary assets, the weights being estimated empirically. Not surprisingly, the opportunity-cost rate in fact turns out to be a simple weighted average of the LA and adjusted inter-bank rates. In the case of reserve assets, the opportunity-cost rate is of course partially offset by the own rate of return, demand being related to the logarithm of the *differential* interest-rate cost.

For simplicity we will refer to the non-precautionary assets as speculative, even though some of them are likely to have similar speculative-risk characteristics to reserves and cash. Their demand functions adopt the symmetric linear form which is familiar from mean-variance models such as that developed by Parkin *et al.* (1970). The only novelty here is the presence of the logarithmic terms which show the spillover or financing effect of changes in the precautionary items. Given their similar money-risk-free characteristics, it turns out to be the case empirically that these terms are only significant in the LA and wholesale bank-deposit relationships so that changes in the precautionary items are simply offset in these holdings, without affecting the overall total of money-safe items held in the bank's portfolio. The underlying mean-variance theory implies various restrictions across these demand functions which are discussed and tested in Spencer (1984).

These asset-demand equations were estimated simultaneously with the relationship showing the effect of the SSD scheme [(12)] on quarterly data

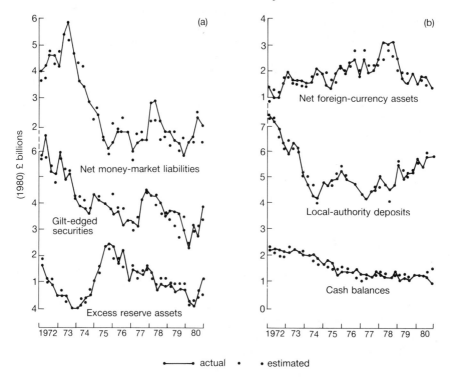

Fig. V.B. Bank portfolio behaviour 1972–1980

for the period 1972(2)–1980(4) using the program ASIMUL (Wymer (1978)). Data for 1975(1) was dropped from the sample in view of the large residuals which this gave.[6] All of these variables were measured in constant (1980) prices. Estimated and actual values for the demand functions are plotted in Figure V.B. The SSD equation was only fitted over the periods 1974(2)–(4), 1977(1)–(2), and 1978(3)–1980(2) when the scheme was of direct relevance, the cost of the scheme (s) being set to zero in other periods.[7] This gave the equation tabulated below. The estimated and actual values for this series are shown as a scatter plot in Figure V.C.

The estimates of the precautionary asset demand functions resulting from this exercise are reported in Table V.3. The weights suggested by the data for the opportunity-cost interest rate (r_0) are shown by the identity at the foot of the table and, as noted above, this may simply be regarded as an average money-market interest rate.

The coefficients in these equations take the sign suggested by the under-lying precautionary theory and these results show that a satisfactory degree of fit can be obtained despite the relatively small number of explanatory variables employed. The chart shows that the excess reserve variable exhibits a high degree of variation, most of which is picked up by the model, the log

Table V.2. The marginal cost of Supplementary Special Deposits (Quarterly, 1974(2)–(4), 1977(1)–(2), 1978(3)–1980(2))

$$s = 0.0425 \; (r_M + t) \; \exp[0.4382 \; (\text{OBL} - \text{LIBL} - N/(1 - \tau))]$$
$$\quad (9.81) \qquad\qquad\qquad (11.19)$$

$$\text{ESE} = 0.2002 \qquad\qquad \text{DW(adjusted for gaps)} = 1.67$$

---

where: $t = \tau(r_M - r_R)/(1 - \tau)$.

The adjusted inter-bank rate used in the demand equations (r_N) was obtained by substituting the estimated value from this equation into the identity (7).

differential term doing most of the work. This reflects relative movements in reserve and money-market rates, but given that this is a logarithm it has some interesting non-linear features. When this differential narrows as it did during 1975, excess reserve liquidity effectively becomes a free good and the banks run this up to a very high level as shown in Figure V.B. The demand for reserves is very interest sensitive in these circumstances. In principle, given this specification, bank reserves would become infinite if T-bill rates were ever to equal the opportunity-cost rate.[8] On the other hand, as this differential opens up as it did during the early years of CCC and (reflecting the effect of the SSD scheme) during 1979, excess reserves fall to minimal levels, as shown in the figure. As this happens they also become less interest-rate sensitive, this specification helping to ensure that they remain non-negative no matter how large the differential.

Table V.3. The demand for the precautionary items (Quarterly, 1972(2)–1974(4), 1975(2)–1980(4))

$$\text{CB} = 0.155 - 0.255 \log r_o - 0.098 \, \text{AB} + 0.042 \, \Delta\text{AB} + 0.155 \, \text{BD} + 0.033\Delta\text{DB}$$
$$\quad (4.41) \quad (2.22) \qquad (4.66) \qquad (3.31) \qquad (8.41) \qquad (2.52)$$

$$\qquad\qquad \text{ESE} = 0.163 \qquad\qquad \text{DW} = 1.430$$

$$\text{X} = 0.144 - 0.9164 \log \, (r_o - r_R) - 0.146 \, \text{AB} - 0.015 \, \Delta\text{AB} + 0.143 \, \text{DB} + 0.038 \, \Delta\text{DB}$$
$$\quad (2.14) \quad (8.21) \qquad\qquad (5.41) \qquad (0.76) \qquad (5.52) \qquad (1.78)$$

$$\qquad\qquad \text{ESE} = 0.250 \qquad\qquad \text{DW} = 1.837$$

---

where: $r_o = 0.522 \, r_N + 0.352 \, r_L + 0.134 \, r_F - 0.011 \, r_G$
$$\quad (6.52) \qquad (4.21) \qquad (2.60) \qquad (0.33)$$

$\quad$ = opportunity cost of holding precautionary balances.
r_R = 3-month Treasury-bill rate.
r_N = 3-month inter-bank rate, adjusted for requirements (equation (7)).
r_L = 3-month LA deposit rate.
r_F = 3-month covered Eurodollar rate.
r_G = 5-year gilt par redemption yield.

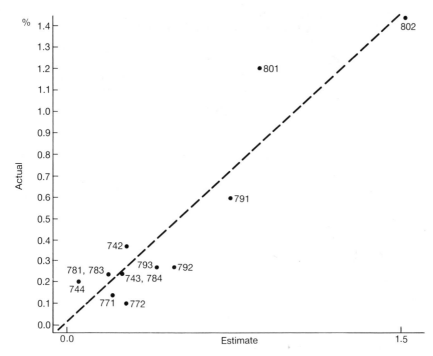

Fig. V.C. The cost of SSD scheme plotted against estimated values

Cash balances exhibit a much smaller range of variation, as is clear from the figure. They are also much less interest elastic, because the high cost of maintaining them keeps them permanently close to the effective minimum. Most of the variation in this item is explained by movements in deposits and advances.

The equations describing the behaviour of the two parallel market items are set out in Table V.4. They track the data well and the coefficients again take the signs expected. As noted above, the logarithmic terms showing the effect of financing the precautionary balances are most significant in these equations. The 'deposit-freezing' effect of a call for special deposits (shown by the variable T) is also concentrated here, for similar reasons. This, together with the non-linear excess-reserve response noted above, has important implications for the behaviour of short-term interest rates and the money supply in model simulations such as those reported in the next chapter. For example, they suggest that a call for special deposits will in the first instance be financed in the parallel money markets, pushing the associated interest rates up. If the situation is one in which the differential between T-bill and money-market rates is low, so that bank reserves are excessive, banks will run these off as they become more expensive, moderating the rise in money-market rates whilst at the same time pushing up T-bill rates (and, at least if the formula is in operation, MLR and base rates).

Base rates are likely to keep up with market rates in this kind of situation, minimizing the danger of perverse round-tripping effects on the money supply. However, if the initial situation is one in which the differential between T-bill and other rates is large, so that bank reserves are already close to the minimum requirement, there is little scope for a further depletion in response to a widening differential. So in this case a call for special deposits will just push up money-market rates, encouraging overdraft arbitrage and other perverse monetary responses if the 'formula' is operative.

The significance of the advances (and retail deposits) terms in these equations is also interesting in this connection since it suggests that, once initiated, such arbitrage processes will be cumulative. Indeed, the mathematical analysis of Appendix II shows that the system will be unstable once this kind of situation develops.

The interest-rate responses in the equations in Table V.4 reveal a high degree of substitution between the two parallel money-market terms, which we would expect given their similar speculative-risk status. There is also a significant degree of substitution between these assets and the remaining, arguably riskier, portfolio items: foreign-currency deposits and gilts. The equations describing the behaviour of these items are tabulated in Table V.5.

The own-rate coefficients in these equations take the right sign and are very significant. Strictly speaking, in view of the mean-variance theory underlying these relationships these rates should be *expected* rates of return

Table V.4. The demand for parallel money-market items (Quarterly, (1972(2)–1974(4), 1975(2)–1980(4)))

$$N = 0.006 + 0.133 \log r_o + 0.478 \log (r_o - r_R) - 0.122\, r_G - 0.144\, r_F + 0.669\, r_N$$
$$(0.03)\quad (1.49)\qquad (5.98)\qquad\qquad (1.96)\qquad (1.83)\qquad (3.40)$$
$$- 0.404\, r_L - 0.149\, \text{AB} - 0.275\, \Delta\text{AB} + 0.077\, \text{DB} - 0.100\, \Delta\text{DB} - 0.522\, \text{T}$$
$$(2.78)\qquad (1.89)\qquad (4.89)\qquad (0.95)\qquad (3.85)\qquad (6.52)$$
$$+ 0.540\, \text{BB} + 0.466\, \text{WB}$$
$$(4.89)\qquad (3.78)$$

$$\text{ESE} = 0.366 \qquad\qquad \text{DW} = 1.748$$

$$\text{LB} = 0.004 + 0.090 \log r_o + 0.322 \log (r_o - r_R) - 0.108\, r_G - 0.218\, r_F - 0.4037\, r_N$$
$$(0.02)\quad (0.99)\qquad (3.96)\qquad\qquad (1.90)\qquad (3.11)\qquad (2.78)$$
$$+ 0.730\, r_L - 0.217\, \text{AB} + 0.181\, \Delta\text{AB} + 0.221\, \text{DB} + 0.056\, \Delta\text{DB} - 0.352\, \text{T}$$
$$(5.29)\qquad (3.98)\qquad (3.69)\qquad (4.86)\qquad (2.01)\qquad (4.21)$$
$$+ 0.168\, \text{BB} + 0.203\, \text{WB}$$
$$(3.05)\qquad (2.00)$$

$$\text{ESE} = 0.218 \qquad\qquad \text{DW} = 2.187$$

---

rather than *observed* yields. However, experiments with gilt-edged expectations using the McCallum (1975) method described in Section VIII.3 made little difference to these results. The reason for this is that capital gains on these items are on average small, given their very short maturity, and more difficult to predict than gains on long-term gilts. So the results reported here just use the 5-year redemption yield as an indicator of the expected return.

A similar difficulty must be faced with the expected return on foreign-currency items. Since these were in the main covered against currency risk, it is reasonable to use a covered eurodollar rate as a first approximation to the overall expected return, as in the reported results. However these items are subject to default and other residual risks which have been very significant at times (for example, following the Herstatt banking crisis of June 1974) and were until October 1979 limited by exchange controls. The problem is that variations in such risks and the restrictiveness of exchange controls may be reflected in the covered interest differential, tending to bias the interest-rate response towards zero. However, the use of dummy variables to allow for the Herstatt crisis and the end of exchange controls had no perceptible effect on the results, suggesting that this bias is not serious in this case.

These results suggest that, in equilibrium, changes in deposits and advances will largely be reflected in the gilt and LA-debt portfolios.[9] However, the first difference terms suggest that the immediate impact is concentrated in holdings of precautionary and money-market items, so that the initial effects on gilts and LA deposits are much smaller. The foreign-currency position does not appear to be affected by such influences. The

Table V.5. The demand for other speculative items (Quarterly, 1972(2)–1974(4), 1975(2)–1980(4))

$$GB = - 0.003 \log r_o - 0.010 \log (r_o - r_R) + 0.267\, r_G - 0.037\, r_F - 0.122\, r_N$$
$$\quad\;\; (0.06) \qquad\quad (0.03) \qquad\qquad\quad (5.62) \qquad (1.03) \qquad (1.90)$$
$$\quad - 0.108\, r_L - 0.271\, AB + 0.149\, \Delta AB + 0.149\, DB - 0.015\, \Delta DB + 0.011\, T$$
$$\quad\;\; (1.90) \qquad (5.13) \qquad (3.52) \qquad\quad (7.01) \qquad\quad (0.52) \qquad\quad (0.33)$$
$$\quad + 0.087\, BB - 0.244\, WB$$
$$\quad\;\; (1.19) \qquad\;\; (2.57)$$

$$\qquad\qquad ESE = 0.389 \qquad\qquad DW = 2.010$$

$$FB = 0.001 + 0.035 \log r_o + 0.126 \log (r_o - r_R) - 0.037\, r_G + 0.399\, r_F - 0.144\, r_N$$
$$\quad\;\; (0.01) \;\; (0.67) \qquad\quad (2.70) \qquad\qquad\quad (1.03) \qquad (5.09) \qquad (1.83)$$
$$\quad - 0.2181\, r_L - 0.119\, AB - 0.04\, \Delta AB + 0.038\, DB - 0.013\, \Delta DB - 0.138\, T$$
$$\quad\;\; (3.11) \qquad (2.45) \qquad\; (1.04) \qquad\quad (0.82) \qquad\quad (0.30) \qquad\quad (2.80)$$
$$\quad + 0.205\, BB + 0.575\, WB$$
$$\quad\;\; (3.40) \qquad\;\; (6.14)$$

$$\qquad\qquad ESE = 0.311 \qquad\qquad DW = 1.696$$

model is based upon the assumption that the banks have adjusted fully within three months of any such change taking place and the DW-statistics (together with more specific tests) suggest that this specification is adequate.

The effect of changes in the banks net wealth or share capital looks at first sight a little odd, tending to reduce holdings of gilts and increase holdings of foreign-currency assets and parallel money-market assets. Perhaps we should not read too much into this effect, which could be a quirk of the particular data period being investigated. However, it is interesting that an increase in shareholders funds increases the banks exposure to inflation, at least on an inflation-accounting basis. And as I note in Appendix I (in the context of non-bank behaviour), changes in the rate of inflation are likely to be negatively correlated with capital gains on gilts so that it would in fact be sensible to hedge against this effect by running down holdings of gilts when wealth or the capital base increased.

7   The effect of the SSD scheme on the structure of bank portfolios

The effect of applying the SSD scheme was, of course, highly non-linear, depending upon how close the IBELs ceiling was set in relation to the average bank's IBELs. However, once this is translated into an interest-rate equivalent, the effect on the portfolio can be calculated in a straightforward manner. The effect on excess reserve holdings is, as has been demonstrated, still non-linear—depending upon whether these are initially excessive. The effect on this part of the portfolio can be very marked in this case, and detailed inspection of the data reveals that in this instance the scheme caused banks to reclassify secured lending to the discount market (a reserve asset) as unsecured lending (an offset to IBELs). The model suggests for example that the scheme pushed up the marginal cost of money-market deposits by 1.5 per cent (p.a.) by 1980(2) and that this had the portfolio effects set out in Table V.6.

In addition to these effects, the banks' portfolios and the money supply would have been affected by any changes in market and lending rates which occurred as a consequence of this kind of reallocation. The analysis of such effects is deferred to the next chapter.

Table V.6. Estimated portfolio effect of SSD scheme in 1980(2) (£ millions, 1980)

Cash balances	−20
Reserve assets	−480
Gilt-edged securities	−190
Foreign-currency assets	−150
LA deposits	−430
Net money-market liabilities	−1,270

Notes

1. I will usually refer to this item loosely as 'reserve assets' and similarly use the term 'required reserves' to represent reserves required under the $12\frac{1}{2}$ per cent rule and special deposits.
2. Although the fc and money-market positions have been net liabilities it is convenient to consider them as net assets.
3. Strictly speaking, eligible liabilities include net fc liabilities $(-F)$ where these are positive. But since banks have in aggregate maintained a net asset position, the effect of this rule has been negligible.
4. The large gap observed empirically between 7-day retail deposit and market rates suggests, prima facie, that banks are able to pass reserve-asset costs back to these depositors. Yet similar regressions using the retail-deposit rate failed to reveal any significant reserve-requirement effect. Work on base lending rate was also inconclusive. As was noted in the previous chapter, the tax-incidence model predicts that base rates should exceed money-market rates if these exceed reserve-asset rates, but this was overwhelmed by the effect of a relatively low MLR when the 'formula' was in operation. When the adjusted cost of money-market deposits was introduced as an additional variable into base-rate equations run over the administered MLR period, this variable was found to be insignificant. Interestingly, however, there was a noticeable drop in the significance of MLR, reflecting the fact that when the SSD scheme was in place (increasing the adjusted relative to the unadjusted market rate) MLR tended to be high relative to money-market rates. This could either have been because MLR was increased as part of the overall monetary-control package, or (as will be illustrated in the next chapter) due to the depressive effect of the SSD scheme on money-market rates.
5. This was also checked at a later stage using a Hausman (1978) m-test.
6. The largest error was in the gilts equation, suggesting that these large residuals were associated with the rebound of confidence which occurred in this quarter.
7. It is possible that the scheme affected 1974(1), 1976(4), and 1978(2) as banks adjusted their portfolios during the period of grace following the announcement. I checked this assuming that such effects would work in the same way as a rise in r_N and introducing dummies for these quarters in this restricted way. The last was the only one of (marginal) significance. However, this took a negative sign, perhaps reflecting anticipation rather than announcement effects.
8. The feedback effect of bank behaviour prevents this happening in the Treasury model.
9. Again the exogeneity of these variables has been checked using a Hausman (1978) m-test.

VI

Monetary Control and the Problem of Bank Liability-management—some Policy-simulation Results

Introduction and summary

The econometric results presented in the preceding two chapters reveal quite a lot about the pressures on the early CCC system and about the reactions of individual sectors, but do not immediately tell us much about the characteristics of the system as a whole. They do, however, furnish the building blocks with which an interactive model of the system can be constructed. This allows some of the ambiguities remaining from the theoretical analysis of Appendix II—designed to throw light on the working of the financial system under different control regimes—to be pursued.

Of course there are many aspects of the system which have not yet been discussed. I have hardly touched upon the non-bank private-sector's demand for gilts, for example, or the speculative shadow this casts over the demand for money. So far only the precautionary or arbitrage demand for money (as reflected in the demand for bank advances) has been analysed. However, Appendix I shows that it is reasonable to view the precautionary and speculative demands separately, putting the latter to one side when discussing the former. This is very convenient since it allows the behaviour of the short-term asset markets to be investigated without worrying too much about the long-term markets and expectations, or the celebrated Lucas critique of policy simulation. (The discussion of these points is deferred to Chapter IX.) The simulations reported here are conducted in this spirit. Although they were obtained by running the complete financial sector of the Treasury model, the policy specification and model structure are such that there are no speculative effects on the demand for money.

Two sets of results are reported. The first contrasts the effect of a PSBR cut when the supply of reserves is fixed (a caricature of the proto-CCC system) with one in which this is varied to keep Treasury-bill rates in line with other rates a (characterization of the later CCC system). The initial situation is one in which reserve assets are tight. Reflecting the theoretical analysis set out in Appendix II, the effect of the cut is perverse in the first instance, since the banks react to the implied loss of reserves by bidding rates in the wholesale markets up and (at least in relative terms) Treasury-bill rates down. Given the MLR formula and base-rate specification, this encourages overdraft arbitrage, which soon destabilizes the system. On the other hand, if the authorities keep short-term rates in line, this facilitates an upward movement in base rates, avoiding perverse differentials, so the monetary effect of a cut in the PSBR is reinforced by a fall in bank lending. This seems to be the way in which the authorities had originally intended the system to operate.

A slightly different background situation is then investigated—one in which banks enjoy moderately large excess reserves and, reflecting the analysis of the previous chapter, tend to keep short-term interest rates in line even without official intervention. It is, moreover, assumed that the authorities manipulate MLR by administrative decision, making sure that it keeps abreast of wholesale deposit rates. The analysis of the Appendix shows that this specification is unambiguously stable. The simulations illustrate the effect of a Special Deposit call and an SSD scheme against such a background situation. The model suggests that the effect of a Special Deposit call on the monetary aggregates comes through very slowly, due to the lags observed empirically in the behaviour of bank lending. This consequently limits its use as an instrument of short-term monetary policy. On the other hand the SSD scheme worked very quickly, involving an initial overshooting of interest rates as banks attempt to reshuffle their portfolios to avoid penalty costs. Of course, many (but certainly not all) of these adjustments were cosmetic, making it difficult to interpret the behaviour of the monetary aggregates when the scheme was in force. This, together with the 'eurosterling leak' opened up by the abolition of exchange control in October 1979, led the authorities to abandon the scheme in June of the following year.

This chapter ends with a brief résumé of the theoretical and empirical results as they relate to the experience of the early CCC years and a general discussion of the problems which bank-liability management by banks and industrial companies present for the monetary authorities.

1 The model and policy assumptions

The version of the Treasury model used in this particular exercise is described in Spencer and Mowl (1978). The company-borrowing and bank-portfolio equations were earlier versions of those discussed in the previous two chapters. Although the coefficients may differ somewhat, the characteristics of these equations are essentially the same.

This specification incorporates a general equilibrium model of the short-term financial markets, which distinguishes retail and wholesale items as well as reserve assets. Reflecting the analysis of earlier chapters, it solves for interest rates in the following way:

(i)   Retail loan and deposit rates are set by the banks with reference to MLR and parallel money market rates.

(ii) Banks then accept all retail deposits and meet any reasonable loan demands made at these rates.

(iii) Given these demands, the banks finance any surplus or deficiency of funds in the parallel-money and reserve-asset markets, the allocation between these markets being effectively determined by their initial reserve-asset position.

(iv) The ebb and flow of funds in these markets then determine parallel-money market rates, MLR, and hence, via (i), retail loan and deposit rates.

For the purpose of this exercise it was assumed that the authorities adopted a neutral gilt-edged market policy, maintaining the *expected* return on gilts in line with short-term rates, in order to prevent speculative effects on the demand for money. In the interests of diagnostic simplicity, feedbacks from the real sector are neglected at this stage, so prices, financial surpluses, and the like are held constant. In keeping with this assumption, official intervention was used to fix the exchange rate—although the early CCC period was of course characterized by 'dirty floating' so that some of the external feedbacks would in fact have been reflected in the exchange rate and hence prices and activity. The external side of this version of the model was based on the Beenstock–Bell (1979) capital-flows model discussed in Chapter XI, implying a rather low degree of capital mobility. Finally, it was assumed that the discount houses were constrained by their undefined assets multiple or some similar device, so that their ability to take advantage of the various interest-rate differentials which open up is negligible.

2 The effect of different reserve-asset supply policies on the stability of the early CCC system

The theoretical analysis of Appendix II is designed to shed light on the working of the financial system under various different control regimes, particularly its behaviour under CCC. The main results can be summarized as follows:

(i) If *either* there are no reserve requirements *or* banks act as asset rather than liability managers then the usual sectoral gross-substitutability assumption assumed in theoretical work (and confirmed in the empirical results) are sufficient to ensure stability.

(ii) A *competitive* banking system is stable no matter what the reserve-asset supply policy adopted by the authorities. This highlights the role played in unstable processes by sticky base rates and other imperfections in the retail banking system.

(iii) If the authorities keep MLR or reserve-asset rates in line with money-market rates this ensures stability even with the kind of sticky base-rate behaviour observed empirically.

(iv) If on the other hand MLR is fixed in line with reserve-asset rates (as under the 'formula') then stability depends critically upon the initial conditions of the system, particularly the liquidity situation of banks and non-banks. If initial holdings of excess reserves and cash are high, the system will be locally stable. However, if they are depleted the system will be unstable.

The last of these results leaves open the stability of the proto-CCC system. This ambiguity can only be resolved using an empirically based model. The first set of simulations reported is designed to throw further light on this issue.

These were run using a historical data base for the early CCC perod (1972(1)–1977(1)) in which the interest-rate relativities were such that arbitrage operations were either profitable or on the verge of being so. In order to characterize the behaviour of administered rates it was assumed that MLR was a simple mark-up on the T-bill rate given by the 'formula' and that bank-base rate was determined by an equation similar to those discussed in Chapter IV, estimated using quarterly data for this period:

$$r_B = 0.108 + 0.134\,r_R + 0.509\,r_M + 0.306\,r_{B(-1)}$$
$$(1.9)\quad\ (2.9)\qquad\ (3.7)\qquad\ (2.1) \tag{1}$$

$$R^2 = 0.981 \qquad\qquad \text{ESE} = 0.711 \qquad\qquad \text{DW} = 1.42$$

Given this base-rate specification and starting point, the stability of the system will depend critically upon the authorites' reserve-asset supply policies. Two alternative specifications are therefore investigated, which, although perhaps a little extreme, would seem to bracket the range of policies pursued at different times by the authorities. As we have seen, the original intention was to squeeze bank liquidity, thereby forcing up market yields. This kind of reserve-asset squeeze naturally forced reserve-asset rates below other short rates—by as much as 4 percentage points on occasion. The simplest way to model this effect is to suppose that the authorities fix the supply of reserve assets to the system, so that the only way the banks can expand their balance sheets is by bidding them away from non-banks. Since this is a rather extreme representation—it is difficult to find episodes in which such policies seem to have been pursued—this must be regarded as a limiting case.

The mathematical model suggests that the stability of this regime depends critically on the banks' initial holdings of reserves. If these are significant they may act as a buffer, absorbing the effect of minor shocks. However, if they are low, as they were during the early CCC years, the system will be unstable given the kind of base-rate formula I have assumed. This is essentially because, as banks expand their wholesale deposits, they will simultaneously need to bid for reserves, tending to depress base rates in relation to wholesale money rates and opening up an incentive to overdraft-arbitrage movements. The first result gives a clear example of such an unstable process.

By way of contrast I will consider another extreme, in which there is no attempt to restrict the supply of reserve assets. The authorities might, for example, vary their supply in order to preserve the differential between reserve asset and other rates. One or two early instances of this type, in which a Special Deposit call was combined with an increase in the Treasury-bill tender and MLR, were noted in Chapter III. Similarly, the authorities have in recent years tended to release Special Deposits in order to relieve such pressures. This latter specification was employed in the second simulation. The mathematical analysis shows that this will be stable under a variety of base-rate formula including the one used here, so our second result provides an example of such a stable supply specification. The Appendix also looks at the case in which the supply of reserves is varied in order to peg T-bill rates, suggesting that this will be unstable in these circumstances. This may be confirmed by model simulations but there would be little point in discussing such results here.

In both of these simulations reserve-asset pressure was induced by reducing the PSBR (by (1975) £1 billion spread over the first two years). This is perhaps a little counter-factual in relation to the early CCC period when there was little emphasis on controlling the PSBR for monetary reasons. It is perhaps more relevant to the 'overfunding' policy of more recent years. It may, however, be regarded as illustrative since reserve-asset pressure caused by other influences, for example a balance of payments deficit, would have similar effects.

For simplicity there are no expenditure effects associated with this cut. It was assumed that this reduced the non-bank sector's demand for money, gilts, and other public-sector debt in the same way as a reduction in its net financial wealth.

Figure VI.A shows the effect of this under the fixed reserve-asset supply policy. The upper panel shows the effect on non-bank portfolios. The initial fall in net wealth is clear, and since bank borrowing is not directly affected this implies a similar fall in gross wealth and asset holdings. Nearly half of this is reflected in a reduced demand for money (mainly time deposits), the rest being reflected in holdings of public-sector debt.

The central panel shows the effect of this on bank balance-sheets. The banks react to the outflow of retail deposits by selling a wide range of assets, forcing up market interest rates, as shown by the bottom panel. As demonstrated in the previous chapter, the initial effect is concentrated in the parallel money-market deposits, but as rates in this market rise, this causes banks to reduce their excess reserves, transmitting the effect to the reserve-asset market. However, in this example the latter effect is rather weak since excess reserves are initially low. Indeed, the fall in bank reserves shown in the figure largely reflects the fall in required reserves. Consequently, there is little to stop parallel money-market rates rising relative to reserve-asset rates and MLR. Given the base-rate equation used here this means that they also rise relative to base rates.

Once this open up an arbitrage differential the response is inevitably per-

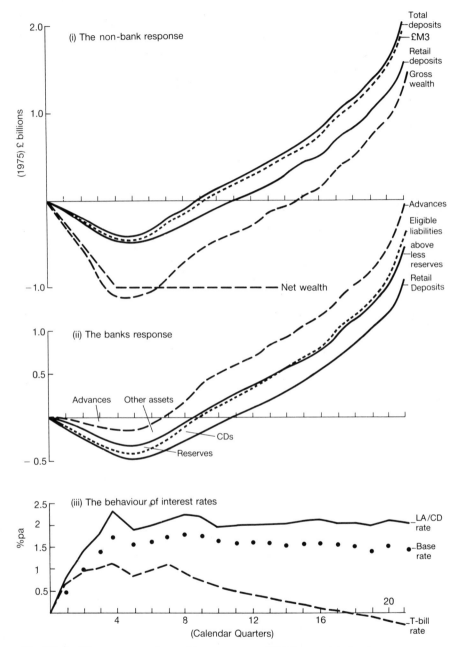

Fig. VI.A. The anatomy of an arbitrage process (PSBR cut with fixed reserve-asset supply) (£ billions 1975)

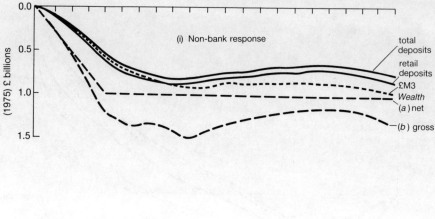

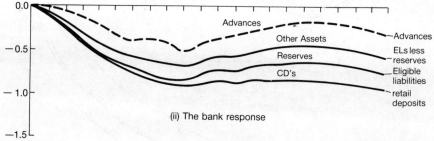

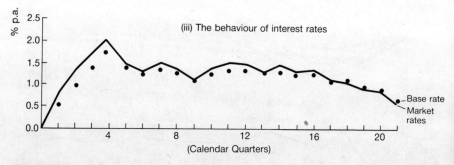

Fig. VI.B. Special deposits as a smoothing device (PSBR cut with constant market differentials) (£ billion 1975)

verse. This happens after three quarters in this run, turning the demand for bank borrowing, time deposits, and CDs sharply upwards and increasing the pressure on bank portfolios through the leakage into required reserves. Since the banks cannot finance this secondary outflow out of excess reserves, they are forced to respond by reducing their net parallel market position, largely by issuing CDs. The effect of this, together with their renewed purchases of reserve assets, is to increase the gap between parallel money rates and base rates.

The estimates reported in Chapter IV suggest that there is quite a significant lag in the non-bank response to arbitrage differentials, which means that the momentum of this merry-go-round takes several years to build up. The figure reveals that the effect on £M3 does not become perverse for two years, and that these processes do not become explosive until the final two years of the run. However, it is likely that these lags are biased upwards by measurement error and that in practice such processes would become explosive much more quickly. On the other hand, the specification of administered-rate behaviour is entirely mechanical, and rules out any stabilizing reaction on the part of the banks or the authorities.

Figure VI.B shows what happens when the special deposit call is relaxed in order to keep T-bill rates in line with other market rates as the pressure on bank-balance sheets increases. This allows the reduction in the PSBR to be reflected in a fall in sterling M3 without any perverse side-effects. Taken together, these simulations suggest the paradoxical result that the reserve-asset shortages induced under the proto-CCC system in fact increased the monetary aggregates. This reflects the mathematical fact that an unstable system will always react 'perversely' to exogenous shocks.

Figure VI.B illustrates one or two further points. It shows that providing perverse differentials can be avoided; a squeeze on the bank's resources, for whatever reason, will cause them to sell short-term securities, leading to a rise in short-term interest rates and a fall in lending to non-banks. This is presumably the kind of mechanism the authorities had in mind when they originally devised the CCC system. But unfortunately it is very difficult to squeeze bank resources if initiatives on the PSBR and gilt sales are ruled out, whilst special deposits are used to control interest-rate differentials. Technically, if the MLR or the SSD scheme is available as an additional policy instrument, this restores the authorities freedom of action—but in practice the scope for such a squeeze must remain limited.

Of course in this run the fall in non-bank borrowing—largely reflected in holdings of time deposit and CDs—reinforces the initial cut in the PSBR. So the reduction in the demand for £M3, which directly reflects about a half of any change in net wealth, is almost as large as the cut in the PSBR itself. The reduction in the monetary aggregates is moderated by bank sales of CDs in response to the initial outflow, although this effect is small.

3 The effect of a Special Deposit call on the late 1970s system

The next two simulations attempt to represent the behaviour of the late 1970s version of the CCC system. it is initially assumed that base rate moves in line with parallel money-market rates. This could either be because the authorities set MLR in this way, and are followed by the banks (as seems to

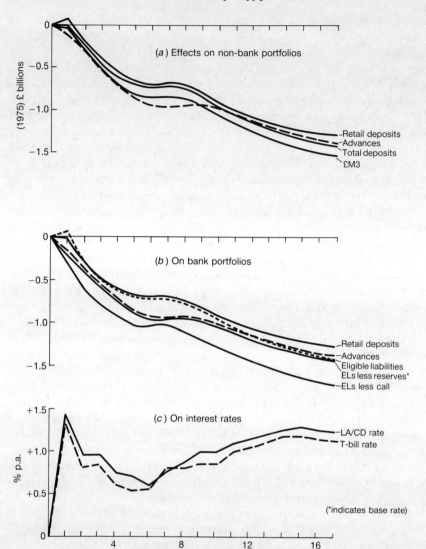

Fig. VI.C. The effect of a one per cent Special Deposit call (£ billions 1975)

have happened under the administered MLR version of CCC) or because the banks themselves behave in this way (as appears to be the case under the August 1981 arrangements). This in itself means that the system will respond in a stable manner, as the Appendix shows. I also employed a data base (1976(1)–1980(1)) in which interest rates did not immediately encourage round-tripping and banks enjoyed moderately high levels of excess reserves. T-bill rates were then left to find their own level given an unchanged supply

Table VI.1. The effect of a Special Deposit call on the late 1970s system (Effect after two years in 1975 £ millions, first-quarter effects in parentheses)

Financial instruments	Public sector	Commercial banks	Banking dept; B of E	Non-bank residents	Overseas residents
1. Notes and coin	+172	−81		−91	
	(+74)	(−34)		(−40)	
2. Bank balances at B of E		−4	+4		
		(+9)	(−9)		
3. Interest-bearing reserve assets	0	−170		+125	+45
	0	(−89)		(+28)	(+61)
4. Special deposits		+386	−386		
		(+348)	(−348)		
5. Gilt-edged stocks	+28	+5		−36	+3
	(+14)	(+1)		(−16)	(+1)
6. Non-marketable public-sector debt	+35			−35	
	(+86)			(−86)	
7. Banks £ lending		−946		+946	
		(−169)		(+169)	
8. £ retail bank deposits		+758		−776	+18
		(−15)		(−14)	(+29)
9. CDs and inter-bank deposits		+57		−62	+5
		(−40)		(+33)	(+7)
10. Local-authority temporary debt	+16	+28		−45	+1
	(+18)	(−1)		(−21)	(4)
11. Net government indebtedness to B of E	−382		+382		
	(−357)		(+357)		
12. Other non-bank private-sector liabilities				−49	+49
				(−47)	(+47)
13. Foreign-currency bank deposits		−33		+23	+10
		(−10)		(−6)	(+16)
14. Official foreign-exchange reserves	+131				−131
	(+165)				(−165)

Sign convention: increase in assets (+) increase in liabilities(−).

but move broadly in line with other market rates, reflecting the high rate of substitution of reserves and money-market assets in bank portfolios.

Figure VI.C shows the effect of making a 1 per cent SD call against this kind of background situation. Table VI.1 shows some of the numbers involved. In the first instance, the banks again sell parallel money-market instruments, but as this pushes up the associated rates, they tend to run off excess reserves as well. This also causes borrowing to fall. The table shows that the first-quarter effect on £M3 is very small (−£21 millions) due to the non-bank take up of CDs. On balance, the banks finance the initial call largely by reducing lending and excess reserves.

Over the next year or so, lending continues to fall as the lagged interest-rate effects come through, accompanied by a fall in retail deposits. The latter reduces the banks required reserves, allowing them to restore their reserve ratios to the original level. As the lagged effects work through, interest rates ease back significantly. But this in turn interrupts the reduction in lending, so that the fall in rates is only temporary. The lags in the response of non-bank portfolios mean that the interest-rate response is cyclical.

It is worth emphasizing the role which reserves assets play in this run. According to my estimates, the response of bank lending to interest rates takes time to come through. So excess reserves act as a buffer in the first couple of quarters, absorbing the effect of the call. This has the side-effect of keeping T-bill rates in line with other rates. Against this background situation it is immaterial whether the authorities set MLR in line with T-bill or other market rates. However, if, as in the previous simulation, reserves were initially tight, this specification could make a great deal of difference. Technically, the analysis of the Appendix shows that the system is always stable (given my simplifying assumptions) if MLR and base rates are set in line with money-market rates, essentially because T-bill rates are then free to go their own way, without any untoward side-effects. However, this would put the discount houses under enormous pressure to expand their balance sheets, straining the discount-house neutrality assumption. It is by no means clear what would happen in practice if the authorities tried to squeeze a reserve-deficient system in this kind of way.

The reserves sold by banks are taken up by non-bank residents and the overseas sector as shown in the matrix. Residents finance this through a rundown in their net position with the banking sector and by demanding less cash from the public sector. The non-resident take-up of reserve assets is faciliated by inflows into sterling, responding to higher UK interest rates, matched by a small increase in the reserves. So on balance the monetary authorities' increased Special Deposit liabilities are matched by reduced cash liabilities and higher foreign-exchange reserves.

Finally it should be stressed that even if the banks do have room for manœuvre as they do in this simulation, the effect of an SD-call takes some time to come through, due to the lags in non-bank behaviour. These results suggest that the first-quarter impact on £M3 is negligible and, depending upon the exact circumstances of the call, often perverse. This effectively rules out the use of Special Deposits as a way of exercising short-run control of the money supply, since it implies instrument instability.

4 Disintermediation and the effect of the Supplementary Special Deposit scheme

As we have seen, the problems experienced with the Special Deposit call lead the authorities to experiment with supplementary schemes, first in late 1973, then again in late 1976, and finally in June 1978. These devices were intended to work by raising the marginal cost of deposits, thus reducing bank intermediation and in particular the kind of wholesale liability management which had so badly upset the initial CCC arrangements. The idea was that such schemes would be imposed temporarily, usually as part of a larger package designed to stop monetary growth. The econometric results discussed in the previous chapter suggest that the scheme was in this respect very effective at times. In the second quarter of 1980, for example, just before it was removed, it would appear that the scheme raised the cost of wholesale deposits to the banks by 1.5 per cent, reducing them by perhaps £1¼ billion. However, this kind of estimate does not take into account the effect of any consequent changes in interest rates on lending and retail deposits. Nor does it take into account any of the more cosmetic effects of the scheme.

These econometric results suggest that the way which the banks responded to the scheme was crucially dependent upon their initial reserve-asset position. If this was excessive, this obviously gave them some room for manœuvre, but the exact degree of flexibility depended upon the initial discount-market position and the reactions of the authorities. If, for instance, the discount houses also found themselves with a flexible balance-sheet position, banks could simply reclassify their secured loans to the market (which qualify as a reserve asset) as unsecured loans, (which count as inter-bank lending and reduce IBELs). So banks could reduce their reserve assets and net money-market liabilities at the stroke of a pen, with minimal effect on interest rates, the money supply, or anything else of importance. This kind of adjustment is reflected in Table V.6, which suggests that given an initial excess-reserve position and unchanged interest rates the adjustment would take the form of a rundown of this excess position. The discount market had therefore to come up against its undefined assets multiple before any SSD scheme could really begin to bite. The behaviour of this multiple is therefore an indication of the effectiveness of the scheme, one which I have found helpful as a check on the econometric results.

The banks employed several other book-keeping devices in order to adjust their money-market position. There was in addition a wide range of potential forms of disintermediation. (A useful background discussion of these is to be found in the Bank of England (1982) article on the scheme.) These devices diverted wholesale deposit and lending business through less convenient or high-cost channels. The best known of these was the commercial bill leak which involved wholesale borrowers issuing trade bills instead of taking out bank loans. These were then accepted by a bank and sold on to a wholesale depositor instead of a CD, all of this taking place 'off balance sheet'. Similarly, the eurosterling leak, made possible by the abolition of exchange controls in October 1979, routed this kind of business through offshore markets.[1]

In practice the potential for this kind of leakage greatly reduced the effectiveness of the scheme and made it increasingly difficult to monitor and interpret the behaviour of the monetary aggregates. However, although there was no official limit to the extent of this kind of process, there was a natural limit in the form of increasing inconvenience and other costs. So reflecting this, following the final application of the scheme, first the commercial-bill issue and then the eurosterling statistics increased as the pressures on the banking system intensified and the implicit costs rose. Of course, the fact that significant numbers of banks had to pay penalties reveals that not all of the effects of the scheme were cosmetic.

In order to investigate these non-cosmetic effects, another model simulation was conducted. It was again assumed that the discount market was initially up against its undefined asset constraint, so that there was no significant scope for leakage of this kind. Since the model says little about the interest-rate sensitivity of the eurosterling and commercial-bill leaks, it is convenient to abstract from these and concentrate on the effect of the scheme on the rest of the banks' business. This is done most simply by assuming that the scheme is imposed at a level which reduces the banks' IBELs by £1 billion compared to the initial situation, before adjusting for any cosmetic effects.

This assumption is a little artificial since in practice an IBELs ceiling is set and the effects depend upon the way in which the pressures on the system develop. However, this is just a convenience since there will always be some IBEL ceiling which generates any specified effect on the banks' actual IBELs. Technically, these results were obtained by adding a residual to the identity generating the adjusted marginal cost of funds to the banks. (Equation V.(7), where 's' represents the residual.) The computer was programmed to vary this residual until IBELs were reduced by the required amount.[2]

It was assumed that the banks were given a six-month period of grace when the scheme was announced but that they would immediately begin to rearrange their affairs, so that half the adjustment was seen over the first quarter. This 'scheme' was removed three years after announcement in order to see how quickly the system took to return to the initial equilibrium.

The data base used in this exercise was the same as that used in simulating the SD call. However, in this case different base-rate/MLR setting assumptions are appropriate. This is because money-market rates tend to fall as banks adjust their position, and it would be perverse to suppose that base rates fell in line with these. Indeed, a competitive banking system would mark these rates up in line with the marginal costs of the scheme. And as was noted in Chapter V, the empirical evidence suggests that MLR and base rates rose relative to observed money-market rates when the scheme was in force, although this probably reflects the influence of relatively high T-bill rates. This analysis suggests two slightly different specifications. The first is that the authorities set MLR in line with T-bill rates and are followed by the banks, and the second is that the banks set their rates in line with the marginal cost of deposits adjusted for the effect of the scheme (and other

Table VI.2. The effect of the Supplementary Special Deposit scheme (Effect after two years in 1975 £ millions, second-quarter effects in parentheses)

Financial Instruments	Public sector	Banking sector	Banking dept; B of E	Non-bank residents	Overseas residents
1. Notes and coin	0 (+27)	−20 (−19)		+20 (−8)	
2. Bank balances at B of E		−10 (−11)	+10 (+11)		
3. Interest-bearing reserve assets		−64 (−39)		+70 (+48)	−6 (−9)
4. Special Deposits		−30 (−33)	+30 (+33)		
5. Gilt-edged stocks	−146 (−182)	+120 (+168)		+26 (+14)	
6. Non-marketable public-sector debt	−1 (−38)			+1 (+38)	
7. Banks £ lending		−392 (−276)		+392 (+276)	
8. £ retail bank deposits		+371 (+272)		−367 (−266)	−4 (−6)
9. CDs and inter-bank deposits		+646 (+838)		−645 (−837)	−1 (−1)
10. Local-authority debt	−4 (−7)	−487 (−710)		+492 (+718)	−1 (−1)
11. Net government indebtedness to the B of E	+40 (+44)		−40 (−44)		
12. Other non-bank private-sector liabilities				+11 (+17)	−11 (+17)
13. Foreign-currency bank deposits		−134 (−190)			+134 (−190)
14. Official foreign-exchange reserves	+111 (+156)				−111 (−156)

Sign convention: Increase in assets (+), increase in liabilities (−).

requirements). Given the high level of excess reserves in banks portfolios, the two rates move in line so these specifications give almost identical results. In this run, base rates and MLR move in line with T-bill rates.

The results of this exercise are displayed in Table VI.2 and Figure VI.D. The required residual adjustment is reflected in the difference between the unadjusted and adjusted money-market rate shown in the lower panel.[3] Initially this has to rise sharply given the lags in non-bank borrowing, but as the effects of the higher base rates begin to work through, this relieves the strain on bank portfolios, reducing the cost of the scheme.

Given the discount-market neutrality assumption, the banks can only

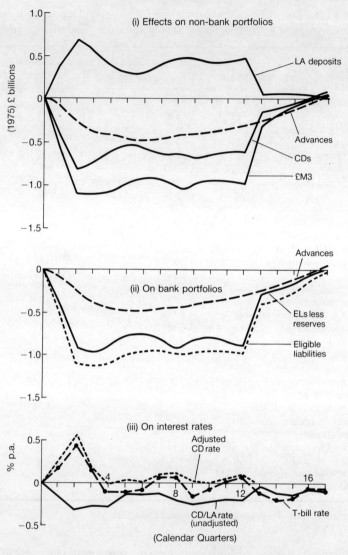

Fig. VI.D. The effect of an SSD scheme (£ billions 1975)

adjust their money-market position by unwinding transactions with non-banks. They attempt to do this partly by running off their excess holdings of reserve assets. These are to some extent taken up by non-bank residents, but their demand for such instruments is not very interest elastic. In contrast to the previous run, there are overseas outflows from sterling—although in practice inflows might occur due to confidence effects which are not considered here—so non-residents tend to reduce their holdings of reserve assets.

The main effect in these circumstances is to force T-bill rates up in line with the adjusted cost of funds to the banks, with only modest falls in bank reserves. Allowing for the effect of changes in market interest rates can therefore make a big difference to the effect on bank portfolios.

In strong contrast, the parallel money-market model suggests that non-banks are indifferent between CDs and LA deposits, so the banks can most easily reduce their money-market deposits by selling LA deposits. This is shown clearly by the upper panel of the figure which shows that the initial non-bank response consists mainly of a rundown of CDs mirrored by an increased uptake of LA deposits. In view of the results of the previous chapter, this adjustment is entirely cosmetic, only being limited by considerations of portfolio balance on the part of banks. However, the empirical results suggest that these frictions are important, so that given the lags in the behaviour of lending a large short-run residual adjustment to the shadow price of money-market finance is required. This builds up to 0.7 per cent by the second quarter and is clearly reflected in the behaviour of T-bill and lending rates. As the effect of this comes through on to lending, the need for bank portfolio adjustments is diminished and the residual is reduced. As in the previous simulation, the bank-lending responses are cyclical, although in this case the scheme is removed before this becomes apparent. Interest-rate adjustments on the kind of scale exhibited in this run would perhaps have some effect on activity, though this could go either way, depending upon whether this was more sensitive to market or bank rates.

Finally I would note that both Zawadski (1981) and Hall (1983) have suggested that the effect of imposing the scheme is to allow a general *lowering* of the level of interest rates. This will indeed be the case if there is scope for cosmetic adjustment, allowing the banks to continue with the rest of their business, but even then we would expect to see some accommodating movement in relative rates of return. Once the scheme begins to affect the rest of the bank's business, however—as it undoubtedly did during 1979–80—the system must respond by pushing lending rates up relative to wholesale deposit rates and on my estimates this will imply a *rise* in the absolute level of lending rates.

5. Conclusions: bank liability-management and the problem of monetary control

These results illustrate the difficulties of controlling the monetary aggregates through short-term market operations when banks act as liability managers. In such a situation banks can cover any increase in their lending by simply bidding for funds in the wholesale markets. Attempts by the authorities to control this process by restricting the supply of reserve assets or calling for special deposits are futile, and in some circumstances counter-productive. The management of such a system is clearly a subtle affair.

The experience with the early CCC system clearly underlines this point. The initial relaxation of credit control, together with the reintroduction of personal interest relief, implied a very large increase in bank lending to the private sector. This was estimated at £7.5 billions—about half of the overall increase during 1972–3. Some of these funds would have been reinvested with the banks, given lags in expenditure and investment decisions, but the leakage from this system and the reserve requirement quickly led to a tightening of the banks reserve-asset positions, causing the banks to bid these back through aggressive sales of CDs and other wholesale deposit items. The authorities reinforced the pressure on the banks' reserve assets by calling for special deposits. Yet the banks again responded by issuing wholesale deposits, rather than by selling secondary reserve assets as the authorities had originally envisaged.

The authorities' open-market operations were intially confined to switches between reserve assets and cash. They therefore had little means of preventing the differential between parallel money-market rates and reserve-asset rates from widening in response to the banks' behaviour. Under the MLR formula this opened up a differential between money-market rates and prime lending rates, encouraging perverse arbitrage transactions. The effect of this on company borrowing alone was estimated at £2.5 billion. This in turn amplified the pressure on bank portfolios and the money markets. The model suggests that this kind of process is unstable given an unchanged supply of reserve assets and an MLR linked to T-bill rates.

The SSD scheme, introduced in December 1973, was designed to break into this spiral by making bank-liability management prohibitively expensive. As a consequence, the round-tripping process unwound during 1974, permitting a general reduction in interest rates and a release of Special Deposits. The scheme was suspended in February 1975 but has been used frequently since then, being particularly effective during 1979 and the first half of 1980. The scheme had various effects, many of them cosmetic, but it did tend to increase bank base rates both absolutely and relative to money-market rates. The abolition of exchange controls in October 1979, opening up an efficient 'eurosterling leak', led this scheme to be abandoned in June 1980.

In the intervening periods when the SSD scheme has not been in place, the authorities have relied upon discretionary changes in MLR—backed up by calls for Special Deposits and open-market operations—as a way of controlling bank credit and the monetary aggregates through the general level of interest rates. Although these measures tend to work rather slowly, they can, as we shall see, be reinforced by more active gilt-edged market policies, allowing a reasonable degree of short-run monetary control whilst avoiding the perverse side-effects associated with a squeeze on bank portfolios. The Treasury has tended to view these policies as acting on the demand for money (see, for example, HM Treasury (1980b)), although 'disequilibrium money' theorists have argued that this amounts to a supply-side control (Artis and Lewis (1981) pp. 29–30)). The name is perhaps a matter of taste. But putting these labels to one side, this kind of policy should obviously be distinguished from one which is designed to operate primarily through a reduction in the reserve-asset base of the banking system. It is also quite different from a measure—such as the SSD scheme—which attempts to control bank portfolios directly. As we have seen, these policies may have perverse side-effects and—since the abolition of exchange controls—would cause UK banks to lose business to their eurosterling and other competitors. However, a 'demand-side' approach—by which I mean one directed at the counterparts of money in the portfolios of non-banks rather than banks—is not handicapped in this way.

Notes

1. These items offer another cross-check on the econometric estimates discussed in the previous chapter. They are strongly correlated with estimates of the cost of the scheme indicated by equation V.(7).
2. It is in principle possible to work back to the implied level of the ceiling using an equation such as (12) of the previous chapter (together with one for the bill leak and any other cosmetic effects which are thought to be relevant). The overall effect of a historical application of the scheme can be analysed quite conveniently by introducing econometric estimates of the interest-rate cost equivalent (such as those derived from our estimates of this equation) as fixed residual adjustments in the adjusted-rate identity (7). However, such results are more difficult to understand than the one presented here.
3. This differential is also affected by the relative rise in T-bill rates. This tends to reduce the adjusted cost of funds, although the effect is very small.

PART TWO
Monetary Targets, the Exchange Rate, and the Role of Expectations in an Open Economy

VII

The Experience of Monetary Targets

Introduction and Summary

The architects of the CCC system believed that the demand for money and credit was sufficiently interest elastic to allow fiscal and monetary policies to be pursued independently. To the extent that conflicts between these policies emerged, as they did in the 1973 budget, for example, the emphasis placed on demand management meant that monetary policy was naturally subordinate to fiscal policy. Yet the events of the 1970s lead to an increasing degree of pessimism about these interest elasticities and to worries about the effect of high and volatile interest rates on the private sector. At the same time, doubts about the efficacy of demand-management policies and concern about the effect of inflation on the economy mounted. So, by the end of the decade, fiscal and monetary policies were regarded as being almost inseparable, with former being subordinate to the latter.

At the same time the dramatic behaviour of sterling led to a renewed interest in the connection between monetary policy and the exchange rate. The monetary theories initially used to explain this behaviour were very simple and suggested that monetary policy promised a relatively quick and reliable means of controlling prices in an open economy, with minimal side-effects upon activity. As experience accumulated and these theories developed it became increasingly apparent that these exchange-rate effects, though clearly very powerful, were not as straightforward as had initially been thought. It is the purpose of the second part of this work to look at UK macroeconomic policy in the second half of the 1970s against this theoretical background and examine some of the complexities involved.

This chapter begins with a brief review of this experience, beginning with the agreement with the IMF of December 1976. This brought an end to the fall in the exchange rate and ushered in a regime of published monetary targets, seen initially as a way of buttressing the incomes policy. The rebound of confidence in 1977 soon lead to a conflict between the authorities' exchange-rate objectives and the monetary targets agreed with the IMF. In the event they decided in favour of the latter, the 'uncapping' of sterling in October of that year underlining the commitment to a more determined counter-inflationary policy stance.

The pressures on the monetary targets under the first two years of the Thatcher administration are then examined. These included the wage increases which followed the breakdown of the incomes policy and the oil-price rise which followed the Iranian revolution. The effect of such inflationary pressures under a regime of monetary targets is to push up interest rates and the exchange rate as shown by the Dornbusch (1976) exchange-rate overshooting model which is discussed briefly, together with the work of Minford, Buiter and Miller, and other commentators. The debate about the effect of the North Sea oil discoveries—the Kay and Forsyth thesis—is also reviewed, together with various contemporary estimates of the effect of these developments on the exchange rate. Finally, the links between fiscal and monetary policy are examined in the context of the Medium Term Financial Strategy and the philosophy underlying the 1981 budget.

1   The uncapping of sterling in October 1977

The rebound of confidence in the exchange rate which followed the IMF agreement was initially welcomed by the authorities as a chance to rebuild the exchange reserves. However, as the inflows continued they came to pose an acute policy dilemma, forcing a choice between the newly published monetary targets and the authorities' exchange-rate and competitiveness objectives. This chapter begins with a look at the nature of this dilemma and the way in which it was resolved.

Monetary policy had been more or less dictated by the need to maintain the exchange rate until this was floated in June 1972. As we have seen, the decision to float the exchange rate was taken largely in order to allow more freedom of action on domestic economic policy. But in the event, monetary policy continued to be influenced by external considerations—not so much during 1973 and 1974, when the perverse behaviour of the monetary aggregates was the prime concern, but certainly during 1975 and 1976. The exchange rate was also supported on a large scale by official intervention, largely financed by foreign-currency borrowing. Indeed, the behaviour of the authorities over this period induced a very significant correlation between the exchange rate and both the reserves and (in a negative direction) UK interest rates. The strength of these reactions make it extremely difficult to identify sensible exchange-rate or capital-flow relationships over this period, as has been demonstrated for example by Haache and Townend (1981).

This econometric work confirms the general impression given by anecdotal evidence and official statements that monetary policy over this period was strongly influenced by competitiveness or real exchange-rate objectives. (Indeed the slide in sterling which began early in 1975 was initially started by a rumour that the Bank of England had sold sterling in the belief that the real exchange rate was too high.) However, as was noted in the Introduction, monetary economists came to argue over this period that price competitiveness, being a real phenomenon, could not be affected by monetary or nominal exchange-rate policies, which would simply be offset in domestic prices—any attempt to meet an unwarranted competitiveness, output, or other real target would lead to runaway inflation. The slide in sterling during 1975–6 provided support for this belief, causing a marked upturn in the rate of inflation despite the incomes policy which was in place, and in turn imposing a severe strain on the incomes policy itself. A contemporary study by economists using the Treasury model (Odling-Smee and Hartley (1978) suggested that the effect of a devaluation on international price competitiveness would be entirely eroded by domestic inflation within a four to five-year period. At the same time, policy-makers became increasingly concerned about the effect of inflation upon expenditure and employment.

Although monetary growth during the first half of 1977 was not an immediate concern to the authorities, interest rates had by October been reduced to very low levels. MLR stood at 5 per cent. With the almost certain boost that this would give to bank lending in later months, this faced the authorities with a clear choice between the exchange-rate peg and the sterling M3 target. In view of their increasing concern about the effect of inflation on expenditure and the doubts about their ability to influence competitiveness, they opted for the latter, lifting the cap. In the event this hardly affected the rate. But its removal underlined the comitment to a much more determined counter-inflationary policy stance. The logical connection between monetary policy, inflation, and the exchange rate dictated that the exchange rate be left to find its own level in the market.

In the event, the worries about bank lending to the private sector proved well-founded. At the same time the CGBR was unexpectedly high and there was a pause in sales of gilts to non-banks. Consequently sterling M3, only slightly above its target growth range (of 9–13 per cent) in October 1977, ended up 3 per cent above target by the end of the financial year 1977–8. This was due in part to a last-minute change in seasonal adjustment factors. Although the overshoot was largely due to the attempt to cap the exchange rate, the initial experience with monetary targets was therefore a slightly unfortunate one.

The experience with the monetary targets during the financial year 1978–9 was a rather happier one, at least in terms of the final outcome. The exchange rate came under downward pressure during the Spring of 1978, reflecting worries about the rate of monetary growth and the fiscal relaxation announced in the April budget. This coincided with another pause in sales of gilt-edged stocks. In this instance there was no conflict between monetary and exchange-rate considerations, which both pointed in the same direction. Interest rates were increased and there was a substantial amount of intervention in support of sterling (£2 billions during the second calendar quarter). Yet these measures were not very effective in restoring confidence—especially in the gilt market—and had to be reinforced by a package of fiscal and monetary measured in June 1978. This included the restoration of the corset. This package had he desired effect and the rest of the financial year was marked by large sales of gilts and a rising exchange rate, with minimal intervention. Sterling M3 ended the period just above the middle of the target range of 8–12 per cent.

2   The PSBR and funding arrangements

Although the initial experience with monetary targets was not an easy one, eventually forcing the authorites to reimpose the corset in June 1978, this experience was certainly not as traumatic as those of 1976 or 1973–4. The resilience exhibited by the exchange rate in the face of doubts about the PSBR and, towards the end of the period, the incomes policy, can be attributed directly to the safety net afforded by the monetary targets, together perhaps with the build-up of oil production. I have already argued that the avoidance of market instabilities was partly due to the adoption of a new *modus operandi* in the short-term money markets. It was also due to the increased reliance upon control of the PSBR and gilts sales as weapons of monetary policy. This meant that the authorities could afford to adopt a less anxious attitude towards adverse movements in bank lending to the private sector.

The main worry about a high PSBR is that it will ultimately lead to a high rate of inflation. But in the short run, before the necessary portfolio and inflationary adjustments have taken place, the problem is that a high PSBR will swell the growth of the monetary aggregates and that interest rates will have to rise to prevent this. This is in part because—as we saw in Chapter II—the private sector will naturally tend to increase its holdings of both money and gilt-edged stocks as its wealth increases. Some of the empirical evidence relating to these portfolio effects is examined in the next chapter.

The monetary authorities can in principle offset such effects on the demand for money by raising the rate of return on non-monetary assets. This will tend to raise the cost of bank credit and reduce the demand by the private sector. But as we have seen, by the time that monetary targets had been adopted the authorities had come to realize that they could not rely upon such effects to work smoothly or quickly. They therefore came to place an increasing degree of reliance upon the gilt-edged market (and the national saving media) as a way of funding the PSBR and influencing monetary growth in the short term.

Of course, the use of long-term markets to fund debt can never be entirely straightforward. It is difficult to persuade investors in such markets to buy large tranches of stock when they are uncertain of future developments and in particular future demands upon the market. In the case of the gilts market, the government broker can sell more or less what he likes when the market is in a confident mood, but his room for manœuvre is extremely limited when it is uncertain. He cannot move his tap price ahead of the market for fear of upsetting the apple cart. Sales of gilts by tender would have similar effects in such an uncertain situation. In the absence of hard information such a market will stagnate, or drift downwards, until it is generally felt that the downside risk is small, and it starts to recover. Monetary control is a rather haphazard affair in this kind of environment.

This problem was most acute during the early years of CCC when the authorities were slow to keep their MLR up with market rates and the markets were perhaps uncertain of their intentions. Despite the pressure on the monetary aggregates, very few gilts were sold over these years. The authorities manipulated MLR a lot more actively following this experience, both in order to induce a favourable response from the gilt-edged market and avoid an unfavourable short-term market response. This policy soon became predictable, being known as the 'Duke of York' tactic. (Dennis (1982) gives a good description of the way in which this tactic worked and suggests that the rise in MLR in October 1975 constitutes the first example of its use.)

The adoption of monetary targets and the concern in more recent years for the size of the PSBR has had the effect of making the authorities' demands upon the gilt market much more specific and of minimizing the longer-term uncertainties about inflation and interest rates. There is therefore an essential synergy between the move towards financial targets and the increased reliance upon funding policy and these should not be regarded as separate developments.What seems to happen in this situation is that following the announcement of these objectives, the market marks gilt-edged prices (and hence expected returns) up to a level at which it is prepared to take up the implied amount of stock. This process generally works quite smoothly, although it may take a few days for prices to adjust to the appropriate level. There have, however, been occasions upon which the prices which investors felt necessary were well out of line with actual prices and this brought the market to a standstill. In this situation, the authorities had had to judge whether or not the existing level of prices was broadly appropriate. When this was the case they have tended to sit pat and let the situation resolve itself naturally. On other occasions (June 1978, for example) they have taken an initiative on public expenditure as a way of resolving the situation.

Despite this qualification, it is reasonable to characterize this situation as one in which the authorities set the quantity of gilt sales via a monetary target and let the market decide the price which will validate this. The simulations reported in Chapter X are based upon this assumption. Chapter VIII takes a look at the extent to which the authorities have been able to influence the rate of return on gilts and the effect which this has had on sales to non-bank residents.

These developments have been backed up by improvements in the flexibility of funding instruments. The reintroduction of part-paid gilts in March 1977 has allowed the authorities to secure finance several months in advance of the date at which it is needed, obviating the need to sell gilts on a continuous basis. This has also been convenient for investors, and most new issues are now conducted on this basis. The introduction of variable-rate stocks in May 1977, largely as a way of maintaining sales in an uncertain or falling market, has been less successful, partly because the interest rate on these stocks has been linked to Treasury-bill rather than money-market interest rates. Finally, the introduction of index-linked stocks in May 1980 has allowed investors to avoid the risk of adverse inflationary developments and these have at times offered the authorities a useful way of keeping the funding programme going.

3   Wage inflation and the collapse of the incomes policy

Monetary targets were initially adopted by the Labour government to support the incomes policy which had been in place since the Autumn of 1975. They certainly did not constitute the only pillar of counter-inflation policy. It was thought that the monetary targets would at least prevent the kind of strains which the incomes policy had come under with the collapse of sterling in 1976. This had implied a significant drop in real earnings. Indeed, many economists—notably those at the London Business School (LBS)—had argued against the capping of sterling in 1977, maintaining that an exchange-rate appreciation would moderate the pressure for higher money wages.

As it was, the pressure on the incomes policy increased, and the attempt to impose a 5 per cent norm in the Autumn of 1978 lead to the 'Winter of Discontent' and its eventual collapse. It is not entirely clear to what extent monetary policy was itself responsible for this pressure. The rapid growth in sterling M3 during 1977 and the first half of 1978 has already been discussed, and although it moderated following the reintroduction of the corset in June 1978, this slowdown may well have been due to cosmetic effects. With the benefit of hindsight, it is now quite evident that the corset severly distorted sterling M3 during 1979 and the first half of 1980—by more more than it was thought at the time. These distortions may well have affected the other aggregates. Sterling M3 jumped by over 5 per cent in the two months following the removal of the corset. In view of the rapid expansion of bank lending which took place in subsequent months, this kind of figure probably understates the effect the corset had in suppressing the signs of monetary diequilibrium and inflationary pressure building up in the economy in the late 1970s. There seems, nevertheless, to have been a strong autonomous element in the inflationary wage pressures seen over this period.

Whatever the reason for this, the breakdown of the incomes policy faced policy-makers with the choice of financing these increases in wages or taking measures to reign back the consequent growth in the monetary aggregates. In the event this decision was left to the Conservative administration which

came into office following the fall of the Labour Government in the Spring of
1979

4   The medium term financial strategy

The incoming administration was firmly committed to monetary targets,
backed up by a tight control of government expenditure and reductions in
government borrowing. This commitment was underlined by the June 1979
budget which reduced the (annualized) target-growth range for sterling M3
to 7–11 per cent for the rest of the financial year (albeit based on the high
June figure) and published a PSBR forecast of £8.3 billions for that year, this
representing a reduction on previous projections. At the same time MLR was
raised to 14 per cent. The SSD scheme was retained as a temporary
expedient whilst these measures took effect. The budget also involved a
major switch from direct to indirect taxation in an effort to restore incentives
and improve the 'supply side' of the economy. The effect of this switch in
inflationary expectations was countered by the publication of the 'tax and
price' index which took account of the effect of the income-tax reductions on
real take-home pay.

The June 1979 budget marked the first stage of a gradualist programme of
reductions in the rate of monetary growth, borrowing, and inflation. This
programme was formalized in the Medium Term Financial Strategy
(MTFS) announced in the budget of March 1980. The sterling M3 growth
range was to be reduced progressively from 7–11 per cent in 1980–1 to 4–8
per cent in 1983–4 whilst the PSBR was to be reduced from $3\frac{3}{4}$ per cent of
GDP to $1\frac{1}{2}$ per cent.

In the event, wage inflation accelerated further during 1979. Together
with other inflationary developments in the economy this made the
government's monetary objectives much tighter than they would otherwise
have been. Wage bargainers failed to appreciate the resolve of the new
administration and presumably believed that a high level of settlements
would be accommodated by monetary policy as it always had been in the
past. This experience has lead macroeconomists to become interested in the
informational and game-theoretic structure of macroeconomic policy, and to
emphasize the need for this policy to be 'credible'.

These policies appeared fully credible in the financial markets, however,
especially when they were backed up by increases in interest rates: MLR was
raised to 17 per cent in November 1979. So the exchange rate, instead of
falling in the face of these developments as it had done on previous occasions,
tended instead to rise. This appreciation was reinforced by the UK's
possession of North Sea oil which left it well placed in the wake of the Iranian
revolution and the ensuing uncertainty about oil prices. The effective
exchange rate rose by 22 per cent between the end of 1978 and the end of

1980 whilst UK labour costs rose by 45 per cent compared to those of her competitors (measured in common-currency terms.)

5   Alternative explanations of the rise in sterling

A loss of competitiveness on this scale was unprecedented in the UK and quite unforseen. It is difficult to rationalize fully even in retrospect. It was clear to contemporary observers that monetary and oil-related factors were largely responsible, but there was considerable dispute as to the relative influence of these factors.

The first of these explanations had several different strands. The basic view, put forward notably by Buiter and Miller (1981), was that monetary targets were tight in relation to the underlying level of inflation in the economy. A slightly different version, put forward by J. Forsyth (1980) amongst others, saw monetary policy as tight relative to fiscal policy. Both versions saw this relative tightness being reflected in high interest rates and, through the effect of this on the capital account, the real exchange rate. The policy implications were, however, quite different; the Miller–Buiter school arguing for a relaxation of monetary policy, and the Forsyth school for a tightening of fiscal policy.

Miller and Buiter provided some interesting estimates of these competitiveness effects based on the model developed by Dornbusch (1976) discussed in Chapter IX. The basic assumption in this kind of model is that the domestic labour market looks backwards when forming its expectations and is slow to adjust, whereas financial markets are forward looking and quick to react. So, in contrast to simple monetary models, it is interest rates and not prices which bring the short-run demand for money into line with the supply. Consequently a once-and-for-all reduction in the money supply—or equivalently an autonomous increase in wages and the demand for money—means a rise in interest rates which attracts capital inflows. This causes the exchange rate to 'overshoot' the equilibrium value dictated by relative money supplies and implies a loss of competitiveness which persists until prices and interest rates have adjusted. In contrast a reduction in the rate of monetary *growth* as in the MTFS tends to reduce nominal interest rates through its effect on the rate of inflation. But the net effect is to cause a rise in the demand for money and a temporary rise in real interest rates which again causes a temporary rise in the real exchange rate through its effect on capital inflows.

The original Buiter and Miller estimates suggested that a 1 per cent p.a. reduction in the rate of monetary growth would reduce competitiveness by $1\frac{1}{2}$ per cent. On this basis Miller and Buiter calculated that the reduction in the target monetary growth rate during 1979–80, together with the abolition of the SSD scheme and the rise in VAT, had reduced the level of competitiveness by $7\frac{1}{2}$ per cent. In addition they argued that the reductions announced in the MTFS would have affected competitiveness, though this was much more uncertain and they did not offer any estimates of this effect.

There were also several strands to the oil-based explanation of sterling's strength. The first was that North Sea production had been building up rapidly: with obvious benefit to the current account. This influence was stressed by Forsyth and Kay (1980) who estimated that the build-up of production would reduce UK competitiveness by 20 to 25 per cent. This study used pre-1979 oil prices as the basis of the calculation and was based upon an examination of the trade account, omitting capital-account considerations. The analysis was based upon the observation that an increase in oil output would on balance save imports and increase the exchange rate until current-account equilibrium was restored. Such an estimate depends critically upon the base date and the competitiveness elasticity of the non-oil trade account employed—the higher the elasticity the lower the rise in competitiveness necessary to achieve current-account balance. Forsyth and Kay took as their estimate of this elasticity the central value from a range of studies.

The Forsyth and Kay paper was the subject of much discussion. Critics pointed to the neglect of offsetting capital flows. Others used higher estimates of the competitiveness elasticities to obtain smaller value for the impact of rising output. For example, Professors Miller and Williamson wrote an article in the Guardian newspaper, suggesting that an estimate of 5 per cent was more realistic. Professor Niehans came to a similar conclusion (Niehans (1981)). Yet despite its interest, this debate was not entirely relevant to the problem of explaining the rise in sterling. This is because a properly functioning exchange market should have anticipated these developments well before they occurred. The bulk of the effect (at 1978 prices) should have been built into the exchange rate by the beginning of 1979, as I demonstrate in Chapter X, so that any appreciation during 1979 and 1980 due to the increase in production must have been small. Had real oil prices remained at their 1978 levels it is difficult to see why the increase in production should have had a dramatic effect on the exchange rate.

Of course, the doubling of the real oil price over this period was unexpected. The effect of this on the current account was at the time broadly neutral since the UK was only just self-sufficient in oil. Yet sterling probably did benefit from the effect on expectations and capital flows of the UK's position as a potential net exporter during the mid-1980s. The capital account also benefited from the effect of higher OPEC surpluses. Some estimates of these effects were made at the time using the Treasury macroeconomic model and were reported in a Treasury working paper (Byatt *et al.* (1982)). These calculations suggested that a $1 per barrel rise in the price of oil led to a permanent loss of competitiveness of $\frac{1}{2}$ per cent. On this basis, the rise of $15 a barrel which took place between 1978 and 1980 in

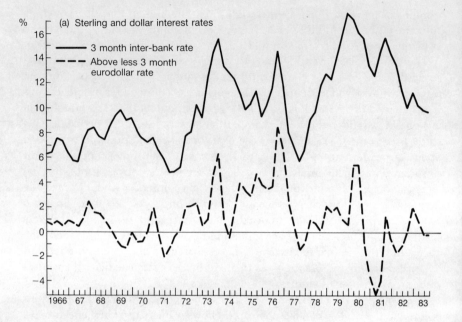

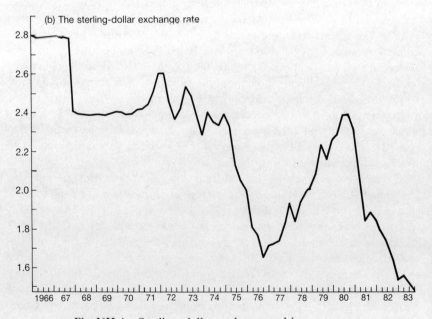

Fig. VII.A   Sterling–dollar exchange and interest rates.

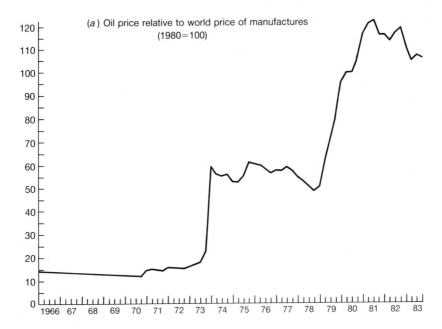

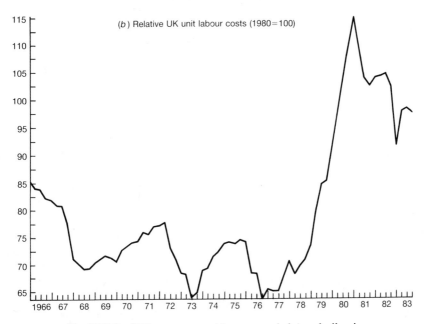

Fig. VII.B   UK cost competitiveness and the real oil price.

the price of North Sea oil would have caused a permanent loss of competitiveness of $7\frac{1}{2}$ per cent.

These simulations suggested that the short-run loss of competitiveness could be significantly greater than this long-run effect. This is because the response of the non-oil trade account to changes in competitiveness tends to be a slow one, requiring a larger change in the short run than the long run to produce a given effect on trade flows. In principle such dynamic effects should be offset by speculative capital movements, depending upon the degree of capital mobility, but in practice they may have led to a temporary overshooting of the real exchange rate. In addition, it was suggested that the build up of North Sea oil output gave sterling the status of a petrocurrency, in that it acted as a hedge against oil-related uncertainties. This may have caused a portfolio shift into sterling but it is difficult to evaluate the loss of competitiveness which this may have caused.

In short, none of these explanations, taken individually or in sum, adequately explain the rise in sterling and the loss of competitiveness during 1979 and 1980. This may have reflected a failure to identify important effects (such as the effect of autonomous wage-pressures) or the difficulty of quantifying those influences which were identified (such as the MTFS). Despite more recent attempts to analyse the factors at work (my own results being reported in Chapter X) it must be admitted that we are little the wiser now than we were at the time. As it happens the rise in sterling has been overtaken by a rise in the US dollar, seemingly related to an imbalance between US monetary and fiscal policy. This has made it very difficult to analyse the behaviour of sterling since 1980 and to judge whether the high exchange rate seen during that year was in fact warranted.

6 The 1981 budget strategy

The combined effect of the inflationary pressures felt during 1979 and 1980 and the non-accommodating monetary policy was to produce a very sharp recession in output. This was compounded by the world recession which was itself partly the result of the rise in oil prices. The rise in the exchange rate had the effect of moderating the rise in inflation, helping consumers to maintain both their incomes and the value of their savings. Yet it intensified the effect of the squeeze on the company sector, especially those manufacturing companies exposed to international competition. Profitability and liquidity levels in manufacturing industry, which were already very low, fell to even lower levels as the competition intensified. Manufacturing companies responded by drastically cutting employment, as well as stocks and investment plans, leading to a sharp rise in unemployment.

In the face of this recession it proved impossible, given existing expenditure plans, to keep to the PSBR trends announced in the MFTS. There had originally been some debate as to whether or not it was appropriate to allow the PSBR to vary in a counter-cyclical way about this trend, but this soon became quite academic. These problems came to a head during the financial year 1980–1. They became clear early on in the year, when a PSBR figure for the second (calendar) quarter of £4½ billion emerged, compared with a full-year projection of £8½ billions. Despite attempts to retrieve this situation, the full-year PSBR overshot substantially, amounting to 5½ per cent of GDP, compared with the original objective of 3¾ per cent. Although sales of gilt-edged stocks held up remarkably well, this greatly increased the pressures on the monetary aggregates, particularly the sterling M3 indicator, swollen as it was by reintermediation effects following the abolition of the corset in June 1980. This aggregate increased by 18½ per cent between February 1980 and April 1981, against the background target range of 7–11 per cent.

The recession had clearly blown the MTFS off course. Although the resilience of the gilts market allowed some leeway on the original projections, the Chancellor faced a choice between yet higher interest rates or a cutback in borrowing in order to get back on track. The eventual decision taken in the 1981 budget was to trim the PSBR by £3 billion compared to what it would otherwise have been. This gave a PSBR figure for 1981–2 of £10½ billion or 4¼ per cent of GDP, compared with the original MTFS projections of 3 per cent. It was also announced that the behaviour of the exchange rate would in future be taken into account when interpreting the thrust of monetary policy.

It was thought that the reduction in borrowing would give enough headroom to continue the interest-rate reductions which had begun on a modest scale in June 1980. In the event, however, the tightening of monetary conditions in the US, and the marked rise in dollar exchange and interest rates which this implied, delayed these reductions. These developments have made it as difficult to judge the success of the 1981 budget as they have the recent behaviour of the exchange rate. Nevertheless, it is difficult to see how the reductions in inflation and interest rates which took place in 1982 and 1983 could have been possible had the MTFS not been brought back on course in 1981. And, contrary to many predictions, the 1981 budget coincided with the turning-point of the cycle, marking the beginning of a sustained economic expansion.

VIII

The Gilt-edged Market and the Speculative Demand for Money

Introduction and summary

This chapter looks at some of the links between the PSBR and the monetary aggregates which work through the effect of the associated changes in the financial wealth of the private sector on the demand for money. At the empirical stage, this question is pursued indirectly, by investigating the effect of changes in wealth on the demand for gilts and the other counterparts to money in private-sector portfolios. I will also look at the scope for bond-financed fiscal policies by investigating the extent to which the authorities can successfully manipulate the relative rate of return on long-term securities and will try to determine the effect that this has on the demand by resident non-banks. This leaves the impact effects of fiscal policy on activity and prices, both of which will tend to affect the demand for money. These depend upon the composition of the expenditure and financing effects of the package. For this reason fiscal policies which have the same effect on the PSBR and the financial wealth of the private sector may have very different consequences for the monetary aggregates. This point is, however, pursued by Middleton *et al.* (1981) and is not taken up here.

The analysis starts with a simple illustrative model of the gilts market in which both demand and supply depend upon various current-dated variables, notably the overall return on gilts including expected capital gains (relative to that on wholesale money-market instruments). I show that this 'expected return' clears the market and I solve for two simple reduced forms which explain this, together with the quantity traded, in terms of the *current* values of variables impinging on the market. The only way in which this model differs from the conventional market equilibrium one is that the market-clearing variable is unobservable—a problem which can be handled in a fairly straightforward way using the McCallum (1975) substitution method.

I next ask what happens if demand or supply depends upon the separate components of the expected return, so that this variable cannot be seen unambiguously as clearing the market. I use as an example the case in which the authorities lean into the wind. In this case there are at least three endogenous variables: the quantity traded, the long-term gilt-edged yield, and the associated expected gain. This model must be solved by forward substitution and the reduced forms for these variables will involve expectations about the *future* values of the variables impinging upon the market. I point out the various conceptual and technical problems which this involves and derive a reduced form for the expected differential return which depends upon current-period variables representing these expected future values (the information set).

The various possible simultaneity and measurement-error biases are illustrated using the correspondence between the simple model and the conventional market-clearing model. In the more complex case it is appropriate to estimate the demand function directly, replacing the *ex ante* expected differential return by the out-turn, but instrumenting this with the value predicted from a first-stage regression of the out-turn on the relevant information set. Some simple econometric results of this type, drawn from my (1981) *Economic Journal* paper on the gilts market, are then presented.

These results suggest that during the 1960s and 1970s, at least, it was possible to predict a non-zero differential return using a fairly simple regressive-expectations model in which gilt yields followed short-term UK and overseas interest rates and the expected rate of inflation. These differential returns could be as high as 20 per cent (p.a.) for short periods of time. The lag was almost certainly due to a leaning into the wind effect. These expectations apparently had a powerful effect on the demand for gilts and, by implication, the demand for money. There seems, therefore, to be some considerable scope for the authorities to manipulate expectations in order to fund public-sector deficits. But such conditions imply rising gilt prices, which cannot be sustained indefinitely. So the scope for bond-financed deficits in the long run is rather limited. This chapter concludes with a comparison of these results with those obtained by Bennett and Grice (1984), using a similar set of explanatory variables to explain the demand for money directly.

1 The PSBR, financial-asset accumulation, and the demand for money

Kaldor (1970) showed that the short-run statistical relationship between the monetary aggregates, interest rates, and the PSBR was a rather tenuous one. More recently Llewellyn (1982, pp. 104–9) has noted that the sharp rise in the PSBR since 1974 has coincided with an equally sharp increase in gilt sales to the private sector, reducing the proportion financed by monetary expansion. Yet this should come as no surprise. To some extent, the other so-called money-supply counterparts would be expected to offset movements in the PSBR automatically, due to the portfolio behaviour of the private sector. Gilt sales should also tend to act as an offset given the emphasis placed by the authorities since 1974 on funding operations. If the fiscal and monetary authorities pursue separate objectives and if moreover the relevant interest rates are difficult to measure, one should not expect to find any simple *ex post* relationship between the monetary aggregates, interest rates, and the PSBR. The only way of proceeding in this kind of situation is through a careful econometric study, distinguishing between demand and supply factors and taking account of the likely expectational effects.

The approach employed here focuses upon the proximate determinants of the demand for money viewed as part of the balance sheet of the non-bank private sector (NBPS). One of the major objectives of this work has been to look at the connection between the PSBR and the monetary aggregates working through the net financial-asset position of the NBPS. To recap, this analysis sees the net financial wealth of the NBPS as being largely exogenous to its decisions in the short run, the result of asset-accumulation effects which work very slowly. For this kind of reason portfolios will typically be in disequilibrium. This disequilibrium will extend to holdings of financial assets generally and will not be confined to money balances. In this framework a change in the public-sector financial deficit—to the extent that this is reflected in an NBPS rather than an overseas-sector financial surplus—will change its net financial wealth and this will spill over into the short-run demand for money. This disequilibrium effect will disappear over time as the NBPS readjusts its financial-asset position through its expenditure. Yet it is important from a short-to medium-term perspective to establish just how strong these disequilibrium wealth effects are.

2   Gilt-edged expectations and the speculative demand for money

In the short-run, when financial wealth is given, bank advances and the demand for gilts and similar assets may be seen as the counterparts of money in the balance sheet of the NBPS. For this reason the demand for broad money is likely to be complex—acting as a buffer in the portfolio—taking up the slack between these items and the overall size of the portfolio, and therefore reflecting a variety of speculative precautionary and transactional influences. However, given certain plausible assumptions about the nature of speculative and precautionary risks, its counterparts may be shown to have relatively simple, separable demand functions. The demand for advances will depend only upon precautionary factors and the demand for gilts (and other non-monetary assets) only upon speculative considerations. This argument is set out in Appendix I. In this sense the demand for bank borrowing may be seen as the obverse of the precautionary demand for money and the demand for gilts as the obverse of the speculative demand for money. Moreover, the demands for these items, taken together with financial wealth, effectively determine the short-run demand for money through the balance-sheet identity of the NBPS.

In view of this it is convenient to model the demand for money indirectly—through its counterparts in the NBPS balance sheet. Bank borrowing was discussed in Chapter IV, and so it remains to develop a model of the NBPS demand for gilts and other long-term public-sector debt.

In view of my introductory remarks, I will be primarily interested in investigating the degree of substitution between these long-term items and short-term monetary assets and their sensitivity to changes in financial wealth.

The basic model underlying this work is a linear specification derived from mean-variance theory. This relates the NBPS demand for gilts (G, deflated by some scale variance S such as wealth or income) to the *expected* differential rate of return between these and short-term instruments ($(r_G + \mu_g - r_M)$, where r_G and r_M are the observed yields on gilts and money-market instruments and μ_g represents expected capital gains on gilts). In order to allow for hedging behaviour, the general specification also includes a hedging term $h'Z$ (a linear function of a vector of variables (Z) such as the investor's perceived correlation between unexpected gains on gilts and changes in the price level):

$$G/S = h'Z + k(r_G + \mu_g - r_M) + e_d. \tag{1}$$

This equation is derived and discussed in Appendix I. The term e_d is an additive-error term with zero mean, assumed to be uncorrelated with the exogenous variables impinging upon the market. The term (k) is a parameter reflecting the degree of uncertainty about returns on gilts, and the risk aversion of the typical investor. If either of these influences is negligible this parameter will become infinitely large and the gilts market will be dominated by speculators. In this special case the equilibrium market solution will be one in which the expected differential return is zero:

$$(r_G + \mu_g - r_M) = 0. \tag{2}$$

This is the case of the 'Expectations Hypothesis' (EH), familiar from the theory of the Term Structure of Interest Rates (Malkiel (1966)). In general, however, we need to make some assumption about the behaviour of other market participants—particularly the authorities—in order to investigate the equilibrium solution.

Suppose, for example, that we represent the authorities' supply of gilts by a similar linear expression in the expected return (or differential return) and a vector of other predetermined supply-side variables (X):

$$G/S = a'X + b(r_G + \mu_g - r_M) + e_s \tag{3}$$

Then (neglecting for simplicity the demands of other sectors) we may solve (1) and (3) to give the quantity of gilts and the expected differential return as functions of *current* exogenous (or predetermined) variables:[1]

$$(r_G + \mu_g - r_M) = p_x'X + p_z'Z + u_R \tag{4}$$

$$G/S = q_x'X + q_z'Z + u_G \tag{5}$$

where

$$p_x = Da' \quad p_z = -Dh' \quad u_R = D(e_s - e_d) \quad D = (k - b)^{-1}$$

$$q_x = Dka' \quad q_z = -Dbh' \quad u_G = D(be_s - ke_d)$$

The error terms (u_R, u_G) in these reduced-form equations are uncorrelated with the predetermined explanatory variables given that we assume that this is true of the structural-error terms (e_s, e_d).

These equations are of interest in that they are the analogues of the reduced forms which are obtained for observed prices (or interest rates) and quantities in a conventional situation, in which the former clear the market. The only difference is that in this case the market-clearing variable—the expected return—is not directly observable. Some relatively simple ways of getting around this problem are reviewed in the next section.[2]

The problem becomes much more complicated if the supply function (or for that matter the reaction function of any market participant) is not homogeneous in the expected return, so that capital gains and interest returns on gilts do not have the same impact. In this case, expected returns on gilts (or the differential return) cannot be viewed unambiguously as clearing the market. Suppose, for example, that the authorities lean into the wind, so that the supply of gilts depends upon the change in gilt prices or yields:

$$G/S = b(r_G - r_{G(-1)}) + a'X + e_s. \qquad (3)'$$

In this case we may obtain a relationship between r_L, μ_g, r_M and the predetermined variables of the system (using (2) and $(3)'$), but this is no longer homogeneous as in (4):

$$r_G = p_x'X + p_z'Z - D(br_{G(-1)} + k(\mu_g + r_M)) + u_R. \qquad (4)'$$

The expected capital-gain term μ_g in this equation is negatively related to the change in the gilt-edged yield (r_G) which the investor expects over the current period $(Er_{G(+1)} - r_G)$. So equation $(4)'$ must be regarded as a forward-looking difference equation in $(Er_{G(+i)} \; i \geq 0)$. Such equations are difficult to solve and involve the problem of multiple solutions, or as they have become known, 'speculative bubbles'. A unique solution can, however, be obtained if these are eliminated on rationality grounds (see Minford *et al.* (1979), Blanchard and Watson (1982), and also the discussion of the next chapter). In this case forward iteration of $(4)'$ shows that (r_G) and (μ_g) depend upon current and expected *future* values of all of the variables impinging upon the market $(X, Z, \text{and } r_M)$.

In order to handle this situation, it is necessary to specify how expectations of such variables are formed. In general, we would expect these to depend upon the full information set available to the investor. However, in order to make the analysis tractable it is necessary to restrict this to some small but relevant set (I). In this case we may represent his view about the expected differential return to gilts in the form:

$$(r_G + \mu_g - r_M) = p'I + u \qquad (6)$$

of which (4) is a special case.

3   The McCallum substitution technique

As we have seen, a major problem with equations of this type is that expectations are not directly observable. Yet under the Rational Expectations Hypothesis (REH), the *ex post* out-turn value of any variable will equal its *ex ante* expectation plus an error term which has zero mean and is uncorrelated with any *ex ante* observable variables (including those represented by Z, X, or I). If we represent the *ex post* capital gain on gilts by $(g = \mu_g + v)$ we have in this case:

$$(r_G + g - r_M) = (r_G + \mu_g - r_M) + v \tag{7}$$

This may then be substituted into the left-hand side of an equation such as (6). After rearrangement, we have the equation:

$$(r_G + g - r_M) = p'I + w \tag{8}$$

where w represents the combined error term $(w = u + v)$ and is therefore uncorrelated with I and has zero mean. The parameter vector (p) may therefore be estimated consistently by an OLS regression of the out-turn on the exogenous variables. This is the well-known 'substitution method' due originally to McCallum (1975).

In the homogeneous case we may in fact substitute (7) into (4) and estimate this together with (5). In other words, we may proceed (as in a conventional market-clearing situation) to estimate reduced-form equations relating prices and quantities to current-period demand and supply variables. Assuming the system is identified in the conventional sense, we can then calculate the structural parameters. Expectations do not present any special problems in this case. Of course, in the special case of the Efficient Markets Hypothesis (EMH), the logical combination of the EH (2) and the REH (7), we would expect the parameters (p) to be insignificantly different from zero.

If we wish to estimate the demand function (1) directly, a slight variation of this technique is appropriate. This is because it is not valid to estimate a structural-demand equation by ordinary least squares (OLS) after substituting an *ex ante* market-clearing expectation by its *ex post* out-turn. There are two reasons for this. The first is that the expectation is a market-clearing variable (the analogue of a price in a conventional situation) and will thus be negatively correlated with the structural-error term, biasing the associated coefficient downwards. The second is that the substitution method introduces an additional measurement-error term which is negatively correlated with the out-turn variable, biasing this coefficient further in a downward direction.

In order to avoid this bias it is therefore necessary to use instrumental methods to estimate the demand relationship, assuming this to be identified in the conventional sense. The obvious way to proceed in this case is to estimate (1), replacing the expected differential return by its *ex post* value and instrumenting this using an estimate from an equation of type (8).

For the demand equation to be identified, there must be at least as many predetermined variables which affect the market but which do not appear in the equation as there are endogenous explanatory variables in the equation. In this context, identification is made difficult by the high level of aggregation. For example, a major factor affecting the supply of gilts is likely to be the indebtedness of the public sector, or in flow terms, the PSBR. Unfortunately, these will tend to be associated with the financial wealth of the private sector and its net acquisition of financial assets, making it dangerous to rely upon such variables in order to identify the demand function. Of course, the openness of the UK economy tends to distort the relationship between these statistics, so that the degree of correlation between them is in fact surprisingly low, as has been noted. Autonomous balance of payments flows constitute useful instrumental variables for this reason, and also because they may influence the reactions of the authorities. In addition, overseas interest rates may influence UK rates and the demand for gilts, either through the behaviour of the authorities or non-resident capital movements. Since exchange controls limited their effect on residents' behaviour—other than through expectations—these are also valid instrumental variables over the estimation period used here.

4   An empirical model of gilt-market expectations

The empirical investigation began with an attempt to estimate equations of the form (4) and (6), explaining the *ex post* differential return in terms of *ex ante* observable variables. This was initially intended as a test of the EMH. I found that it was surprisingly easy to find a significant correlation between this variable and relevant supply- and demand-side variables. A typical result is reported in Table VIII.1.

The demand-side variables in this equation include the term G/W which denotes the beginning-of-period stock of gilts relative to financial wealth. The other variables represent supply-side (equation (4)) or perhaps more general

Table VIII.1. The expectations-generating equation (quarterly, 1967(3)–1977(4))

$$
\begin{aligned}
(r_G + g - r_M = {} & 1509 - 0.010 \text{ BAL}_{-1} - 2.24 \text{ PE}_{-1} - 1.58 \text{ PE}_{-4} - 0.87\, r_{F(-1)} \\
& (3.45) \quad (1.8) \qquad\qquad (2.56) \qquad (1.71) \qquad\quad (1.2) \\
& - 3.72\, r_{F(-3)} + 5.40\, r_{F(-4)} + 10.5\, r_{G(-1)} - 1.85\, r_{M(-1)} + 1.62\ (G/W) \\
& \quad (2.3) \qquad\quad (3.1) \qquad\quad (3.7) \qquad\quad (1.8) \qquad\qquad (1.7)
\end{aligned}
$$

$$\text{ESE} = 11.98 \qquad\qquad R^2 = 0.620 \qquad\qquad \text{DW} = 1.718$$

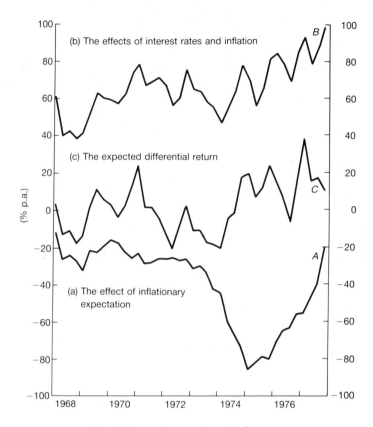

Fig. VIII.A Expectational influences.

expectational effects (equation (6)). The variable PE is a leading indicator of price inflation, a weighted average of import and wage-cost inflation. Together with the lagged long- and short-term interest-rate variables it is almost certainly acting as a supply-side variable. What appears to have happened over this period is that long-term interest rates followed the rate of inflation and short-term rates, but with a lag—induced perhaps by the authorities' leaning into the wind, or by inertia on the part of other non-bank market participants. As these lags worked through, returns on gilts (both actual and, under the REH, expected returns) were first depressed and then inflated relative to short-term rates. The effect of these variables is shown in Figure VIII A. Whatever the reason for this, a regressive expectations model with a variable 'normal rate' depending upon the rate of inflation would have yielded significant profits over this period.

The significance of these lagged interest-rate and inflation variables suggests that we are looking at a general reduced-form equation of the form

(6) rather than one which involves only current values of the predetermined variables (4). This may also explain the curious lag pattern on the eurodollar rate (r_F) in this equation.[3] The overall effect is small. Yet the initial effect is negative, presumably reflecting capital losses resulting from leaning into the wind or other inertial effects. However, one cannot be confident about such rationalizations, or distinguish rigorously between models (4) and (6), without undertaking a full structural analysis, looking jointly at the reaction functions of all participants and the determination of expected returns via a complete systems such as (1) and (3) and (4) and (5)). The term BAL shows the effect of autonomous balance of payments (largely current-account) flows. The negative coefficient may show the effect of confidence in the UK, a structural payments surplus causing capital inflows into sterling and in particular the gilts market, reducing the required rate of return. But here again it is difficult to interpret this result without undertaking a much more structural investigation. It is perhaps worth noting that current supply-side candidates such as the PSBR were insignificant over this period.[4]

The ability of simple regression techniques to detect relationships between *ex ante* observable variables and *ex post* differential returns constitutes strong evidence against the Efficient Markets Hypothesis. It forces the investigator to develop more general models to explain the data and opens the way for these by indicating variables which might be employed by rational speculators when forming expectations of the rate of return. As we have already shown, the predicted values from such relationships can be used as instruments for expectations in a demand equation using the method due to McCallum. The statistical efficiency of these proxies then depends upon how closely they approximate the expectations actually held by the market.

5   An empirical model of the non-bank demand for gilts

These results lead naturally into a structural investigation of the NBPS demand for gilts. This was based on a dynamic version of equation (1). The basic series used in this study consisted of quarterly flows and end-quarter stocks at current market prices. These data are shown in Figure VIII.B and discussed in Spencer (1981). The figure reveals a clear contrast between the period 1968–74 and more recent years. In the initial period, net purchases were low and, with the exception of 1971, offset by capital losses so that the market value of stocks remained fairly flat. This implied a very significant downward trend in the real value of holdings which fell by a half between 1972 and 1974. Since 1974 purchases have been much larger and accompanied by capital gains induced by falling long-term interest rates.

It is clear from the graph that the stock series reflect interest-rate revaluation effects for some considerable time after they have occurred. Since these revaluation effects are an exogenous influence on the portfolio I used transactions flows (T_r) rather than the market-valued stock (G) as the basic

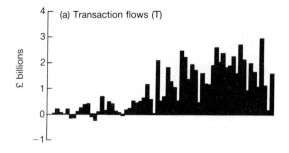

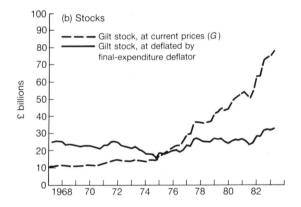

Fig. VIII.B   The non-bank demand for gilt-edged stocks.

dependent variable at this stage of the analysis. In order to handle the dynamics I initially employed the error-correction (EC) class of model developed by Davidson *et al.* (1978).[5] In a discrete time framework this model assumes that the control variable (in this case T_r) will be related to the change in the desired value (G^*) of the target variable during the decision period as well as the difference between the desired and actual values outstanding at the beginning of the period. The model may be represented algebraically as:

$$T_r = k_1(G^* - G^*_{-1}) + k_2(G^* - G)_{-1}. \qquad (5)$$

The EC model may be estimated by regressing the control variable on current and lagged values of the explanatory variables, and also the lagged value of the target variable. However, when this technique was tried very few of these variables were significant and the parameters were unstable. A restricted form of the model was therefore adopted, one suggested by Friedman's (1977) observation that new savings flows can be invested more quickly than existing investments, since the latter adjustments implies a two-rather than a one-way adjustment cost. This intermediate model uses both savings flows and the stock of wealth as regressors. The other explanatory variables appear only as current or lagged levels (as in the stock or partial-adjustment model).

This stage of the empirical work used GIVE, an instrumental-variable estimation package developed by Hendry and Srba (1980). The expectations, interest rate, and flow adjustment terms were instrumented using the same variables as used in the regression reported in Table VIII.1. Initial experiments revealed that it was important to allow the flow adjustment model to distinguish between changes in the real value of financial wealth due to financial surpluses and revaluations induced by inflationary and interest-rate changes. The latter were not significant when instrumented and they were therefore excluded from the model. It was also found that the flow adjustment model was best specified in real terms, giving the restricted model:

$$(t_r - \dot{d}) = q(\dot{s} - \dot{d}) + k[f(r_G + g - r_M) + h - G/S]$$

where:

r_G = redemption yield on 20-year gilts (instrumented)
r_M = 3-month inter-bank rate (instrumented)
g = capital gains on gilts (proxy for expectations, instrumented)
T_r = quarterly purchase of gilts by NBPS
G = beginning of period NBPS holding of gilts (at market prices)
$t_r = T_r/G$
D = TFE price deflator
$\dot{d}$ = rate of price inflation (percentage change in D averaged over previous year)
S = beginning of period-scale variable (Y or W)
$\dot{s}$ = percentage change in S (excluding, in the case of W, the effect of revaluations) averaged over previous year
Y = TFE
W = Financial wealth of NBPS (at market prices)

Several alternative scale variables were tried, including TFE and financial wealth. Both yielded quite reasonable results. The specification employed in the simulation model is presented in Table VIII.2.

The stock and flow adjustment coefficients in this equation are significant and take plausible signs. The standard error compares well with OLS regressions employing more complex dynamic specifications and others using the instrumental variables themselves explicitly in the equations as 'confidence variables' (as a check upon the restriction implicit in the McCallum technique). In order to reveal the equilibrium holding of gilts I will examine a steady state in which the growth of income, expenditure, wealth, and the rate of inflation settle down to constant values, denoted by

Table VIII.2. The NBPS demand for gilts (quarterly 1967(3)–1977(4))

$$(t_r - \dot{d}) = 0.1077 + 0.00169 \ (r_G + g - r_M) + 0.888 \ (\dot{w} - \dot{d}) - 0.3564 \ G/W$$
$$(2.95) \qquad (4.44) \qquad\qquad\qquad (2.10) \qquad\qquad (1.85)$$

$$R^2 = 0.611 \qquad\qquad \text{ESE} = 0.0345 \qquad\qquad \text{DW} = 2.04$$

asterisks. In such a state there would be no reason for interest rates (expected or actual) to change systematically over time. Consequently we have (using $g = 0$):

$$(t_r - \dot{d}) = -0.1077 + 0.00169 \ (r_G - r_M) + 0.888 \ (\dot{w} + \dot{d}) - 0.3564 \ (G/W)$$

This is a stable first-order difference equation with a steady state solution for $(G/W)^*$ which depends upon $(r_G - r_M)^*$ and the rates of change $\dot{w}^*$, $\dot{d}^*$, and t^*.

$$(G/W)^* = 0.3022 + 0.0047 \ (r_G - r_M)^* + 2.49(\dot{w} - \dot{d})^* - 2.80(t_r - \dot{d})^*$$

This expression suggests that a one-point rise in the equilibrium-yield gap $(r_G - r_M)^*$ will raise the proportion of gilts in the portfolio by only 0.5 per cent. This is much lower than is indicated by OLS reduced-form regressions obtained using lagged values of the yield gap and the level of the long rate, but excluding proxies for expected capital gains. This is almost certainly because these variables act as proxies for capital gains and revaluation effects in such specifications and attract large coefficients for this reason. If the result of Table VIII.1 is substituted into the demand function reproduced in Table VIII.2 to give the restricted reduced form of the model, this gives a similar result to that emerging from such unrestricted reduced-form regressions. However, on the present interpretation almost all of the effect of a change in interest rates in this equation is due to the effect on expected differential return between gilts and money will reduce the state.[6]

Many of the properties of this equation can be inferred directly from its equilibrium form. In particular it is worth noting that a once-and-for-all increase in the general level of prices (or real incomes) increases the desired nominal stock once inflationary expectations have returned to their original level. This leads to a temporary increase in gilt sales. Similarly, a steep rise in interest rates causes a reduction in the market value of gilt-edged portfolios, which implies an increase in gilt sales (in addition to any effect resulting from higher expected rates of return) as investors attempt to make this up.

6 Implications for the demand for sterling M3

These results have important implications for the short-run demand for money function. Although the approach is indirect, it does confront the speculative aspects of the problem directly, without being complicated by precautionary or other effects. It suggests that gilts and wholesale money items are rather imperfect substitutes. Their expected rates of return have diverged considerably in recent years, reflecting the effect of inflation and the supply behaviour of the authorities. On these estimates, the differential expected return has on occasion exceeded 20 per cent p.a. The effect of such differentials on the demand for gilts is significant, so there is apparently scope for the authorities to engineer such situations in order to induce sales of non-monetary debt. However, these conditions imply rising gilt prices which cannot be sustained for very long. The authorities' influence over differentials and sales of gilts in the long-run is therefore limited. These results suggest that the long-run effect of changes in the yield curve on the demand for gilts is very small, especially when compared with the short-run effect resulting from regressive expectations. Taken together with the low interest-rate elasticity of the demand for private credit noted in Chapter IV, this means that the scope for pursuing purely bond-financed fiscal policies is in the long run very limited.

Of course, the NBPS holds assets other than gilts and money and it is important to say something about the behaviour of these items. Acquisitions of National Savings instruments have been particularly significant in recent years, as the monetary authorities have made their terms more attractive as a way of helping to reduce the growth of the monetary aggregates. Econometric equations describing the demand for these items may be found in Spencer and Mowl (1978). The NBPS also hold local-authority deposits which are closely substitutable for wholesale bank deposits, a complication which was considered in Chapters V and VI. Moreover, since the abolition of exchange controls in 1979, residents have been able to switch freely between UK and overseas securities, introducing the complication of international currency substitution (Girton and Roper (1976), McKinnon (1982)). It is difficult to quantify this particular effect. But allowing for these complications on the basis of pre-1979 estimates (using the result of Table VIII.2), it may be shown that half of any increase in the net financial assets of the NBPS will be held in the form of £M3 at unchanged interest rates.[7]

These results have been broadly confirmed by work conducted by Bennett and Grice (1984). They use a similar quarterly pre-1979 data sample (1963–78) and similar explanatory variables and techniques as those used in my study of the demand for gilts to explain the demand for £M3 directly. (They also allow the overall level of interest rates and a CCC shift dummy to affect the demand for money.) Their results suggest that a 1 per cent expected differential return between gilts and money will reduce the long-run stock of £M3 by 0.4 per cent. This is numerically similar to my estimate of 0.6 per cent for the effect on the gilt stock since the money stock was on average $1\frac{1}{2}$ times the size of the stock of gilts over this period. The long-run elasticity of £M3 with respect to gross wealth is 1.4 when estimated directly. This is consistent with my finding that the effect of wealth on the demand for gilts is low. It suggests that, on average over the estimation period, about a half of any increase in wealth was invested in £M3.[8]

Notes

1. Of course, if we wish to solve independently for the long-term gilt yield (r_G) and expected gain (μ_g), this is a different kettle of fish. We can only do this by treating (4) as a forward-looking difference equation as in the non-homogeneous case discussed below.

2. A slight complication arises if the demand and supply functions are homogeneous in $(r_G + \mu_g)$ but not (r_M). In this case it will be necessary to solve for the joint equilibrium of the gilt and wholesale money markets, determining both of these variables in the process. However, providing that all the functions involved are homogeneous in $(r_G + \mu_g)$ the solution will still only depend upon current predetermined variables.

3. No evidence of these lagged effects was found in the non-bank demand function described in the next section. Of course since exchange controls were in place, eurodollar rates cannot have impinged upon the gilts market through non-bank resident demands, but must have worked through overseas demand or the reactions of the authorities.

4. Structural stability tests of this relationship reported in Spencer (1981) suggest that it generally performs well, but that a structural break occurred towards the end of 1976, due to the adoption of monetary targets by the authorities. (This does not appear to have occurred on the demand side since the basic demand specification, developed in the next section, is stable over this break.) More recently I have tried fitting relationships of this type to data for the period 1976–84. The lagged interest rate and forward-looking inflation terms are still very significant over this period, and significant coefficients are picked up by hitherto insignificant supply-side variables such as the PSBR, as well as some of the demand-side variables.

5. This formulation has been found to work well in many empirical situations. It encompasses several simpler models as special cases, in particular the familiar partial-adjustment model. This particular specification results when the parameter k_1 is restricted to equal k_2, forcing the adjustment to current disturbances to take place at the same speed as adjustment to the disequilibrium at the beginning of the period.

6. If, for example, the authorities could arbitrarily change the long-run yield gap $(r_G - r_M)$ through their open-market operations the equation of Table VIII.1 would give a misleading forecast of capital gains and would at some stage be discarded by the market. In this case we would expect the long-run effect on the demand for gilts to be smaller, as indicated by the above calculation. This point is taken up in Chapter X.

7. It should be noted that the long-run wealth effect in the gilts equation is not very well determined statistically. Indeed, tests with encompassing specifications showed that income variables out-performed wealth variables if they were both included as long-run scale variables. This could have been due to errors in

measuring the stock of wealth. And yet the wealth terms out-performed income variables in the flow-adjustment terms, suggesting that financial surpluses and deficits are important influences on the short-run demand for gilts. These various tests are reported in Spencer (1981).

8. They also find that the wealth elasticity of the demand for money is significantly lower in the short run (0.77), perhaps reflecting my finding that the short-run elasticity of demand for gilts tends to be higher than the equilibrium elasticity, though both of these effects may simply reflect measurement errors in the wealth variable.

IX

Monetary theory and Policy in an Open Economy

Introduction and summary

This chapter discusses some of the monetary theories which have been used to explain the behaviour of the exchange rate in recent years. These theories were intially very simple and suggested that monetary policy offered a reliable way of controlling prices in an open economy, but as experience accumulated it became apparent that the effect of monetary policy on the exchange rate was by no means as straightforward as had initially been thought. If domestic wages and prices failed to adjust quickly then monetary policy would have a disproportionate effect on the exchange rate and the internationally exposed sectors of the economy.

This chapter begins with a review of some of the simpler models and then looks at the implications of domestic wage and price rigidities using the Dornbusch exchange-rate overshooting model. This abstracts from other dynamic effects which are likely to be important, particularly the evolution of wealth and the current account, analysed by Dornbusch and Fischer (1980), and the dynamics of the productive capital stock, emphasized by Neary and Purvis (1981). Unfortunately, however, analytical solutions to rational-expectations models can only be obtained by looking at the effect of one type of lag at a time. More complicated dynamic situations can only be handled using numerical methods, as in the model-simulation results reported in the next chapter.

The Dornbusch model shows in relatively simple terms how lags in the adjustment of domestic output, prices, or wages can cause a monetary contraction to have a disproportionate effect on the exchange rate and the traded-goods sector. I outline the model using a few standard algebraic equations and diagrams and first look at the properties of the model under the Mundell–Fleming assumption that the expected changes in the exchange rate is zero: so that nominal interest rates are equalized across currencies. In the 'naïve' case the exchange rate is the only variable which can move to equate the demand and supply of money, so violent overshooting occurs, depending (inversely) upon the weight which imports (or traded goods) have in consumption. The effect of assuming rational expectations is then explored. In this case, interest rate movements also help to achieve monetary equilibrium, so that the degree of overshooting is lessened.

I go on to investigate the effect of a North Sea oil discovery using this model, following the recent theoretical papers on this by Eastwood and Venables (1982) and Buiter and Miller (1981). This kind of discovery is equivalent to an increase in overseas income, part of which will be spent on domestic output raising its relative price: the terms of trade or the real exchange rate. This is the celebrated Forsyth and Kay effect. Eastwood and Venables suppose that this rise in output will leave the demand for money unaffected. A fixed money-supply assumption then serves to fix the average price level so that the relative price adjustment is brought about by a rise in the absolute price of domestic output and a fall in the price of overseas output. The latter is brought about by an exchange-rate appreciation, but since a change in the domestic output price can only be brought about through a change in the level of activity in this model, the discovery inevitably causes an expansion of activity.

The rise in expenditure (and wealth) associated with the discovery is, however, likely to increase the demand for money directly, putting downward pressure on the equilibrium price level and activity. This effect has been emphasized by Buiter and Miller. Consequently these effects are ambiguous and empirical evidence is needed to resolve this indeterminacy. This discussion is taken up in the context of the simulation results described in the next chapter.

The final section looks at the effect of relaxing the perfect capital-mobility assumption common to these monetary models of the open economy and outlines some of the wider portfolio-equilibrium effects which then obtain.

1   The monetary theory of the exchange rate

The simple monetary theory of the exchange rate, as expressed in the papers on this subject by Johnson (1976) and Mussa (1976) for example, offers a natural starting point for a discussion of open-economy macroeconomics under flexible exchange rates. This specification is based on the assumption that international trade will equate prices in different countries, expressed in terms of a common currency such as the dollar. So if E represents the exchange rate (expressed throughout this book as the cost of foreign exchange to the home country), and if D and D^* represent the cost of living or general goods-price deflators at home and abroad (expressed in local currencies), then it is assumed that:

$$D^*E/D = 1 \qquad (1)$$

This is the famous 'law of one price'. It is similarly assumed that international currency speculation will equate expected common-currency rates of return, so that if r and r^* represent domestic and overseas (nominal, local-currency) interest rates and x the expected rate of appreciation of the exchange rate, we have the interest-parity condition:

$$x = r - r^* \qquad (2)$$

Together with (1) this implies that expected *real* interest rates are equated internationally:

$$r - \dot{d} = r^* + \dot{d}^* \qquad (3)$$

(where $\dot{d}$ and $\dot{d}^*$ denote expected rates of inflation). There is no role for short-run demand management policy[1] in this model since prices in both domestic and overseas markets are set by overseas suppliers and domestic producers can in principle sell as much as they wish at these prices. With a fixed rate of monetary growth, these assumptions serve to fix the determinants of the demand for real balances—nominal interest rates and activity—independently of the supply of bonds to the system. The latter simply affects the capital account. Consequently if we denote the domestic demand for real balances by K and the money supply by M_s we have:

$$D = M_s/K \qquad (4)$$

and the exchange rate follows by setting up a similar relationship for $D^*, K^*,$ and M^* and substituting these into (1):

$$E = M_s K^*/M_s^* K \qquad (5)$$

It is interesting to note that in this prototype version of the model, causality runs uniquely from the (relative) money supply to prices (via (4)) and hence to the exchange rate (via (1)). It does not run from the exchange rate to prices in the way that it would in a structural model of the economy. This made the original model difficult to accept at face value and, reflecting this, the monetary approach seems to have had little impact upon UK macroeconomic policy in the period immediately following the floating of the exchange rate. Moreover, as experience with the new system developed the model became exposed to criticism on empirical grounds. A major problem was that the law of one price did not appear to hold, at least for general price deflators in the short run (Kravis and Lipsey (1978), Isard (1977)). This was apparent from the simple observation that nominal exchange rates were more volatile than general price indices.

The response of the monetarists to this criticism has been to argue that published price indices are poor measures of the appropriate transactions price deflators (Bilson (1980)). The 'true' price indices should on these grounds be treated as unobservable variables, with a ratio defined to equal the nominal exchange rate. This version of the theory leads *directly* to an equation of the form (5): the exchange rate, being the relative price of two currencies, is simply related to their relative supplies. The volatile behaviour of the exchange rate is then claimed to be the result of the erratic behaviour of the monetary authorities and the rational forward-looking behaviour of the market. This gives the 'equilibrium rational expectations' version of the model due to Frenkel (1976), Mussa (1979), and Bilson (1980).

2 Two-sector models of the open economy

Other monetary theorists, notably Niehans (1975) and Dornbusch (1976), have instead developed the monetary model by relaxing the assumption that the law of one price applies to all markets. This complicates the process of exchange-rate determination and policy formulation considerably. It is necessary, at the very least, to distinguish between domestic and foreign-produced goods and to ask how closely substitutable they are empirically (as I do briefly in Section X.1). Since this degree of substitution varies widely between different types of good, depending upon their homogeneity, portability, and so on it is also useful to disaggregate domestic output. This unfortunately increases the number of items and relative prices in the system, making analytical work difficult.

One scheme which avoids this problem, due originally to Salter (1959), is based on a dichotomy between 'traded' and 'non-traded' goods. It is assumed that the latter do not enter international trade and that residents may only substitute domestically produced non-traded goods for traded goods. They are supposed to be indifferent between those traded goods produced domestically and overseas, equating their domestic currency prices. If P_T represents the domestic-currency price of domestically produced traded goods and P_T^* the foreign-currency price of foreign traded goods this implies the 'law of one price for traded goods':

$$1 = EP_T^*/P_T \tag{6}$$

There is no direct arbitrage mechanism for equating non-traded goods prices in this model, so that the cost of living may differ from one country to another, reflecting differences in these prices. We must therefore ask what determines their equilibrium values and how quickly they will move back towards equilibrium following a disturbance. Depending upon the answer to this question, several different solutions are possible and the next two sections look at some of these alternatives. But once differences in non-traded goods prices can emerge, they will be reflected in the real exchange rate (R) defined as the cost of living overseas, relative to the cost of living at home, both expressed in a common currency:

$$ED^*/D = R \tag{1}'$$

If we denote the local-currency prices of non-traded goods at home and abroad as P_{NT} and P_{NT}^* respectively, and assume for simplicity that they carry the same weight in the respective cost of living indices, that is—

$$D = P_{NT}^w P_T^{1-w}; D^* = P_{NT}^* P_J^{*1-w} \tag{7}$$

—then the real exchange rate may be written as:

$$R = \left\{ \frac{EP^{*NT}}{P_{NT}} \right\}^w \tag{8}$$

These models still maintain the assumption that capital is perfectly mobile. This helps to keep down the number of markets and relative prices in the system, since it is not necessary to distinguish between foreign and domestic bonds. Moreover, since the (foreign-currency) prices of bonds and traded goods (or, in terms of the alternative paradigm, overseas output) are fixed in world markets, their relative price is given and they may be treated as a single composite item or balance of payments aggregate. Transactions which only affect these items (as in the Dornbusch fiscal-policy example discussed in the next paragraph) therefore have no effect on the domestic economy.

The model can be further simplified by ignoring the labour market, or by treating labour as analogous to a non-traded good. If prices are perfectly flexible, then changes in the money supply are offset in inflation and simply act as a tax on the private sector: without affecting relative prices. There is only one relative price in this system—the real exchange rate or the relative price of non-traded goods *vis-à-vis* bonds and traded goods. If prices are sticky, this property still extends to the steady-state equilibrium of the system as has been demonstrated in a domestic/overseas good context by Kingston and Turnovsky (1977) and a traded/non-traded good context by Riley (1982).

Models of this type exhibit closed-economy characteristics since the non-traded good sector is closed but retain many of the features of the basic monetary open-economy model since the traded-good and financial sectors are exposed to international competition. Demand-deficient unemployment can exist if wages and non-traded goods prices are sticky and the former are low in relation to the latter, as has been demonstrated by Dixit (1978). This analysis is similar to the four-regime closed-economy analysis of Muellbauer and Portes (1978) touched upon in the introductory chapter. In this case there is an important role for fiscal policy—providing this affects the demand for domestic or non-traded goods. Fiscal-policy-induced changes in the demand for traded goods have no effect on activity, simply affecting the current account of the balance of payments, as has been noted by Dornbusch (1974). Assuming that this is a pure fiscal policy and thus financed by a bond issue, it will be exactly offset in the capital account, so neutralizing the balance of payments and exchange-rate effects. Money is neutral in a long-run, static sense as Appendix III demonstrates.

The relative efficacy of monetary and fiscal policy in this type of model was originally established in two well-known papers by Mundell (1963) and Fleming (1962). They concluded that in a fixed exchange-rate regime, fiscal policy involving expenditure on domestic goods would have a powerful effect on activity and that monetary policy would have no effect, but that these positions would be reversed under a floating exchange-rate regime with a fixed money supply. Mundell and Fleming assumed that all prices were fixed and that international capital flows would equate nominal interest rates, independently of monetary and exchange-rate policy and expectations (that is, $x = 0$ in (2)). These assumptions dictate the result that fiscal policy is fully crowded-out under a fixed money supply, floating exchange-rate regime since they serve to fix both the price level and interest rates and (with velocity unchanged) nominal and real incomes.

This kind of model resembles the basic monetary specification in that producers in the traded-goods sector face fixed prices and can in principle sell as much as they like at these prices, so that their output is supply rather than demand determined. Their own product real interest rate is fixed at the world rate (using (2) and (6) to obtain an equation analogous to (3)). They thus trade in the product and capital markets on the same terms as their overseas competitors. Yet they face a real wage which may differ from that overseas. In order to complete this two-sector specification some specification of the behaviour of domestic wages and non-traded goods prices is therefore necessary. I will investigate two essentially monetarist solutions in this chapter, both of which have had a great deal of influence upon the policy debate in the UK. The appeal of these models has been due in part to the fact that causality appears to run from monetary developments to the exchange rate and thence to prices and wages, rather than from prices to the exchange rate.

3   The International Monetarist model

The first of these specifications is the 'International Monetarist' model developed largely by an influential group of economists at the London Business School (Ball, Burns, and Warburton (1979)). They saw the real exchange rate as being determined by structural factors affecting the demand and supply of non-traded goods, independently of monetary conditions. Several such influences, including the likely effect of North Sea oil production, are for example considered in Burns, Lobban, and Warburton (1977). In their empirical modelling they focused for simplicity upon the effect of long-term productivity trends, using an approach used previously by Balassa (1964). They then noted that prices would eventually have to be consistent with monetary equilibrium so that (4) holds in the long run. Substituting this into (1)$'$ then allows (5) to be generalized to:

$$E = RM_s K^* / M_s^* K \qquad (5)'$$

The next step is to assume that the exchange markets are dominated by rational, forward-looking speculators who realize that the equilibrium value of the exchange rate is determined by (5)$'$, and move it into line with this value following any change in the money supply. Thus changes in the money supply are immediately reflected in the exchange rate and the prices of traded goods. Competitive pressures on wages and non-traded goods prices are assumed to be powerful enough to ensure that these move quickly into line, thus completing the adjustment and rationalizing the expectations held by the exchange markets.

The International Monetarist model thus offered both a convenient method for determining the exchange rate in an econometric model and a mechanism through which monetary policy could affect inflation. Indeed, this mechanism looked more powerful and reliable than the others which had been identified—and acted directly upon prices, apparently without the long lags and output losses which monetarists had hitherto accepted as a consequence of their proposals. Monetary effects on the exchange rate also began to feature in the Treasury model at this time, though these effects were modelled in a structural way, through the effect of exchange-rate expectations on capital flows. Together with the parallel work on wealth effects in the consumption function these developments radically transformed the mainstream models, making them much more monetarist in character.

4   The Dornbusch Model and the effect of price rigidities on the operation of monetary policy in an open economy

The simplicity of the original LBS approach clearly lay in the assumption that changes in the exchange rate and traded-goods prices were quickly reflected in non-traded goods prices and wages. In effect, the general price level then moves to bring the demand and supply of money into equilibrium as in the basic monetary model. Providing this is the case, there is no need to consider the effect of disequilibrium movements in output and interest rates. But if this price adjustment is frustrated by institutional rigidities in the labour or non-traded goods markets, then something else must adjust to clear the money markets, the most obvious candidate for this role being the domestic interest rate. This in turn is likely to have consequences for the exchange rate, causing it to overshoot its equilibrium value. The exchange-rate overshooting model developed by Niehans and Dornbusch gives a very neat dynamic analysis of the consequences of such rigidities.

In the original Dornbusch (1976) model, the domestic price level did not directly reflect movements in the exchange rate, so prices were entirely rigid in the short run. Since this does not qualitatively affect the response of the system to a monetary shock, this assumption could reasonably be used to simplify the model. But since it can affect the response of the system to a real shock I will employ the Eastwood–Venables (1982) version of the model which makes an allowance for the direct effect of the exchange rate on the price level. This allows the general cost of living index (D) to be a geometric weighted average of domestic output prices (P) and overseas output prices (P^*).[2] The latter are fixed in foreign-currency terms (and are conveniently normalized to equal unity). However, in domestic-currency terms they depend upon the exchange rate, expressed as the cost of foreign currency (E). The cost of living is thus:

$$D = P^w(EP^*)^{1-w} \qquad 0 < w < 1$$
$$= P^w E^{1-w} \qquad\qquad\qquad (9)$$

or letting lower-case letters represent logarithms:

$$d = wp + (1 - w)e \qquad\qquad (10)$$

Using this general price index as the deflator in a neoclassical demand for money function gives:

$$m = \phi y - \Theta r + wp + (1 - w)e \qquad \phi, \Theta > 0 \qquad (11)$$

(where m, p, and y represent the logarithms of the money supply, prices, and output). The exchange rate is determined rationally in the Eastwood–Venables model, being expected to follow a path which equalizes the common-currency returns to foreign and domestic securities. It is important to distinguish between the *actual* rate of change $(\dot{e})$ and the *expected* rate of change (x). Rational expectations thus implies:

$$x = \dot{e} \qquad (12)$$

Substituting this into the arbitrage relationship (2) gives an equation describing movements along a rational path which is uninterrupted by new pieces of information:

$$\dot{e} = r - r^* \qquad (13)$$

The real sector is represented by a simple Keynesian model in which the demand for domestic output depends upon itself (in the guise of income), international price competitiveness $(e - p)$, and the real interest rate $(r - \dot{p})$:

$$y = d(e - p) + gy - \mu(r - \dot{p}) \qquad (14)$$

and a Phillips-type relationship is used to handle price adjustment:[3]

$$\dot{p} = b(y - \bar{y}) \qquad (15)$$

(where $\bar{y}$ denotes full employment output). Before looking at the dynamics of this system I will first outline its long-run equilibrium solution. This is obtained by setting the rate of change variables $(\dot{p}, \dot{e})$ to zero in (13) and (15). This implies that $(r = r^*)$ and $(y = \bar{y})$, which allows (11) and (14) to be rewritten as:-

$$\bar{y} = d(e - p) + g\bar{y} - \mu r^* \qquad (16)$$

$$m = \phi \bar{y} - \Theta r^* + wp + (1 - w)e \qquad (17)$$

The first of these conditions depicts long-run domestic-output equilibrium, and is represented by the IS curve in Figure IX.A.(a). This has a unit slope, indicating a constant level of competitiveness. The second is a long-run monetary-equilibrium condition requiring a constant cost of living index (given a fixed money supply) and is represented by the LM curve in the figure. The slope of this line depends upon the weighting paramter w. These two equations may be solved for the equilibrium values of p and e, indicated by the intersection at point E in the figure. In this model, a reduction in the money supply does not directly affect the long-run goods-market condition but requires a fall in prices to preserve monetary equilibrium, pushing the LM line in a south-westerly direction. With the goods-market condition unaffected, the original level of competitiveness must be preserved, so both domestic and import prices (in terms of domestic currency units) are reduced in the same proportion as the money supply. The equilibrium therefore shifts to a point such as C in the diagram. If domestic prices adjust instantaneously

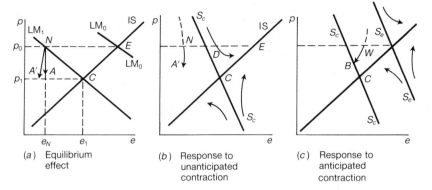

Fig. IX.A   The effect of a monetary contraction in the Dornbusch model.

that is the end of the story. However, if they are sticky a rather complicated adjustment process will ensue. Consider first of all the Mundell–Fleming assumption that the exchange rate is not expected to move ($x = 0$) so that nominal interest rates are equalized internationally ($r = r^*$, using (2)). I will refer to this as the 'naïve expectations' case. Suppose also that (as in the basic Dornbusch model) output is fixed at its long-run value by supply rigidities ($y = \bar{y}$). The long-run monetary-equilibrium condition (17)—derived under precisely these assumptions—must then also hold in the short run. So the system must always lie somewhere along the relevant LM locus. In the first instance, domestic-output prices are fixed at the original level so that the exchange rate is the only variable which can clear the money market. This requires an appreciation (a *fall* in e) which is sufficiently large to move the cost of living index immediately to its new equilibrium value, so in this version of the model, as in the simple monetary model, prices are reduced 'at a stroke'. The exchange rate will overshoot violently, depending inversely upon the weight of overseas goods in the price index.

In terms of Figure IX.A(a), with the original price level (p_0), the system will move to point N on the new LM curve. The cost of imports falls to (e_N), below the equilibrium value (e_1). Since this point is above the IS curve, this implies a loss of competitiveness, depressing demand (y) below output ($\bar{y}$). This in turn causes domestic-output prices to adjust downwards. The system moves gradually back towards equilibrium along the LM locus, because as domestic-output prices fall, this allows the exchange rate to depreciate whilst keeping the cost of living at its new lower value. Exchange-rate speculators consistently make mistakes, however, since they expect the rate to move in the direction of the arrow NA rather than NC.

If exchange-rate expectations are rational so that (12) holds, the overshoot is smaller than in the naïve case. This is because domestic interest rates can then adjust to help equilibrate the markets. Changes in output may also help.

As we have seen, point N is not consistent with a rational expectational equilibrium if output is fixed. If output falls in line with demand, then this will reduce monetary pressures and domestic interest rates. This is only consistent with an expected exchange-rate appreciation (that is, a fall in (e)), a movement in the direction of say NA$'$ in the diagram. If the exchange rate moved in the direction of NA or NA$'$ in order to preserve consistency, this would progressively lower import prices and interest rates causing further expectations of appreciation. This process would be self sustaining, but would push the system progressively away from equilibrium along a path such as NA$''$ in Figure IX.A(b). Rational speculators will, however, avoid such unstable paths and search for one which is consistent and equalizes common-currency returns but which leads towards equilibrium.[4]

This rational equilibrium path will start from a point such as D in the diagram, involving an initial exchange rate which is somewhere between the naïve (e_N) and the original (e_0) levels.[5] The rise in the exchange rate then eases only part of the monetary pressure caused by the contraction, so that domestic interest rates have to rise, consistent with an expected depreciation of the exchange rate. The market initially marks the exchange rate up just sufficiently to ensure that this expected depreciation, taken together with the downward adjustment of domestic prices, moves the system towards equilibrium (at C).

Technically, this kind of response is dictated by a stable saddle-point property. This is a standard feature of such models. Associated with any equilibrium point there is a line—known as the stable manifold—showing the set of disequilibrium points from which the system will converge to this equilibrium. The line $S_c S_c'$ in Figure IX.A(b) shows the stable manifold associated with the equilibrium at C. With the original price level given, the exchange rate 'jumps' in order to put the system on the stable manifold associated with the new equilibrium position whenever an unanticipated shock occurs. The system then moves gradually along this branch towards the new equilibrium. The jump from E to D and move from D to C simply gives an example of such a response. The slope of this stable branch is ambiguous, but Eastwood and Venables argue that we would expect it to be negative on empirical grounds, implying that the exchange rate overshoots in response to an unanticipated monetary shock.

So far I have assumed that the monetary contraction is unanticipated (i.e. that it is implemented immediately upon announcement). The effects of anticipated monetary shocks are a little more subtle, making it important to distinguish the separate effects of announcement and implementation. The first point to note is that as long as the announcement is credible, discontinuous movements in the exchange rate can only occur upon the point of annoucement. The second point is that during the interregnum between annoucement and implementation the LM curve does not move, so that the dynamic behaviour of the system is dictated by the equations of motion associated with the original equilibrium point at E, not the new one at C. These directions of motion are indicated by the arrows in Figure IX.A(c), associated with the original stable manifold $S_eS'_e$.

This situation was first analysed by Wilson (1979). He showed that the rational adjustment path consists of two phases, showing the response of the system both before and after implementation. On the point of announcement, the exchange rate rises to shift the initial equilibrium from E to a point such as W in Figure IX.A(c). This actually eases monetary pressures during the interregnum, causing domestic interest rates to fall relative to those overseas, and is consistent with a continued appreciation. The loss of competitiveness causes domestic prices to fall during this phase. The combined effect is to move the system in a south-westerly direction along a path such as WB. The rationality assumption implies that the system chooses the path which brings it on to the stable manifold $(S_eS'_e)$ associated with the new equilibrium point at the precise moment when the contraction is due to be implemented. Thereafter, there is a gradual movement towards equilibrium along the new stable branch (BC) as in the case of an unanticipated reduction. It is worth noting that the maximum exchange-rate gain (and loss of competitiveness) occurs on the point of implementation (at point B in the diagram). This involves an overshoot—though this is less than in the basic case. It turns out that the earlier the contraction is announced, the smaller is the overshoot and—*a fortiori*—the initial exchange-rate response. Intuitively, this is because the annoucement allows the system to spread the effects out both backwards and forwards over time.

5   The effect of oil discoveries in the Dornbusch model

Resource discoveries will affect an open economy in many different ways, both real and monetary. As they increase domestic incomes and these are partly spent on domestic output this will push up its relative price, the real exchange rate. To the extent that they absorb domestic factors and output in their exploitation this will also bid up their prices, particularly the real wage. Cordon and Neary (1982) have termed these the 'spending' and 'resource' effects. The former is essentially the effect identified by Forsyth and Kay (1980) in the North Sea context and the one which we will focus upon in this chapter. The 'resource' effects of the North Sea are by comparison small but will be taken into account in the next chapter.

In macroeconomic terms, an oil discovery is equivalent to an increase in income in the form of overseas or traded goods, since dollar oil prices are fixed in world markets. In the Dornbusch model this causes an increase in the demand for domestic non-oil output (y) without increasing its long-run supply ($\bar{y}$). Eastwood–Venables and Buiter–Miller handle this by introducing a shift variable into the domestic-output equation ((14) and

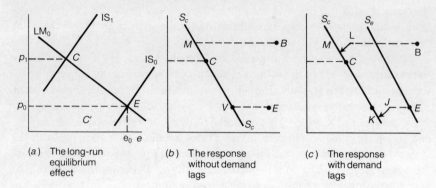

Fig. IX.B   The effect of an oil discovery in the Dornbusch model.

hence (16)). This equals the annuity or permament-income equivalent value of the reserves, multiplied by the propensity to spend on domestic output.

In terms of the steady-state diagram, this pushes the IS curve in a north-westerly direction as shown in Figure IX.B(a) requiring an increase in the relative price of domestic output, or a fall in competitiveness. In their treatment Eastwood and Venables assume that there will be no effect on the demand for money and that the supply of money is fixed. This serves to fix the overall cost of living so that the relative price adjustment is brought about by a fall in the absolute price of overseas output offset by a rise in the absolute price of domestic output. I will call this domestic-output price-effect the EV or indirect monetary effect. Diagramatically, the LM curve does not shift and so the equilibrium point also moves in a north-westerly direction from E to C, requiring an increase in the equilibrium price of domestic output.

If the rise in GDP associated with the discovery increases the demand for money directly then the effect on the price of domestic output becomes ambiguous. This effect can be captured by introducing shift variables into (11) and (17). In this case the LM schedule shifts downwards, making it possible that the new equilibrium position is below the previous one (e.g. at C'). This effect has been emphasized by Buiter and Miller (1981). In their model the exchange rate does not directly affect prices ($w = 1$) so that there are no indirect effects and the rise in activity unambiguously requires a fall in the price of domestic output. I will therefore label this the Buiter–Miller (BM) or direct monetary effect. The net effect on the domestic price level depends on whether the leftward shift in the IS schedule is greater or less than the leftward shift in the LM schedule. Given the connection between domestic activity and inflation implied by (15) this is of crucial importance to the dynamics.

If both prices and the exchange rate were flexible and there were no lag in the effect of the oil revenues on demand the system would immediately adjust to the new equilibrium position. But when domestic output prices are sticky this introduces dynamic effects. We will analyse these assuming expectations to be rational, starting with the basic Eastwood–Venables case.

With the price level set at its initial level (p_0) the exchange rate will then have to 'jump' to put the system on the stable manifold ($S_cS'_c$ in Figure IX.B(b)) associated with the new equilibrium. This is steeper than the LM curve and is assumed to have a negative slope, so the short-run exchange rate lies somewhere between the old and new equilibrium values. In other words, the exchange rate will undershoot its long-run value (in both nominal and real terms). This is because an exchange-rate appreciation has the effect of reducing domestic monetary pressures and interest rates, requiring an exchange-rate appreciation during the adjustment phase. The long-run effect will be discounted for this reason. The short-run equilibrium is represented by point V in the diagram. This represents a position of excess demand for domestic output, consistent with an increasing price of domestic output. The initial loss of competitiveness only partially offsets the spending effect. From this point the system moves along the stable manifold towards C. This involves a gradual loss of competitiveness as domestic prices rise and the exchange rate appreciation continues.

If there is a direct impact upon the demand for money this will have an additional effect, identical to the effect of a reduction in the money supply in the Dornbusch model. If this effect dominates so that the old equilibrium is to the north east of the new one, at point B for example, then the dynamic effects will be quite different from those outlined by Eastwood and Venables. This is because domestic output prices must fall, and this requires a recession given (15).

The exchange rate will initially overshoot and interest rates will rise, moving the system from B to M. Domestic output prices will then gradually adjust downwards and the exchange rate will fall back, moving the system progressively along the stable manifold from M to C. Since we do not know anything a priori about the effect on domestic prices we cannot say anything about the dynamic response.

Eastwood and Venables are primarily interested in the case in which there is a lag in the effect of the oil discovery on domestic demand. They suggest that this could occur either because consumers fail to perceive the future tax cuts associated with future government oil revenues or because credit-market imperfections prevent them from doing this. In this case, they point out that there will be an 'interregnum' between the dates at which the discovery is made and the revenues increase demand. During this period, demand will be depressed by a high exchange rate and domestic prices will be falling. This is the only way an oil discovery can cause a recession under their assumptions.

The stable adjustment path will in this case be given by a path such as EJKC. The exchange rate will jump in order to move the system from E to J. During the interregnum the system will move gradually from JK as domestic prices fall and the exchange rate appreciates, governed by the equations of motion associated with the pre-oil equilibrium at point E. The path is such that the system will arrive at point K as soon as the oil revenues begin to boost demand. Thereafter the system will move into an expansionary phase, moving along the stable manifold as in the basic case.

In general, direct demand for money (BM) effects are likely to be superimposed upon these EV expenditure effects. I have argued that they will be associated with expenditure rather than oil production and so they too are likely to be subject to delays. Consequently, one would expect the effect of an *anticipated* monetary tightening, discussed in the previous section, to be superimposed on the EV delayed-expenditure effect. The essential point to recall is that the initial rise in the exchange rate is smaller the further into the future the contraction takes place. So delays in the demand for both goods and money work to reduce the initial jump in the exchange rate. For this reason, the exchange rate need not at any time overshoot, even if the BM effect dominates the steady-state solution. However, an exchange-rate overshoot is possible and such a case is illustrated in Figure IX.B(c). The nominal exchange rate jumps from the initial equilibrium at B to L. This is followed by an interregnum during which domestic prices fall and the exchange rate continues to appreciate, governed by the equations of motion associated with B. In this case the development delays and direct monetary effects are such that the economy reaches the stable manifold at a point above C, just as the revenues begin to be spent. This implies a further deflationary phase similar to that of the basic BM case, as the system moves down the manifold to C. If on the other hand the lags are longer, this reduces the initial jump so that the economy finds itself on the stable manifold at the end of the interregnum at a point below C, requiring a final expansionary phase as in the EV case. The dynamic effects are quite ambiguous if both direct-monetary and lagged-adjustment effects are allowed for.

6   The implications of imperfections in international capital markets

So far, all of the models examined in this chapter have relied upon the assumption of perfect capital mobility. As we have seen, this results in a purely monetary theory of the exchange rate. However, this is no longer the case if capital is imperfectly mobile internationally, due to the diverse risk characteristics of different currencies or perhaps exchange controls. The exchange rate is then determined as part of a wider portfolio-equilibrium process, involving money, domestic and overseas bonds, and physical capital assets. A steady-state equilibrium model of such a system is set out in Appendix III. It is useful at this stage to draw out a few points which emerge from this analysis as background to the simulations reported in the next chapter, which were run under both perfect and imperfect capital-mobility assumptions.

Some of the characteristics of the monetary models carry over immediately to the more general portfolio model. The real rate of return on overseas bonds (or, analogously with traded goods: traded bonds) is fixed at the world level in the long run and so may be viewed as exogenous to the system. By the same token, changes in the domestic demand and supply of overseas or traded bonds are met through the capital account of the balance of payments, as in monetary models.[6] This essentially leaves a closed financial system in which domestic bonds, physical capital assets, and money are traded. This is very similar to the portfolio model of the closed economy developed by Tobin and Buiter (1976), Niehans (1974), (1978), and others.

The long-run properties of this kind of model are largely dictated by the assumption that financial assets are denominated in nominal terms, so that the demand for these items increases proportionately with the domestic price level (as in equations (8) and (9) of the Appendix). For example, if the monetary authorities accommodate a one-shot fiscal expansion, keeping relative rates of return unchanged, it follows that all financial holdings and the price level will eventually increase by the same proportionate amount as the nominal national debt. This will restore the system to its original real equilibrium position. But if the authorities change the proportions of money and domestically traded bonds supplied to the system, whether by fiscal policy or open-market operations, then this prevents it returning to the initial real equilibrium and implies a change in relative rates of return, depending upon the degree of substitutability between these two assets. The rate of return on capital goods may be disturbed by this adjustment, in which case the long-run level of activity will be affected, as the Appendix demonstrates.

Unless the demand for money is independent of interest rates and activity, the simple monetary theory of the price level and the exchange rate will not hold in such a model. (A more precise description of the conditions under which it will hold is to be found in the Appendix.) This is because changes in the composition of financial portfolios imply changes in rates of return and activity, affecting the long-run demand for real balances and hence the relationship between money and prices. Indeed, if money and bonds are very close substitutes the price level will be proportional to the overall supply of domestic financial assets, independently of its composition. Unless some very special assumptions are made, only a balanced expansion of the bond and money stocks will have neutral effects in such a system.

Notes

1. At least in the traditional demand-management sense. Yet monetary policy may still affect the supply of output and the demand for labour in the short run if wages are sticky and labour is immobile. In this case labour acts in the same way as a non-traded good does in the models outlined in Section 2. If the demand for money depends upon wages and the level of activity, (5) should then be viewed as a steady-state relationship.

2. Alternatively we might consider P and EP^* to be the domestic-currency prices of domestic non-traded and traded goods.

3. The question of credibility in the labour and goods markets does not arise in the Dornbusch model since these markets are assumed to respond only to the current pressure of demand.

4. Such unstable paths are often referred to as 'speculative bubbles' (by Minford (1981), for example)). But this terminology is misleading because bubbles proper generate supra-normal profits as long as they continue, whereas the arbitrage condition rules this out in this kind of model. Rational speculators will never ride these unstable paths knowingly because if they do they are on a 'hiding to nothing', gaining nothing as long as the 'bubble' continues but making losses when it eventually bursts.

5. The initial 'jump' in the exchange rate will cause a break in the expectational-consistency condition but this is a natural consequence of new information. The loglinearity of the model implies that the system will move exponentially towards equilibrium, so that the locus DC in the diagram is a straight line.

6. The Dornbusch fiscal-policy result also holds: expenditure on traded goods financed by a sale of overseas or traded bonds has no effect on the domestic economy. The Mundell–Fleming fiscal-policy results may not hold in this situation however: depending upon the relative degree of openness of the real and financial sectors a bond-financed fiscal policy may be more expansionary under floating exchange rates than under fixed rates. With a fixed exchange rate, the expenditure effect will cause a deterioration in the current account and the financing effect an improvement in the capital account. The overall effect on the demand for money and the balance of payments (or the exchange rate) is entirely ambiguous. If the current-account effect dominates, as would be the case for example if exchange controls were in place, then a move to a floating exchange rate would cause this to depreciate and make the fiscal package more expansionary. All this assumes of course that the competitiveness effect of a depreciation outweighs any adverse wealth effects on expenditure—a proposition which as I have noted is very doubtful.

X

The Effect of Monetary Pressures and Oil Production on the UK Economy—Some Consistent-Expectations Simulation Results

Introduction and summary

The Dornbusch model discussed in the previous chapter is based on the view that the financial markets are efficient, forming their expectations in a forward-looking way and clearing instantaneously. On the other hand, the non-financial markets are assumed not to clear, responding only to the current pressure of demand. Such models offer a useful insight into the effect of monetary and supply shocks on an open economy but they neglect wealth and other influences which tend to make the effects ambiguous. Indeed, in the case of an oil-related shock the effects are entirely ambiguous even in this simple model. in this chapter, I present some simulations of a version of the Treasury model in order to help resolve some of the ambiguities and throw light on the magnitudes involved.

Although this model is of course much more detailed than the theoretical model, its general structure is similar. Expectations in the financial markets are modelled explicitly, making it possible to solve the model in a consistent forward-looking way. These markets are also assumed to be in continuous equilibrium, with interest and exchange rates moving instantly to ensure this. On the other hand, operators in other markets are assumed to form their expectations in a backward-looking (typically autoregressive) kind of way and prices do not immediately clear these markets.

Such econometric models are designed to give quantitative estimates of the various responses and lags which are likely in the real world. However, these estimates must be taken with a large pinch of salt since the coefficients and even the structures upon which they are based are uncertain. Alternative models will often give quite different results for this reason. In this exercise I used a modified version of the December 1980 edition of the Treasury model incorporating the estimation results discussed in earlier chapters—(HM Treasury 1980). This version has now been superceded, and the current version has properties which differ in several important respects (Barber 1984). Moreover, the assumptions which I make about policy and the formation of expectations in this exercise differ considerably from the ones normally used at the Treasury. It should also be noted that the method used to identify the appropriate consistent-expectations solution in this kind of model inevitably involves a degree of approximation. Consequently, although the short- and medium-term response is numerically well determined, the long-run results may not be very accurate and should only be regarded as illustrative. Long-run properties can in any case be derived using simpler techniques and often follow directly from theoretical principles such as those addressed in the previous chapter.

The first set of simulations shows the effect of a reduction in the stock of money brought about through a rise in interest rates with an unchanged fiscal stance. This is initially assumed to be unanticipated. As in the theoretical model, the exchange rate and interest rates do a lot of the work initially. Thereafter they come back as domestic output and prices adjust. Most of the adjustment occurs within the first three years. After this, the model tends to cycle around its new equilibrium, the cyclical movement more or less disappearing after about ten years. By this time interest rates are back to their original levels. As a variant on this run, the perfect capital-mobility assumption is then relaxed in order to demonstrate various points made in the previous chapter. Money is no longer neutral, even in the long-run static sense, once this assumption is relaxed, and it turns out that interest rates rather than prices and the exchange rate do most of the adjustment in this case.

The use of a forward-looking expectations model makes it possible to simulate the effect of anticipated disturbances. I demonstrate the effect of announcing a reduction in the money supply a year before it is due to take place, illustrating various dynamic effects suggested by the theoretical treatment. This is a chance to explore the way in which the model discounts future events. It turns out that even under the efficient-markets assumption, the discount rate is very significant: a rise in the exchange rate tends to ease monetary pressures and lower interest rates and is to this extent self-moderating.

I then turn to the effect of oil discoveries, initially abstracting from development delays by supposing that existing wells turn out to be more productive than expected. The model suggests that the BM direct monetary effect (discussed in the previous chapter) dominates the indirect EV effect, requiring a downward adjustment of domestic output prices and wages. This is, however, facilitated by reductions in income taxes and falling import prices (given the wage equation employed) so that it is not necessary to have a recession in activity to bring this about. I then go on to explore the more interesting case of a new discovery, with all of the associated gestation lags. Again, despite the efficient financial-market assumptions, a high discount rate is attached to the discoveries. I discuss the effect of the various assumptions employed and note that with the exception of the sticky-price assumption, relaxing them would have the effect of increasing the discount rate.

Despite the recent academic interest in numerical solution-methods for rational-expectations models, there are very few results that can be used to contrast with this work. Yet surprisingly, results obtained using the

Liverpool model by Minford (1981) also suggest that the market attaches a high discount rate to North Sea discoveries, even though wages and prices are assumed to be more flexible. This strengthens the general impression that the North Sea had very little effect on the exchange rate until production actually built up during the late 1970s, when the effect was of course compounded by a major rise in oil prices.

1 Open-economy aspects of the model

As we saw in Chapter IX, the openness of an economy to international influences substantially affects the way it responds to macroeconomic policy. Unfortunately there has been a degree of disagreement between the major UK modelling groups on this point and this has been clearly reflected in their policy prescriptions. On the one hand groups such as those at the LBS and Liverpool have emphasized the open nature of the UK economy and in particular the effect of the exchange rate on prices, and on the other the CEPG (and other Cambridge economists) have emphasized the effect of domestic costs on prices.

It seems to be generally accepted that the law of one price applies to food and other basic commodities, so that a change in the exchange rate immediately affects their sterling prices. The main area of disagreement has been over the prices of finished manufactured goods: are these set by overseas suppliers in line with overseas costs and the exchange rate or by domestic suppliers in line with UK costs? Until recently, research at the Treasury suggested that UK manufacturer's home-market prices were determined by domestic costs, the model equation being based on simple cost mark-up relationships. This research also suggested that overseas suppliers' prices depended upon the costs facing domestic producers (these had a 40 per cent weight in the model used here) as well as their own costs and the exchange rate (these both having a 60 per cent weight). Consequently, the main impact of the exchange rate on the domestic price level in this version of the model works through imports of basic commodities and semi-manufactured goods. Although some more recent research has indicated that overseas competition has some effect on the price of UK manufactured goods, this remains, broadly speaking, the case.

Differences between the various modelling groups over the degree of openness of the financial sectors have been less apparent, largely because the exchange rate has in most cases been set judgementally, or via an equation which leaves the degree of international capital mobility implicit. The approach adopted by the Treasury modellers was until 1981 to make this explicit via a model of the capital account of the balance of payments. Together with the model of the current account and official exchange intervention, this could then be solved for the exchange rate which cleared the market (HM Treasury 1979). Since 1981 the model has incorporated a direct exchange-rate equation and the capital account has been determined indirectly as the residual item in the balance of payments identity (HM Treasury 1981).

Neither of these approaches have yielded satisfactory empirical results, at least in recent years. This is largely due to the problems of structural change, simultaneity bias, and measurement error which have been severe in the case of the UK. For example, if capital flows are regressed directly on relative interest rates and indicators of exchange-rate expectations, these biases tend to reduce the associated coefficients, suggesting a very low degree of international capital mobility. In the first case this is because the authorities have tended to raise UK interest rates in response to capital outflows, introducing a simultaneity bias. In the second case this is because expectations are measured poorly.

Similar problems affect the estimation of direct exchange-rate equations as has been demonstrated by Haache and Townend (1981). It is in fact difficult to develop exchange-rate relationships which predict better than the forward exchange rate does. Indeed, sterling exchange rates seem to satisfy the kind of 'efficient market' criteria discussed in Chapter VIII, suggesting a very high degree of capital mobility (Frenkel 1981). Yet this could be due to the high variance of the exchange rate itself, reflected in the residual variance of econometric equations, which makes it difficult to construct a powerful test of such a proposition.

In view of these empirical problems, it is difficult to assess the degree of capital mobility appropriate in the case of the UK. The historical evidence is in any case less relevant now that exchange controls have been removed, tending to make the UK financial markets more open. I have therefore adopted an eclectic approach in these simulations. Since it does not appear to be possible to rule out the 'efficient markets' case of perfect capital mobility and rational expectations on empirical grounds and since these are the assumptions used in theoretical models, this offers one obvious set of assumptions, viewed perhaps as a limiting case. On the other hand we may regard the kind of estimates which emerge from work on capital-flows equations as a lower bound on the possible degree of capital mobility. So as an alternative I also ran these simulations using the capital-flows equations built into the model, but maintaining the rational-expectations assumption. The capital-account equations imply an inflow of £750 million (in 1980 prices) in response to one point rise in UK interest rates and are discussed in HM Treasury (1979). They were originally based on the work of Beenstock and Bell (1979). The method used to solve the model under these various assumptions is discussed in Spencer (1985a).

2   Monetary-policy assumptions

I assumed that a fixed money-supply rule was in operation, supposing that sterling M3 was at its desired or target value in the base run and programming the model to vary policy instruments so as to bring it back to this level during the simulation. As we have seen, the demand for sterling M3 is modelled indirectly in this version of the model. It is determined as the residual in the balance sheet of the non-bank private sector, the difference between its total financial wealth, bank borrowing, and the demand for gilt-edged stocks and overseas assets. This demand for money function is thus more complex than the simple neoclassical formulation adopted in the theoretical model. In particular, the demand for sterling M3, reflecting the speculative motive, appears to be strongly influenced by the differential between the expected return on gilt-edged stocks (including capital gains) and that on short-term assets. So in order to streamline the assumptions and make them comparable with those employed in the theoretical work it was assumed that the authorities would manage the gilt-edged market in a way which ensured that the expected return on gilts equalled that on short-term assets. They were assumed to manipulate the overall level of interest rates in order to control £M3, varying 3-month holding-period yields on long- and short-term assets equally, without attempting to 'twist' the term structure in this sense. Of course, the term structure of interest rates (that is, observed yields to maturity) does vary in these runs, reflecting expectations of capital gains. It was assumed that the supply of reserve assets was varied in order to keep the Treasury-bill rate (and thus MLR and base rates) in line with other money market rates, in order to avoid the instabilities examined in Chapter VI.

The demand for sterling M3 also depends upon the expected differential return between UK and overseas money-market assets. However, the estimated impact of this 'currency-substitution' effect is very weak, due perhaps to the effect of exchange controls or the empirical difficulties mentioned above. In order to make the results clear-cut I eliminated this effect for the purpose of this exercise, building in the different assumptions about capital mobility by varying the sensitivity of non-resident capital flows.

These fixed money-supply assumptions naturally go hand in hand with a floating exchange-rate assumption. So I assumed that the exchange rate varied in order to keep the balance of official financing (the change in the official exchange reserves net of foreign-currency borrowing) at its base-run level. I also assumed that changes in debt interest payments were offset by changes in income taxes. Otherwise, given the fixed money-supply assumption, they will be financed through extra borrowing and this has the effect of making the model unstable[1] reflecting the discussion of Appendix III. The base-run solution was constructed from a historical data base for the years 1974–82. This was projected to 1985 and modified to allow for a constant (1974) oil price.[2]

3   Simulating the effect of monetary pressures on the exchange rate

The effects of a 1 per cent reduction in sterling M3 under these assumptions is shown in Table X.1. It is important to stress at the outset that these simulations illustrate the effect of a reduction in the money supply for a given fiscal-policy stance. They are therefore not immediately relevant to an analysis of the MTFS which involved reductions in the rate of monetary growth brought about through reductions in the PSBR. They show the effects that monetary pressures are likely to have if they are reflected in interest rates (as for example in 1979 and early 1980) and the role which the exchange rate, wages, and prices play in the ensuing adjustment. Treasury-model simulations[3] which contrast the use of interest rates and fiscal-policy instruments to secure reductions in the money supply are presented in Richardson (1981).

The first of these simulations shows the effect of such a reduction assuming that it is completely unanticipated and that capital is perfectly mobile internationally as in the Dornbusch (1976) paper. The results are shown in Table X.1(*a*) and the associated figure. Not surprisingly, the initial impact is felt largely by exchange and interest rates. There is very little initial effect on consumer prices or earnings, so the rise in the nominal exchange rate implies a similar rise in the real exchange rate, indicated here by relative unit labour costs in the central panel of the figure.

The rise in the exchange rate causes a substantial fall in prices in the second quarter, easing the monetary pressures. With the lagged effects of the high interest rate seen in the first quarter this allows exchange and interest rates to fall back. The timing of these effects depends critically upon the various lags involved, but in this specification short-term interest rates fall below their original level temporarily. The interest-rate movements necessary to attain the monetary objective in later quarters are relatively small compared to the initial adjustments, as is clear from the lower panel of the figure.

In practice inflationary and monetary pressures tend to develop gradually over time, implying a rather smoother adjustment than that indicated by this stimulation result. This is essentially of a 'diagnostic' character, designed to point out the various factors at work as simply and as clearly as possible. Moreover, in order to allow these adjustments to take place more smoothly the authorities attempt to control the aggregates on a financial-year rather than a quarterly basis.

The effect of allowing the system more time to adjust can be seen from the second simulation (Table X.1(*b*) and Figure X.A(*b*)). Technically, this shows the effect of announcing in the first quarter that sterling M3 is to be reduced by 1 per cent one year later (that is, in Q5), assuming that financial operators find this credible and again that capital is perfectly mobile. This is essentially the theoretical case analysed by Wilson (1979) and discussed in the previous chapter. As this analysis leads us to expect, the exchange rate jumps initially, though by rather less than in the previous case. This tends to reduce prices and ease monetary pressures over the first four quarters, that is before the monetary contraction takes place. Short-term interest rates fall below their initial level, and this dictates an appreciating exchange rate over this interregnum. The maximum appreciation occurs after a year, just as interest rates are raised in order to secure the reduction in the money supply. These exchange- and interest-rate effects are naturally less than in the case of an unanticipated cut. Thereafter they adjust back quickly towards their equilibrium values as in the basic case.

The initial overshooting of the exchange rate depresses output over the first four years in both of these runs, through the effect competitiveness has on trade volumes. The current account improves initially due to the well known *J*-curve or currency-invoicing effect. Yet the economy is not unambiguously depressed since real wages and wealth rise and this leads to an increase in consumers' expenditure. Indeed, in contrast to the simple Dornbusch model which abstracts from wealth effects, the fall in prices causes an additional boost to consumer expenditure. This is sufficient to push the system into an expansionary phase after real earnings have adjusted. In more recent versions of the Treasury model (Barber (1984)) these wealth effects have been more than enough to offset the adverse competitiveness effects, so that an appreciation of the exchange rate is expansionary even in the short term. This reflects a downward revision of the competitiveness elasticities following the experience of the early 1980s.

As I noted in Chapter II, wealth effects on consumers' expenditure in the UK appear to be subject to extremely long lags, explaining why this continues at a buoyant level throughout these simulations. The downward adjustment of wealth is clearly reflected in the current account. A more detailed examination of the results nevertheless shows that private-sector financial wealth falls by only half a per cent by the end of the simulation period (in both runs) and thus still has some way to go before returning to equilibrium. The movement towards equilibrium is not monotonic (as it is in the Dornbusch model) but cyclical, due to the presence of complex roots in the model.

Given the assumption of perfect capital mobility the equilibrium solution will, as I have shown, be one in which the nominal exchange rate appreciates and prices fall by one per cent and interest rates return to their original levels. So the behaviour of prices and exchange rates during the last few years of these runs also suggest that the system is still in disequilibrium, especially in the case of the second simulation in which the reduction in the money supply is delayed by a year. This behaviour is again explained by the wealth effect which (together with the high level of activity it implies) tends to maintain the demand for money at an artificially high level, depressing prices below their equilibrium values. Consequently these simulations tell us very

Table X.1. Simulated effects of a 1 per cent reduction in sterling M3 under alternative assumptions

	Real GDP at factor cost	Real personal disposable income	Consumer's expenditure	Unemployment	Current balance	PSBR	Consumer expenditure deflator	Average earnings	Exchange rates	UK unit labour costs	Interest rates short-term	Interest rates long-term
	%	%	%	000s	£m (1975)	£m	%	%	%	%	points	points
(a) Unanticipated reduction in Q1 with perfect capital mobility												
Q1	-0.18	-0.11	-0.19	4.0	29	-13	-0.02	-0.04	2.82	2.79	4.70	0.21
Q2	-0.13	0.28	0.05	8.8	32	-11	-0.25	-0.05	1.60	1.56	-0.32	0.00
Q3	-0.06	0.22	0.21	11.3	16	-4	-0.40	-0.07	1.66	1.62	-0.35	0.02
Q4	-0.07	0.17	0.16	12.3	3	-12	-0.52	-0.17	1.75	1.61	-0.04	0.04
Q5	-0.05	0.09	0.26	11.7	-3	-25	-0.57	-0.29	1.76	1.47	-0.24	0.04
Q9	-0.13	0.09	0.09	15.0	-48	24	-1.10	-0.87	1.43	0.59	-0.36	-0.02
Q13	-0.08	0.04	0.14	13.1	-41	31	-1.25	-1.25	1.44	0.21	0.25	-0.01
Q17	-0.06	-0.04	0.13	7.5	-34	36	-1.18	-1.57	1.51	-0.06	0.34	0.00
Q21	0.06	0.04	0.19	-3.0	-22	30	-1.35	-1.72	1.44	-0.81	-0.01	-0.02
Q25	0.09	0.08	0.21	-13.6	-35	38	-1.37	-1.70	1.41	-0.33	-0.35	-0.03
Q29	0.15	0.21	0.22	-33.7	-31	0	-1.32	-1.57	1.51	-0.09	-0.12	-0.02
Q33	0.10	0.16	0.18	-30.0	-16	31	-1.24	-1.47	1.63	0.09	0.05	0.00
Q37	0.02	0.12	0.16	-10.2	-9	45	-1.24	-1.43	1.65	0.19	-0.01	0.01
Q41	0.00	0.10	0.13	-3.0	-12	50	-1.20	-1.37	1.63	0.24	0.07	—
Q45	-0.01	0.09	0.11	0.0	-5	58	-1.13	-1.31	1.58	0.24	0.13	—
(b) Reduction in Q5 announced in Q1 with perfect mobility												
Q1	-0.06	-0.12	-0.03	1.2	23	-10	-0.03	-0.01	2.33	2.32	-0.21	0.27
Q2	-0.11	-0.11	-0.02	9.4	37	-8	-0.20	-0.02	2.39	2.39	-0.31	0.09
Q3	-0.08	0.08	0.10	7.3	32	-9	-0.43	-0.07	2.47	2.43	-0.49	0.12
Q4	-0.07	0.17	0.18	9.5	23	-10	-0.06	-0.19	2.60	2.43	-0.44	0.17

Q5	-0.20	0.12	0.01	13.7	-2	-20	-0.71	-0.36	2.71	2.37	3.87	0.18
Q9	-0.18	-0.05	0.23	21.7	-47	19	-0.92	-0.98	1.91	0.96	-0.28	0.03
Q13	-0.13	0.01	0.20	22.6	-45	53	-1.16	-1.46	1.64	0.18	-0.25	-0.01
Q17	-0.03	0.03	0.16	11.3	-55	43	-1.37	-1.81	1.56	-0.27	0.21	-0.02
Q21	0.05	0.02	0.17	-3.8	-20	27	-1.54	-1.98	1.64	-0.38	0.42	-0.02
Q25	0.12	0.05	0.23	-17.9	-26	-19	-1.95	-1.95	1.61	-0.39	-0.44	-0.03
Q29	0.18	0.23	0.24	-39.8	-34	2	-1.52	-1.83	1.67	-0.21	-0.28	-0.03
Q33	0.12	0.17	0.19	-36.4	-15	38	-1.46	-1.73	1.84	0.00	0.08	0.00
Q37	0.03	0.11	0.16	-12.8	-7	45	-1.45	-1.69	1.87	0.14	0.04	0.01
Q41	0.01	0.10	0.14	-4.9	-10	85	-1.40	-1.61	1.84	0.19	0.06	0.01
Q45	0.00	0.10	0.12	-1.4	-15	59	-1.33	-1.54	1.77	0.20	0.13	0.00

(c) Unanticipated reduction in Q1 with imperfect mobility

Q1	-0.17	-0.10	-0.18	3.7	27	-12	-0.03	-0.04	2.69	2.65	4.51	0.46
Q2	-0.12	0.28	0.03	8.2	26	-8	-0.22	-0.05	1.20	1.19	-0.51	0.28
Q3	-0.05	0.18	0.18	10.2	11	-1	-0.34	-0.06	1.20	1.15	-0.44	0.34
Q4	-0.06	0.11	0.11	10.7	-2	-9	-0.41	-0.15	1.16	1.03	0.06	0.42
Q5	-0.04	0.05	0.17	10.0	-6	-18	-0.43	-0.25	0.83	0.58	0.58	0.11
Q9	-0.07	0.09	0.14	9.1	-47	25	-0.41	-0.61	0.13	-0.51	0.04	0.34
Q13	0.07	0.09	0.06	0.0	-26	9	-0.25	-0.61	0.03	-0.58	0.53	0.36
Q17	0.08	0.08	0.06	-11.3	0	-1	-0.28	-0.53	-0.02	-0.57	0.58	0.40
Q21	0.15	0.16	0.12	-18.5	-4	-16	-0.20	-0.36	-0.10	-0.48	0.30	0.33
Q25	0.15	0.20	0.15	-21.2	1	-34	-0.11	-0.19	-0.07	-0.26	0.22	0.35
Q29	0.10	0.20	0.13	-20.2	5	-32	-0.02	-0.06	-0.02	-0.07	0.18	0.35
Q33	0.05	0.18	0.12	-13.7	6	-2	-0.04	-0.05	0.05	0.01	0.31	0.35
Q37	0.03	0.18	0.11	-7.0	-1	10	-0.09	-0.01	0.06	0.05	0.37	0.35
Q41	0.02	0.17	0.12	-3.4	-13	19	-0.14	0.05	0.03	0.04	0.40	0.33
Q45	0.01	0.17	0.12	4.4	-20	20	-0.19	-0.02	0.01	-0.20	0.46	0.32

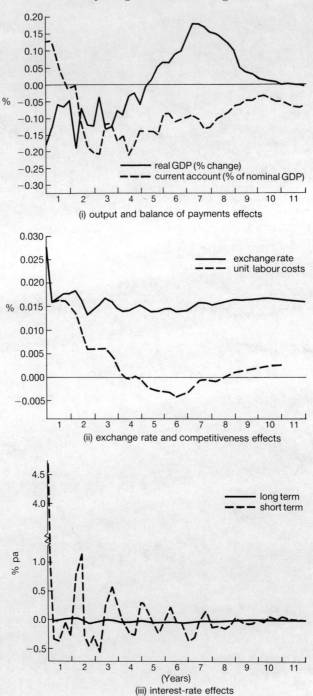

(i) output and balance of payments effects

(ii) exchange rate and competitiveness effects

(iii) interest-rate effects

Fig. X.A. (a) Unanticipated monetary contraction

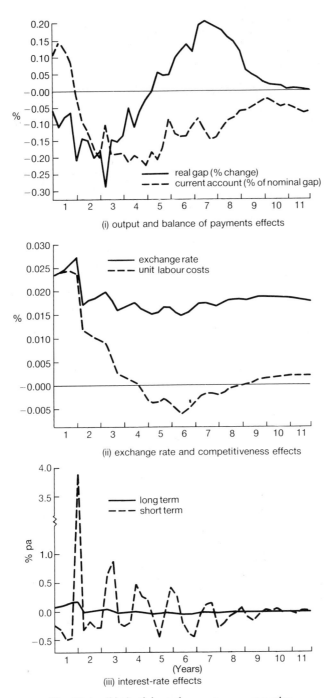

Fig. X.A. (b) Anticipated monetary contraction

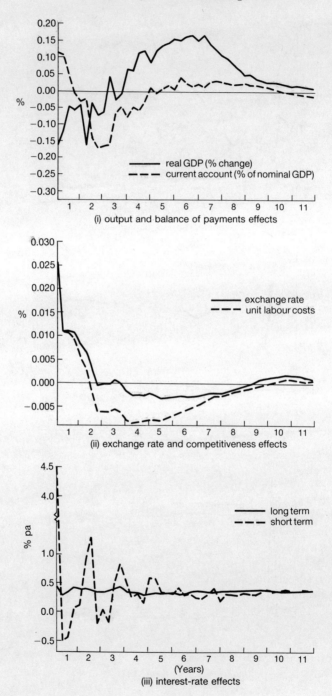

(i) output and balance of payments effects

(ii) exchange rate and competitiveness effects

(iii) interest-rate effects

Fig. X.A. (c) Unanticipated monetary contraction under imperfect mobility

little about the long-run solution. They are primarily designed to illustrate the short- and medium-term adjustments and in particular the degree of exchange-rate overshooting.[4]

As a check on these results the basic case was rerun under the imperfect capital-mobility assumption discussed earlier. The results are displayed in Table X.1(*c*) and the associated figure. This makes surprisingly little difference to the short-run response, the exchange rate and short-term interest rates rising by only slightly less than in the perfect mobility case of Table X.a(*a*).[5] However the long-term interest rate jumps by nearly half a point—much more than under perfect mobility—anticipating the long-run result. Not surprisingly, given the discussion of Section IX.6 and Appendix III, this equilibrium solution involves both a rise in interest rates and a fall in prices, since interest rates are no longer fixed externally. This simulation suggests that most of the adjustment will in fact occur through a rise in interest rates. Given this, goods-market equilibrium dictates a lower real exchange rate and this run exhibits a marked tendency in this direction. Although the net long-run effect on the long-run nominal exchange rate is unclear, this simulation suggests that it will tend to rise following a reduction in the money supply, though under these assumptions the effect is minimal.

4 Simulating the effect of North Sea oil production

Oil discoveries take time and are expensive to develop. This complicates their macroeconomic impact as the paper by Eastwood and Venables (EV) discussed in the previous chapter makes clear. In order to abstract from these complications it is useful to consider a less complicated situation initially, such as would occur if it were suddenly discovered that existing wells were more productive than had previously been thought. This kind of effect often occurs when new fields come on stream. So in the first simulation we suppose that the annual rate of North Sea production is found to be 5 million tonnes higher than originally forecast. This is worth £200 millions per annum in 1975 prices. It is assumed that costs are not affected, so that this increases North Sea profits and economic rent by the same amount.[6] The result obtained assuming perfect capital mobility is shown in Table X.2(*a*) and Figure X.B(*a*). Results 2(*b*) and 2(*c*) show the simulated effect of a new discovery, subject to the various gestation and revenue lags emphasized by Eastwood and Venables, given our two alternative assumptions about the degree of capital mobility. The discovery was assumed to be equivalent to 10 per cent of the North Sea oil reserves as these were projected in the mid-1970s.

The productivity simulation immediately suggests that the effect of higher activity on the demand for money (stressed by the paper by Buiter and Miller (BM) discussed in the previous chapter) dominates the Eastwood–Venables (EV) import-price effect.[7] So domestic prices and

Table X.2. Simulated effects of North Sea oil production

	Real GDP at factor cost %	Real personal disposable income %	Consumer's expenditure %	Unemployment 000s	Current balance £m (1975)	PSBR £m (1975)	Consumer expenditure deflator %	Average earnings %	Exchange rates %	UK unit labour costs %	Interest rates short-term points	Interest rates long-term points
(a) Increase in productivity given perfect capital mobility												
1974 Q1	0.21	0.01	0.02	−2.7	40	−13	−0.02	0.02	0.49	0.50	−0.12	—
Q2	0.20	0.03	0.02	−2.6	54	−30	−0.04	0.03	0.52	0.54	0.06	—
Q3	0.21	0.07	0.04	−2.0	53	−27	−0.06	0.03	0.51	0.53	0.07	—
Q4	0.22	0.10	0.06	−1.0	50	−24	0.07	0.02	0.49	0.50	0.10	—
1975 Q1	0.22	0.10	0.06	0.2	45	−21	−0.08	−0.01	0.46	0.45	0.10	—
1976 Q1	0.16	0.10	0.10	2.6	20	−11	−0.14	−0.17	0.39	0.23	−0.22	−0.22
1977 Q1	0.20	0.13	0.13	2.2	15	−5	−0.26	−0.38	0.43	0.05	−0.16	−0.01
1978 Q1	0.25	0.14	0.14	−1.8	31	−4	−0.42	−0.63	0.54	−0.10	0.25	0.01
1979 Q1	0.32	0.20	0.22	−7.4	27	−10	−0.48	−0.66	0.46	−0.20		−0.01
1980 Q1	0.27	0.26	0.25	−13.0	18	−40	−0.48	−0.56	0.42	−0.16	−0.20	−0.02
1981 Q1	0.31	0.31	0.25	−19.9	19	−30	−0.37	−0.46	0.46	−0.02	0.03	−0.01
1982 Q1	0.25	0.26	0.23	−17.2	26	−21	−0.34	−0.37	0.48	0.12	0.04	−0.01
1983 Q1	0.20	0.25	0.23	−4.2	30	−18	−0.30	0.46	0.14	−0.04	−0.01	−0.01
1984 Q1	0.18	0.25	0.22	−5.6	29	−16	−0.21	−0.24	0.42	0.17	−0.01	−0.02
1985 Q1	0.17	0.24	0.22	−4.1	28	−17	−0.15	0.38	0.19	0.04	−0.02	−0.02
(b) The effect of a new discovery given perfect capital mobility												
1974 Q1	0.02	—	—	−0.5	−3	−4	0.02	0.01	0.48	0.49	−0.01	−0.15
Q2	0.02	—	0.03	−0.09	−11	−1	−0.05	0.02	0.49	0.50	−0.10	−0.16
Q3	0.01	0.04	0.04	−1.2	−19	5	−0.10	0.02	0.52	0.53	0.11	−0.17
Q4	0.03	0.08	0.06	−1.4	−29	15	−0.13	0.01	0.49	0.49	−0.11	−0.21

	C1	C2	C3	C4	C5	C6	C7	C8	C9	C10	C11	C12
1975 Q1	-0.19	-0.37	0.50	0.52	—	-0.16	11	-40	-2.9	0.09	0.07	0.08
1976 Q1	-0.18	-0.19	0.57	0.66	-0.08	-0.21	-19	-67	-10.0	0.09	0.10	0.07
1977 Q1	-0.16	-0.47	0.78	0.98	-0.21	-0.38	-10	-45	-5.9	0.10	0.04	0.10
1978 Q1	-0.08	-0.10	0.94	1.45	-0.53	-0.61	-1	-3	5.1	0.09	0.03	0.15
1979 Q1	-0.06	-0.18	0.93	1.73	-0.81	-0.82	12	4	10.7	0.19	0.15	0.29
1980 Q1	-0.05	-0.49	0.82	1.90	-1.05	-0.98	-33	2	10.9	0.30	0.25	0.22
1981 Q1	-0.01	-0.03	0.86	2.10	-1.19	-1.11	-3	14	-11.6	0.47	0.56	0.56
1982 Q1	0.01	0.04	0.81	2.18	-1.27	-1.21	-5	10	-32.4	0.58	0.68	0.73
1983 Q1	0.01	-0.02	0.77	2.18	-1.33	-1.32	-4	8	-33.0	0.69	0.78	0.76
1984 Q1	—	-0.02	0.72	2.16	-1.33	-1.35	-4	9	-36.5	0.76	0.85	0.84
1985 Q1	—	0.07	0.72	2.13	-1.30	-1.33	-3	5	-40.0	0.83	0.90	0.90

(c) The effect of a new discovery given imperfect capital mobility

	C1	C2	C3	C4	C5	C6	C7	C8	C9	C10	C11	C12
1974 Q1	-0.02	—	0.23	0.23	0.01	0.00	-1	-8	-0.7	—	—	0.03
Q2	-0.02	-0.01	0.21	0.20	0.02	-0.01	-1	-18	-1.4	0.02	0.02	0.03
Q3	-0.02	0.04	0.21	0.19	0.03	-0.04	6	-26	-2.0	0.02	0.03	0.02
Q4	-0.03	0.11	0.19	0.17	0.03	-0.04	16	-33	-2.5	0.03	0.05	0.03
1975 Q1	-0.03	-0.01	0.14	0.13	0.04	-0.03	15	-40	-4.1	0.05	0.07	0.09
1976 Q1	-0.05	0.13	0.12	0.09	0.04	0.01	-18	-58	-12.6	0.07	0.11	0.10
1977 Q1	-0.06	-0.18	0.35	0.31	0.03	-0.04	-3	-34	-11.7	0.08	0.08	0.17
1978 Q1	-0.03	0.06	0.64	0.77	-0.15	-0.19	-13	6	-3.5	0.08	0.07	0.23
1979 Q1	-0.03	-0.06	0.77	1.05	-0.30	-0.35	—	7	4.0	0.18	0.15	0.33
1980 Q1	-0.03	-0.30	0.89	1.33	-0.51	-0.59	-24	12	6.6	0.24	0.22	0.23
1981 Q1	—	0.01	1.11	1.72	-0.70	-0.77	-4	1	-5.2	0.37	0.45	0.48
1982 Q1	-0.01	-0.05	1.14	1.91	-0.84	-0.93	-7	-4	-20.0	0.48	0.57	0.60
1983 Q1	-0.01	-0.02	1.12	1.95	-0.93	-1.65	10	-2	-22.9	0.58	0.66	0.65
1984 Q1	—	-0.04	1.02	1.89	-0.98	-1.10	7	-5	-28.8	0.66	0.74	0.73
1985 Q1	—	-0.12	0.91	1.78	-0.97	-1.11	6	-2	-35.6	0.70	0.79	0.80

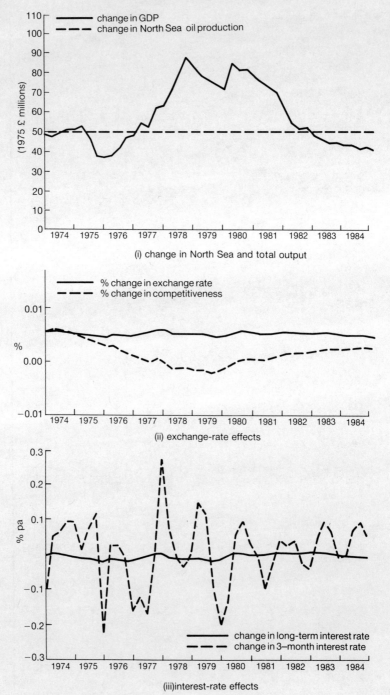

(i) change in North Sea and total output

(ii) exchange-rate effects

(iii) interest-rate effects

Fig. X.B. (a) Simulated effect of an unanticipated increase in productivity

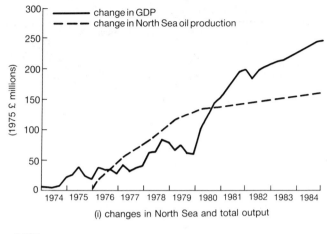

(i) changes in North Sea and total output

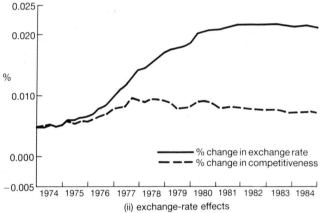

(ii) exchange-rate effects

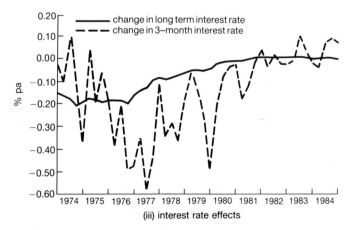

(iii) interest rate effects

Fig. X.B. (b) Simulated effect of North Sea discovery

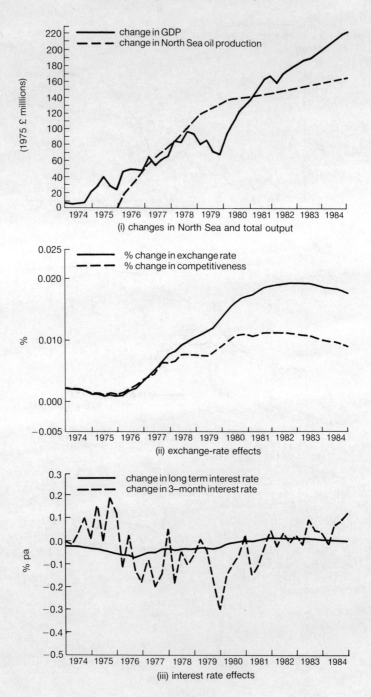

Fig. X.B. (c) Simulated effect of North Sea discovery assuming imperfect mobility

earnings (shown by the difference between real and nominal exchange rates in the central panel of Figure X.B(a) fall as the system moves into equilibrium.[8] However, output does not apparently need to fall below potential for long to achieve this since, given the earnings specification, this is facilitated by the fall in import prices and the reduction in personal income taxes.[9] Indeed, demand expands above potential output after the initial adjustment has taken place.

The next two results illustrate the general point made by Eastwood and Venables quite well—gestation and demand lags will complicate the dynamic response, and can depress domestic demand initially even though the overall impact is expansionary. However, they point out several factors which are missing from their analysis and in particular the importance of the BM effect which again means that domestic prices must adjust downwards rather than upwards. They also reveal the effect of development expenditures and—in case 2(c)—imperfections in the capital market. These expenditures are naturally concentrated in the period immediately following the discovery and are likely to dominate the short-run response given the kind of numbers involved. This means that in contrast to the EV two-phase analysis, we are in practice likely to observe three phases of adjustment:

(a) *The development phase*: On our assumption this lasts for about three years following the discovery. It may be shown that if capital is perfectly mobile the exchange rate must initially rise. If the degree of capital mobility is imperfect, then the development expenditures may cause the exchange rate to fall initially, but both of our results indicate a small appreciation. Domestic expenditures are boosted by the development programme so that the initial phase is an expansionary one, especially in the imperfect-mobility case.

(b) *The interregnum*: This is marked by a strongly rising exchange rate which causes a fall in both interest rates and non-oil output as shown in the figure.

(c) *The expansionary phase*: Once the revenues come on stream this has the effect of expanding demand in the non-oil sectors. This final phase would appear to be of an EV rather than BM variety.

Perhaps the most interesting feature of these results is the way in which interest and exchange rates behave. The theory outlined in the previous section suggests that an efficient market will discount future events impinging upon the exchange rate if domestic prices are in some sense sticky. This is because a rise in the exchange rate will reduce interest rates and will to this extent be self-moderating. These effects are shown very clearly in Figure X.B(b) and suggest that even assuming an efficient market and a tight specification of financial policy the discount factor is considerable. A similar result has been reported by Minford (1981) using the Liverpool model based on very different assumptions about wage determination, suggesting that this is a fairly robust result.

These results lead me to conclude that the direct monetary effect of increasing expenditures provides a significant offset to the indirect exchange-rate effect stressed by EV. This could well require a fall in domestic wage inflation given an unchanged monetary target, as in the variants reported here. But this is a nominal rather than a real adjustment, and should be facilitated by the rise in real incomes associated with the discovery, without any marked fall in non-oil output. Development delays will tend to complicate this adjustment, causing the exchange rate to rise before the increase in real incomes is felt. However, this does not appear to be much of a problem in these simulations which suggest that the market attaches a high rate of discount to future developments, even if it is assumed to be efficient. On the basis of these results we may conclude that the North Sea had very little effect on the exchange rate until the late 1970s. Moreover, there was no formal monetary target until 1977 and until October of that year exchange-market intervention was very significant. In view of this the financial markets may in fact have expected the loss of competitiveness associated with the North Sea to be brought about through UK price inflation as well as exchange-rate appreciation. This would have been another good reason for discounting its effect on the exchange rate.

Notes

1. More precisely, this destroys the stable saddlepoint property of the model, introducing more unstable roots than there are jump variables.
2. This modification was made in order to simulate the effect of oil discoveries sensibly. The macroeconomic impact of such discoveries obviously depends upon the expected difference between their market value and the cost of exploitation. Microeconomic considerations dictate that the expected rate of increase of resource prices should in equilibrium equal the interest rate—the Hotelling Condition. Real interest rates were at times heavily negative during the 1970s and have been strongly positive during the 1980s. But investors would have been unaware of these developments if they viewed the situation from the perspective of 1974, basing their views on their most recent experience. Given this experience it is reasonable to suppose that they expected a zero real interest rate, and thus a constant real oil price. So in this analysis we assumed that the real dollar oil price was fixed at the 1974 level. Of course, recent history would have been very different if the oil price had remained at the 1974 level, and had the 1979–80 oil-price shock not occurred. We might have reconstructed the base to reflect this but since such results are only base-run dependent in a highly non-linear model, we did not consider this to be worthwhile.
3. These simulations were run on the same version of the model as that used here except that expectations were generated by the model's empirically based relationships rather than in a consistent fashion. However, as the discussion of the naïve and rational cases in the last chapter makes clear such differences in specification only affect the dynamics, and not the long-run solution of the model.

4. This point is particularly relevant to rational-expectations simulations. In these runs we selected the solution which gave no change in the expected exchange rate and long-term interest rate over the last four years of the simulation. (This implies that changes in interest rates are zero on average over this period.) This 'terminal' condition' is the analogue of the 'transversality condition' appropriate in infinite time. For this reason the solutions reported here should only be regarded as an approximation to the true solution. However, the nature of the errors introduced through this approximation is such that their contribution during the final part of any run will be infinitely greater than their contribution during the initial part of the run. We may therefore be confident about the accuracy of the approximation during the first few years, even though we may be sceptical about its accuracy over the last few years of the run.

5. This is essentially because the initial improvement in the current-account boosts the exchange rate, making up for the weaker interest-rate effect.

6. The direct contribution of the North Sea programme to the Gross Domestic Product will be increased by these additional profits. These are worth about 0.2 per cent of GDP over this period. However, the direct contribution to Gross National Product and the balance of payments will be somewhat less than this, since these items are struck after deducting profits due abroad which increase in the short run.

7. It might be argued that this simulation exaggerates the BM effect since it is assumed that the rise in activity associated with the North Sea discovery has exactly the same impact upon the demand for money as any other form of activity. However, there can be no doubt that an increase in activity of this type, strongly reflected in consumers' expenditure, would increase the demand for money significantly. It might also be argued that the price equations in the model understate the EV effect by giving a relatively small weight to the exchange rate. The LBS model, for example, would give a much larger weight to this, assuming as it does that overseas competitors rather than UK manufacturers effectively set UK traded-goods prices. Although both of these points are highly debateable they should be borne in mind when looking at these results.

8. The discussion of the last chapter would lead us to expect the exchange rate to overshoot in this case. However, the various dynamic effects on the demand for money broadly cancel out over time so that the exchange rate does not overshoot. In terms of Figure X.A(b) the SS line is vertical so that the system jumps from B to a point immediately above C, then moves vertically down to C as earnings adjust.

9. Although nominal wages are sticky in this model, this is largely due to the fact that expectations are assumed to be formed in a backward-looking way. Wage earners are ultimately assumed to be interested in real disposable incomes rather than money wages. The wage equations are described in Wren-Lewis (1985).

The Monetary-Control Debate: A Conclusion

By way of a conclusion, this chapter takes a look at some of the more interesting developments which took place during the 1970s, viewed from the perspective of the earlier analysis. I will start with the monetary-control debate which raised many interesting issues, most of which are still of great topical interest. I will then go on to look at the way the August 1981 arrangements seem to be working out in practice and to discuss the implications of the increased competition between banks and building societies seen in recent years.

1 The monetary-control debate

Monetary-control arrangements have been the subject of almost continual discussion in the UK in recent years. This debate was given added impetus in June 1979 by two papers appearing in the *Bank of England Bulletin*, the first discussing existing control techniques and the second offering a critical assessment of the main alternative—monetary-base control (MCB). These were followed in March 1980 by a joint Treasury–Bank of England consultative document, the Green Paper on 'Monetary Control' (Cmnd. 7858). These documents clearly reflected the problems which the authorities had experienced since the CCC reforms of 1971.

As we saw in Chapter II, these reforms had been based on a competitive view of the banking system and a belief that the private demand for money and credit was sufficiently interest elastic to allow monetary and fiscal policy to be pursued as independent policies, without recourse to quantitative controls. Private-sector bank borrowing was still implicitly considered to be the residual in the money-supply identity. Yet the authorities were soon forced to reconsider their attitude towards the banking system, falling back on quantitative controls in the guise of the SSD scheme as a way of checking the perverse behaviour of wholesale-deposit issues. Serious doubts then began to emerge about the responsiveness of private-sector bank borrowing to changes in interest rates. As the need for monetary control became more apparent this in turn forced a radical reappraisal of the relationship between monetary and fiscal policy.

Viewed against this background, it is not surprising that the Green Paper expressed serious doubts about the feasibility of monetary-base control. It was felt that the relationship between the base and the money stock would be a rather loose one unless a mandatory reserve requirement were imposed upon the banks. The main worry about a mandatory scheme on the other hand was that it would exert too precise a control, forcing rapid adjustments in both bank and non-bank balance sheets, at the expense of large fluctuations in short-term interest rates. Another worry was that banks would try to avoid the penalties implied by such a scheme through artificial forms of adjustment, as they did when the SSD scheme was imposed. This would simply have distorted the monetary aggregates.

Instead, the Treasury and the Bank of England argued that the existing arrangements, based on fiscal instruments, funding policy, and interest rates, offered a sufficient degree of control over the monetary aggregates in the medium term, by which they meant periods of a year or more. It was argued that a precise month-to-month control over the rate of monetary growth was not necessary to restrain inflation, since this relationship was essentially a medium-term one. Nevertheless, the paper accepted that an improved degree of control was desirable and invited suggestions as to how the difficulties identified with the various forms of MBC could be overcome. In the meantime it proposed a list of reforms which would facilitate short-run control and make it easier to implement MBC if this were felt at some future point to be feasible. These proposals were as follows:

(i)   The SSD scheme would be withdrawn.

(ii) The $12\frac{1}{2}$ per cent reserve-asset ratio would be abolished.

(iii) The banks would, however, hold liquid assets for prudential reasons, subject to Bank of England supervision.

(iv) The arrangement whereby the clearing banks held minimum balances at the Bank of England would be extended to the other banks.

(v)   The Special Deposit scheme would be retained in order to facilitate monetary control in situations of excess bank liquidity.

The proponents of MBC, notably Griffiths *et al.* (1980), replied in its defence that the Green Paper had exaggerated the implied volatility in interest rates. In any case, existing techniques had, they argued, yielded the worst of both worlds, resulting in volatile movements in both interest rates and the monetary aggregates. Milton Friedman, in his evidence to the Treasury and Civil Service Select Committee enquiry into Monetary Policy (Cmnd. 748, 1980) strongly supported MBC, expressing astonishment at the idea that fiscal policy and interest rates should be used to control the money supply. He likened this to controlling the output of motor cars via demand, by controlling incomes and the price of substitutes such as rail travel. How much easier and more effective it would be to control the availability of an essential input such as the monetary base, or in the case of the motor car analogy, steel.

2   Portfolio disequilibrium and the monetary base

Despite their intuitive appeal, such arguments misunderstood the nature of macroeconomic policy as it had evolved in the UK. As we have seen, this policy had been based on the control of broad monetary aggregates such as sterling M3, the idea being that this was related to bank borrowing and other important macroeconomic variables over which the authorities have a fair degree of control. This relationship had traditionally been explained in terms of the 'money-supply identity', and as we saw in Chapter II monetary theorists used this kind of relationship to develop the notion of 'disequilibrium money'. Although it may amount to very much the same thing in practice, I have argued that it is more accurate to describe the wider aggregates as being demand determined, but influenced by the general portfolio disequilibrium or wealth effects of fiscal policy and bank-credit expansion. Either way, these disequilibrium effects are in the first instance reflected in the broad monetary aggregates and perhaps holdings of other financial assets, but are likely as time goes on to affect expenditure decisions and hence inflation. So the broad monetary aggregates, assuming they are not distorted by financial innovation, the corset or similar effects, act as an advance indicator of inflationary developments in the economy. These disequilibrium effects are arguably fundamental to monetary theory, giving it its predictive content.

To stand on its own as the central expression of macroeconomic policy, a system of monetary-base control would therefore have to offer the prospect of an improved degree of control over the broad monetary aggregates. Otherwise it would need to be supplemented by targets for the wider aggregates such as those currently in place, or, less elegantly perhaps, targets for fiscal policy, private-sector credit, and other factors impinging upon non-bank portfolios and expenditure. Since it is unlikely that any measure of the monetary base would reflect these directly,[1] and since the links between the banks' deposits and their holdings of cash are flexible, this linkage would have to be achieved through a mandatory system, with all the attendant risks of disintermediation and distortion.

Left to themselves under a non-mandatory scheme, the banks would tend to hold cash balances largely against sight deposits, since they maintain the viability of their time deposit liabilities through maturity matching and similar techniques. For this reason a non-mandatory form of MBC is broadly equivalent to the control of a narrow monetary aggregate such as M1. It is widely agreed that the narrow aggregates, since they essentially represent short-term transactions balances, will not be significantly influenced by the kind of portfolio disequilibrium effects which are likely to affect the wide aggregates. They largely reflect what is currently happening to prices and economic activity,[2] though in this respect they are very timely and useful statistics. They also reflect perceptions of interest rates and act as leading indicators of nominal income, perhaps for this reason. In recent years the UK authorities have increasingly come to view these as important indicators, particularly when deciding upon the appropriate level of interest rates, and in the 1983 Budget adopted a formal target for M1 which was to stand alongside targets for the broad aggregates £M3 and PSL2.

On the other hand, a mandatory MBC scheme which was ultimately directed at the control of the broad aggregates would also have to confront he problem of private-sector bank borrowing, which has persistently dogged UK monetary-control techniques. There is little to suggest that this item is readily amenable to control via interest rates. To the extent that it is, the evidence reviewed in Chapter IV suggests that such effects are subject to substantial lags. Although the gilt-edged market has become more resilient in recent years, due partly to the adoption of the financial framework, there is no escaping the fact that a strict short-term control of the wider aggregates (for a given fiscal policy) implies large corrective movements in interest rates. The simulations of the previous chapter are indicative of the kind of changes which would be required to control sterling M3 on a quarter-by-quarter basis. It is just possible that the move to tighter short-run control would make the financial markets yet more resilient, but even so it is difficult to see how such an aggregate could be controlled on say a month-to-month basis in the face of such inertia.

Indeed, the evidence of the early 1970s suggests than an MBC scheme would have to be designed very carefully if it was to be stable. It is also suggestive of some of the institutional changes which would be required to make it work. Overdraft facilities would have to be curtailed and their interest rate linked to money-market rates. Otherwise banks would find themselves bidding for deposits in order to acquire monetary-base assets and square their own balance sheets, thereby passing the problem on to another bank as companies supplying the funds ran up their overdrafts. Such institutional changes would in turn affect the way non-banks organized their affairs, perhaps reversing the trend towards liability management seen in recent decades. This would again distort the monetary aggregates, adding to the teething problems likely to be experienced with such a scheme.

Once it is accepted that portfolio-disequilibrium effects on expenditure are of importance, and this is reflected in control arrangements which encompass the broad as well as the narrow monetary aggregates, it obviously becomes necessary to co-ordinate monetary and fiscal policy. In this situation, a fiscal expansion will immediately increase the demand for broad money through its effect on the wealth of the private sector. This effect is absent from Professor Friedman's analysis to which I referred earlier, this presumably being based on a narrow definition of money. Over a longer time horizon such pressures will (except in the rather special circumstances discussed in Section IX.6), impinge on the monetary aggregates however they are defined, working through prices and economic activity.

3   The August 1981 arrangements and their effect on the composition of bank balance sheets

In addition to the reforms they had proposed in the Green Paper, the authorities brought in a further series of changes. These came into effect in August 1981 and included:

(i)   The suspension of MLR

(ii) An extension of the range of banks whose bills would be eligible for rediscount at the Bank of England.

(iii) The definition of a new 'monetary sector', to replace the old 'banking sector', encompassing all institutions acceding to the new provisions.

(iv) The adoption of an unpublished target band for short-term interest rates.

These reforms were designed to allow the Bank of England more room for manœuvre in its money-market operations, allowing the market more say in the determination of interest rates. However, the authorities retained the option of posting an MLR for short periods of time—an option which they availed themselves of in order to make their intentions clear as sterling came under strong downward pressure during mid-January 1985. Although it is perhaps too early to judge their full effect, it is already clear that they are having a major impact upon the balance sheets of the banks and other financial institutions. The most obvious result has been the dramatic increase in bank lending to the private sector—particularly the personal sector—which has taken place since the abolition of the corset in June 1980.

This surge is reminiscent of that which took place following the reforms of 1971, both being shown in real terms in Figure II.A. But history never quite repeats itself. The figure shows that the monetary effects have been quite different given that monetary targets have been in force, and that fiscal and funding techniques rather than short-term money market and interest-rate operations have been used to help implement them. Despite the overshoot which occurred in 1980/1 and 1981/2, the increase in private bank lending has implied a reduction in bank lending to the public sector,[3] which has been fairly static in terms of the nominal amount outstanding. Reflecting this, lending to the private sector increased from 75 per cent of bank assets early in 1980, a figure which as we have seen was artifically depressed by the corset, to 85 per cent by the end of 1983. Figure XI.A shows how the composition of bank balance sheets has been changing in recent years.

This expansion has implied a reduction in the banks' holdings of reserve and secondary reserve assets, as shown by the figure. It has also tended to squeeze the cash balances held with the Bank of England, and the authorities have taken steps to offset this, in order to avoid unwarranted increases in money-market interest rates. This represents a continuation of the short-term smoothing operations examined in Chapter VI. The size of these

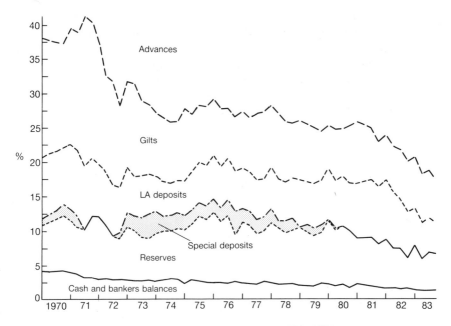

Fig. XI.A. Bank portfolio shares 1970–1983

operations—and the range of techniques employed—has, however, increased with the scale of the problem.[4]

4 Competition and innovation in loan and deposit markets

The removal of the corset opened the way for the banks to complete with the building societies in the mortgage loan and deposit markets. As a result there has been a marked improvement in the range and terms of facilities offered to personal customers, reminiscent of the improvement in corporate facilities which occurred in the early 1970s, and with similar effects.

The entry of the banks into the mortgage market had a catalytic effect upon the behaviour of the building societies. The building societies had until then seen their role as providing inexpensive housing finance by tapping the personal savings market, and had acted collectively to keep the cost of these funds down. This had resulted in a chronic rationing of demand as various empirical studies testify (see, for example, Anderson and Hendry (1984)). The building societies had faced very little competition in this market, except at times (during 1974 and 1975, for example) from local authorites.

There were, however, clear signs of a breakdown in these arrangements during the late 1970s, with the larger building societies seeking an increasingly more independent and market-oriented role. The entry of the banks into the mortgage market appears to have accelerated these developments and marked a significant change in the nature of the market and indeed in the attitude of the building societies themselves. The mortgage and deposit markets are now much more competitive, with the building societies competing both with the banks and between themselves. And the societies now tend to emphasize the need to satisfy the demand for mortgages rather than that of providing inexpensive finance. The following statement of policy, by one of the UK's largest building societies, is quite typical in this respect:

The Society is committed to satisfying the demand for mortgage finance. An interest rate structure has therefore been established at a level at which it is felt that the supply of investment moneys, together with mortgage repayments, will equate with the demand for mortgage funds; whilst at the same time ensuring that the rates paid and changed are fair as between the investor and the mortgagor. (Director's Report and Accounts for the year ended September, 1984, Leeds Permanent Building Society).

Until recently the banks have only felt competitive pressure from the building societies in the retail-deposit market. The building society depositor has traditionally been offered pass-book demand-deposit facilities bearing a rate of interest paid net of tax. These rates have usually been very competitive with bank 7-day deposit rates and recently there have been various attempts to improve the range of chequing facilities available on building society accounts. In the mid-1970s the societies started to raise term deposits at premium rates, which were often competitive with money market rates on a gross of tax basis. More recently they have started to issue term deposits paying interest gross of tax (including marketable certificates of deposit) in order to attract institutional investors. This has brought them into direct competition with the banks in the money markets.

Reflecting the more price competitive edge of the building societies, those monetary aggregates which include their liabilities (M2 and PSL2) have in recent years been growing somewhat faster than those that do not (M1 and £M3). And these wide aggregates have all been growing significantly faster than nominal incomes, implying a steady fall in monetary velocity and making interpretation very different. The fall in velocity can be explained by the general growth in financial asset holdings. partly financed by borrowing from banks and building societies. This has been reinforced by the high level of real interest rates seen during the 1980s, which will have had the effect of increasing the net demand for financial assets (Bennett (1986)).

As in the episode of the early 1970s, it is hard to know to what extent this growth represents the effect of financial disequilibrium, with its implications for the growth of nominal incomes and inflation, and to what extent it simply reflects financial innovation, which could in principle be accommodated without any adverse inflationary consquences. Unfortunately such phenomena can only properly be assessed with the benefit of hindsight and it is difficult to come to any precise conclusion even with the aid of econometric results, as the discussion of Section IV.8 illustrates. In this situation the monetary authorities inevitably came to take into account the narrower aggregates as well as supplementary indicators of monetary conditions such as the exchange rate. Monetary policy became increasingly judgemental as a result. Nevertheless these policies were in the event able to secure a steady decline in the growth of money GDP. Judged in these terms they were remarkably successful.

The banks were of course already very competitive in the money markets and have responded vigorously on the retail side, notably in the provision of interest-bearing sight deposit facilities. The corset, which applied to interest-bearing (ib.) but not non-interest-bearing (nib.) deposits, appears to have dissuaded banks from offering these facilities until it was abolished in June 1979. At that time interest bearing sight deposits were still only 14 per cent of M1, having been virtually static over the previous six months. Banks then made these facilities more competitive and more widely available and they grew steadily, at between 30 and 40 per cent p.a. Nib. deposits grew much more slowly, reflecting substitution into the new interest bearing facilities, so that by the end of 1984 ib. sight deposits constituted about a third of M1, having practically quadrupled over the previous four years.

Most of these interest bearing sight deposits were of a wholesale variety. They were largely drawn in from the money markets by the combination of convenience and competitive interest rates and this had the effect of swelling the overall growth in M1. Yet there was also a growth of ib. sight deposits at the retail end of the market: banks began by offering interest on small budget accounts and then started to offer money market linked rates on sight deposit accounts which maintained a minimum balance (of £2,000). This presumably caused persons and small businesses to switch out of both non-interest bearing balances (representing a reduction in nib.M1) and time deposits (an increase in total M1).

The narrow monetary aggregates were clearly distorted by these developments. The growth of nib. M1 was reduced and that of total M1 was increased. It is also evident that the widespread growth of credit cards and the increasing availability of cash dispensers has affected the narrower aggregates, although these trends have taken place more gradually over time (Johnston (1983b)). It is possible that substitution out of non-monetary assets has reduced the rate of growth of the wider aggregates, although this would not seem very likely. In view of the likely distortion to M1, the 1984 Budget replaced the target for this by one for M0, which has been relatively immune to these developments.

These moves towards increased competition in retail deposit and loan markets are interesting in view of my general thesis that Competition and Credit Control failed because these markets were not sufficiently competitive. On that occasion, the combination of highly competitive wholesale and oligopolistic retail markets caused the system to react to a reserve-asset squeeze in a perverse and unstable way. The erosion of institutional rigidities in retail markets should on this analysis make it easire to implement monetary policy in the future.

Arguably, the problems of more recent years have also been due to institutional rigidities, notably those in the labour market. These have meant that the markets which were responsive to monetary policy, notably the foreign-exchange market, bore the brunt of the adjustment. It is perhaps too early to say whether the pressures of the last few years have led to any significant erosion of these rigidities or to assess the impact of the Government's microeconomic policies. Yet there are clear signs of a movement away from the national wage settlements reflecting such notions as 'the going rate' towards decentralized pay bargaining, reflecting local market conditions. Such developments should again help to make monetary policy work more smoothly and evenly. Nevertheless, the institutional framework will always complicate the operation of monetary policy. This is indeed what makes its study so fascinating.

Notes

1. As it is currently defined, the monetary base M0 largely reflects non-bank transactions influences since non-bank holdings of notes and coin constitute over 85 per cent of the total. It is perhaps best considered as a narow monetary aggregate rather than as a monetary base for this reason. An interesting econometric analysis of the behaviour of M0, non-bank holdings of cash, and their holdings of non-interest bearing M1 has been conducted by Johnston (1983b).
2. The narrow aggregates are similar to nominal GDP in this respect. Authors of various persuasions (notably Meade (1978) and Brittan (1982)) have argued that this offers the best form of intermediate target, noting that such a policy specification would not be affected by unpredictable shifts in velocity. On the other hand it can be argued that monetary aggregates—including the base—should act as leading indicators of nominal incomes and prices. Moreover, nominal GDP is at a disadvantage in that it is subject to long data-collection lags and revisions.
3. It is tempting to view public-sector borrowing from the banks as the residual in the monetary-supply identity in this situation, neatly reversing the situation which prevailed in the 1960s. However, this is only valid to the extent that private-credit is interest inelastic. Otherwise these two items will tend to crowd each other out in a regime of monetary targets.
4. Although a money-market shortage is likely to be associated with 'overfunding' of the PSBR, these phenomena are conceptually different. Overfunding occurs when the demand for bank credit by the private sector exceeds the target increase in sterling M3 (allowing for the external and other technical adjustments) so that given the 'supply' identity (set out in Section II.3) sales of public-sector debt to non-banks must exceed the PSBR in order to offset this. Overfunding therefore relates to the position of the *total* public sector with the banks and will affect the

banks' broad liquidity position as well as the money supply. However, from the point of view of the short-term money markets and interest rates it is the operational balances which the clearing banks maintain at the Bank of England which matter. Overnight and other short-term interest rates are effectively determined as the clearing banks attempt to adjust their holdings of liquid assets in order to achieve a workable balance with the Bank of England. Because the Bank acts as the intermediary between the central government and the rest of the monetary system, bankers' balances (together, of course, with the various central-government accounts held at the Bank) reflect the balance of transactions between the central government and the rest of the system, including transactions in short-term bills. This distinction means that money-market shortages can be offset by a variety of ways which leave the money supply itself unaffected. The technique of releasing special deposits, examined in Chapter V, gives an obvious example of this, as do purchases of Treasury and commercial bills by the Issue Department of the Bank of England (which is part of central government). Direct central-government lending to local authorities achieves the same effect. In order to help alleviate money-market pressures, LA's have been encouraged to borrow from the central government in recent years, and as Figure XI.A shows, this is evident in their reduced dependence upon the banking system. Recent issues of the *Bank of England Bulletin* have included a commentary on money-market influences and assistance, set out in the form of a table showing the way in which these are affected by the central-government accounts.

APPENDIX I

Portfolio Theory and the Demand for Money

Introduction

Most economic agents face a complicated problem when selecting their portfolios, having simultaneously to take account of transactional, precautionary, and speculative risks. In general we should therefore expect asset demands to be complex, reflecting many different contingencies and rates of return. However, if investment opportunities include money-capital-certain assets such as time deposits which yield interest but cannot immediately be used to meet transactional needs, then this is not the case. Providing that the rate of return on such assets is high enough to ensure that they are held in the portfolio, the selection problem can be broken down into separate transactional, precautionary, and speculative sub-problems. This simplifies the asset-demand functions considerably, transactions balances being independent of speculative risk considerations. The demand for such time deposits is nevertheless complex, involving all of these considerations, since it acts as a buffer in the portfolio, taking up the slack between the demand for these speculative and precautionary items and the overall size of the portfolio.

Ando and Shell (1975) originally showed this to be true for a situation in which transaction needs were known with certainty. Of course, in such a situation there is only room for two money-capital-certain items, one held for transactions and the other for speculative purposes. This is because the money-safe item yielding the highest interest rate dominates all other such items in speculative terms, displacing them from the system. In practice, however, we usually observe many such assets in the portfolio, bearing significantly different rates of interest. This phenomenon was originally rationalized by Grey and Parkin (1973) using a model in which transaction needs are uncertain, so that a range of such assets are optimally held, for precautionary reasons. In a similar vein, we frequently observe balance sheets, particularly in the company sector, which contain time deposits which are apparently financed by bank loans bearing a much higher rate of interest. This behaviour can also be explained on precautionary grounds as has been demonstrated by Miller and Sprenkle (1981). In this appendix, I develop a model of this type to show that the Ando–Shell separability result extends to a world of uncertain transaction requirements providing that these are distributed independently of investment returns and point out the consequences for the specification of short-run demand for money functions.

1 The model

I will start by assuming that the individual investor seeks to maximize the expected utility of interest receipts over some finite decision period. Following Miller and Sprenkle I assume that transactions are automatically financed through a bank account. The individual initially sets this at a level A, positive values representing sight deposits and negative values overdrafts. (The notation slightly differs at this point from that used elsewhere in this book.) The account is then drawn down by a random amount x (which may be negative). The balance of $(A - x)$ earns a proportional return of c per cent if it is positive. If it is negative, but within an overdraft limit $(Q \geqslant 0)$ set by the bank, the individual incurs bank charges at the rate of r per cent. Any excess above this limit is charged at a penalty rate[1] $(p > r)$.

In the Miller–Sprenkle model the only other portfolio item is a time deposit-type asset (I) offering a safe nominal return $(i > c)$, but I shall assume following Ando and Shell that there is in addition a long-term asset G offering the nominal yield r_G together with an uncertain nominal capital gain g[2]. I will also assume that the individual is interested in real rather than nominal interest receipts and that the rate of inflation is uncertain, reducing the value of total financial wealth (W) at the rate t. Consequently *ex post* real interest receipts (π), net of bank interest charges (γ) may be written as:

$$\pi = G(r_G + g) + Ii - Wt - \gamma(A - x) \tag{1}$$

where $\gamma(A - x)$

$$
\begin{aligned}
&= c(x - A) & A \geqslant x \\
&= r(x - A) & Q + A \geqslant x > A \\
&= p(x - A - L) + rQ & x > A + Q
\end{aligned}
$$

MS assume that utility $(U$ is a linear function of net receipts. However, this has the unfortunate implication that the investor is indifferent to speculative risk. I will assume that he is speculative-risk-averse, following Ando and Shell in adopting the exponential utility function:

$$U(\pi) = \theta - k \exp\{-\phi\pi\}; \; \theta, \phi, k > 0 \tag{2}$$

Substituting (1) into (2) we see that *ex post* utility may be written as the product of exponential functions of real interest receipts and bank charges:

$$U(\pi) - \theta = k \exp\{-\phi[G(r_G + g) + Ii - Wt]\} \exp\{\phi\gamma\} \tag{3}$$

If real interest receipts and transaction flows are independently distributed then the expectation of this product will equal the product of the expectations of the two exponential terms. If in addition it is assumed that g and t are normally distributed this may be written using the expectations operator (E) as:

$$EU = \theta JP \tag{4}$$

where $P = E \exp\{\phi\gamma\}$

$$= \int_{-\infty}^{A} \exp\{\phi c(x - A)f(x)dx + \int_{A}^{Q+A} \exp\{\phi r(x - A)\}f(x)dx$$

$$+ e^{\phi rL} \int_{A+Q}^{\infty} \exp\{\phi p(x - A - Q)\}f(x)dx$$

$$J = E(-k \exp\{-\phi[G(r_G + g) + Ii - Wt]\})$$

$$= -k \exp\{-\phi[G(r_G + \mu_g) + Ii - W\mu_t} + \tfrac{1}{2} \phi^2[G^2\sigma_g^2 + W\sigma_t^2 + 2WG\sigma_{gt}]\}$$

[1]It is possible that there are in addition lump sum charges for going into overdraft or for allowing the balance to run down below some positive amount. These were investigated by Miller and Sprenkle, who noted that they were likely to be relevant to personal rather than corporate borrowers. They can be introduced without too much difficulty along the lines of the banking sector model set out in Spencer (1984), but will not be analysed here.
[2]If there are several risky assets we may consider G to be an optimally-weighted portfolio of these assets. In principle, holdings of real assets could be handled in this way but we shall ignore this possibility here, confining our attention to the allocation of financial wealth, following Ando and Shell.

and where $f(x)$ is the probability density function for (x), μ_g, σ_g^2 and μ_t, σ_t^2 represent mean values and variances of g and t and σ_{gt} represents their covariance. When determining the optimality conditions for this problem it is convenient to maximize EV, a logarithmic function of EU rather than EU itself, where:

$$EV = \phi^{-1} \log[(-EU + \theta)/k] \tag{5}$$

This is subject to the budget constraint:

$$G + I + A = W \tag{6}$$

and gives the Lagrangian function:

$$L^* = \max_{\{G,I,A,\lambda\}}[G(r_G + \mu_g) + Ii - W\mu_t - \tfrac{1}{2}\phi[G^2\sigma_g^{g2} + W^2\sigma_t^2 + 2WG\sigma_{gt}] - \phi^{-1}\log P(A)$$
$$- \lambda[G + I + A - W] \tag{7}$$

and the first order conditions:

$$\frac{\partial L^*}{\partial G} = (r_G + \mu_g) - \phi[G\sigma_g^2 - W\sigma_{gt}] - \lambda = 0 \tag{8}$$

$$\frac{\partial L^*}{\partial I} = i - \lambda = 0 \tag{9}$$

$$\frac{\partial L^*}{\partial A} = \phi^{-1}\frac{\partial \log P}{\partial A} - \lambda = 0 \tag{10}$$

$$\frac{\partial L^*}{\partial \lambda} = G + I + A - W = 0 \tag{11}$$

2 The demand for precautionary balances

Assuming that an internal optimum obtains, conditions (9) and (10) determine the optimum precautionary balance A independently of (8) and (11). This balance is therefore *not* affected by speculative risk considerations:

$$iP = -\frac{1}{\phi}\frac{\partial P}{\partial A} \tag{12}$$

This may be written in the form:

$$0 = (i - r)w^r + (i - p)w^p + (i - c)w^c$$
$$= h(A; L, r, p, c, i, \phi) \tag{13}$$

where $w^c = \int_{-\infty}^{A} \exp\{\phi c(x - A)\}f(x)dx \geq 0$, $w^r = \int_{A}^{A+Q} \exp\{\phi r(x - A)\}f(x)dx \geq 0$

$w^p = e^{\phi rQ}\int_{A+Q}^{\infty} \exp\{\phi p(x - A - Q)\}f(x)dx \geq 0$; and $P = w^c + w^r + w^p$

Condition (12) has a fairly obvious interpretation. The left-hand side of this equation shows the effect on expected utility of an increase in time deposits and the right-hand side the effect of financing this using the bank account. Three different states are possible *ex post*, depending upon which bank account rate is relevant at the margin and condition (13) sums these two effects across these three states. The w-terms corresponding to each state show the probabilities of this state occurring multiplied by the marginal utility of income (averaged across this state). In sum they are equal to P, the marginal utility of money-certain income. Consequently, rearranging the equation in the form:

$$(i - c)w^c = (r - i)w^r + (p - i)w^p \tag{14}$$

shows that the cash balance will be raised to the point at which the expected marginal utility cost of surplus cash balances equals the marginal saving in overdraft charges. Alternatively, dividing (14) through by P shows that in equilibrium the rate on time deposits is a (utility and probability) weighted average of the three account rates. These results are very similar to those obtained by Miller and Sprenkle which may be reproduced by taking the limit as the coefficient of risk aversion (ϕ) goes to zero (so that marginal utility is constant), in which case this rate is a simple probability-weighted average of the account rates:

$$i = r \int_A^{A+Q} f(x)dx + p \int_{A+Q}^{\infty} f(x)dx + c \int_{-\infty}^{A} f(x)dx \tag{15}$$

The uniqueness of the solution for the optimal account balance A follows from the fact that the second derivative of the logarithm of P is positive. Having established this, the effect of the overdraft limit and the various interest rates on this balance follow by totally differentiating (13) with respect to the relevant variables:

$$\frac{dA}{di} = \frac{-h_i}{h_A} = \frac{-P}{h_A} \leqslant 0 \tag{16}$$

$$\frac{dA}{dr} = \frac{-h_r}{h_A} = -\left[\phi(i-r)\int_A^{A+Q}(x-A)\exp\{\phi r(x-A)\}f(x)dx - w^r \right. $$
$$\left. + \phi Q w^p(i-p)\right]/h_A \geqslant 0 \tag{17}$$

$$\frac{dA}{dp} = \frac{-h_p}{h_A} = -\left[\phi(i-p)e^{\phi rQ}\int_{A+Q}^{\infty}(x-A-Q)\exp\{\phi p(x-A-Q)\}f(x)dx \right. $$
$$\left. - w^p\right]/h_A \geqslant 0 \tag{18}$$

$$\frac{dA}{dc} = \frac{-h_c}{h_A} = -\left[\phi(i-c)\int_{-\infty}^{A}(x-A)\exp\{\phi c(x-A)\}f(x)dx - w^c\right]/h_A \geqslant 0 \tag{19}$$

$$\frac{dA}{dQ} = \frac{-h_L}{h_A} = -\left[\phi(i-p)(r-p)w_p + (p-r)\exp\{\phi rQ\}f(A+Q)\right]/h_A \leqslant 0 \tag{20}$$

where

$$h_A = (r-c)f(A) + (p-r)f(A+Q) - \phi[(i-r)(r-c)w^r$$
$$+ (i-p)(p-c)w^p] \geqslant 0 \tag{21}$$

In words, cash balances are increased (or overdrafts reduced) by increases in the account rates or by reductions in the time-deposit rate or overdraft limit. It is also interesting to note than an increase in the degree of risk aversion unambiguously increases the precautionary balance:

$$\frac{dA}{\partial\phi} = \frac{-h_\phi}{h_A} = -\left[p(i-p)\int_{A+Q}^{\infty}[p(x-A-Q)+rQ]\exp\{\phi p(x-A-Q)\}f(x)dx\right.$$

$$+ r(i-r)\int_{A}^{A+Q}(x-A)\exp\{\phi r(x-A)\}f(x)dx$$

$$\left. + c(i-c)\int_{-\infty}^{A}(x-A)\exp\{\phi c(x-A)\}f(x)dx\right]/h_A \geq 0 \qquad (22)$$

This result suggests that the Miller and Sprenkle conclusion—that relative interest rates will usually favour overdraft borrowing—needs to be qualified to the extent that borrowers are risk averse. They show that if there is no overdraft limit and positive account balances do not pay interest then the overdraft rate must be at least twice the time-deposit rate in order to induce investors to hold positive cash balances.[3] They note that introducing overdraft limits and interest on cash balances tends to increase cash balances. Introducing risk aversion also has this effect.

In their paper Miller and Sprenkle offer some interesting numerical solutions of the model, based on the assumption that transactions flows are normally distributed. Explicit solutions to this kind of model can often be obtained by choosing a density function for $f(x)$ (or in our case $e^x f(x)$) which is integrable. Some interesting examples of this type are offered by Grey and Parkin (1973). For example, suppose that the distribution of outflows is given by a double exponential distribution:[4]

$$f(x) = \frac{\alpha}{2}\exp\{-\alpha|x|\}, \alpha > 0 \qquad (23)$$

The *sign* of the optimum balance (A) can be determined by setting this to zero in (13) and substituting (23):

$$g(0) = \frac{\alpha}{2}\left[\frac{i-c}{\phi c+\alpha}+\frac{i-r}{\alpha-\phi r}+\left[\frac{i-p}{\alpha-\phi p}-\frac{i-r}{\alpha-\phi r}\right]e^{(\phi r-\alpha)Q}\right] \qquad (24)$$

The balance then takes the opposite sign to this expression given (13) and (21).[5] Suppose, for example, that $(-Q \leq A \leq 0)$ as would usually be the case. The integrals in (13) can then be evaluated as follows:

$$w^r = \frac{\alpha e^{-\phi rA}}{2}\left[\frac{1-e^{(\phi r+\alpha)A}}{\alpha+\phi r}-\frac{1-e^{(\phi r-\alpha)(A+Q)}}{\alpha-\phi r}\right] \qquad (25)$$

$$w^c = \frac{\alpha e^{\alpha A}}{2(\phi c+\alpha)}$$

$$w^p = \frac{\alpha e^{(\phi r-\alpha)Q-\alpha A}}{2(\alpha-\phi p)} \quad \text{(assuming } \alpha > \phi p)$$

[3]This may be seen by noting that $A = 0$ is a solution to (15) if $r = p = 2i$, $c = 0$, and if the distribution of outflows is symmetric with zero mean.
[4]For simplicity I can assume that this has zero mean, since a shift in the mean value of any distribution, reflecting the transactions demand for money, has a one-for-one effect on A.
[5]Whether or not $(-)A$ exceeds Q may similarly be checked by evaluating $g(-Q)$.

allowing us to write (13) as:

$$0 = \left[\frac{i-c}{\phi c+\alpha} - \frac{i-r}{\phi r+\alpha}\right]e^{\alpha A} + \left[\frac{2\alpha(i-r)}{\alpha^2-\phi^2 r^2}\right]e^{-\phi rA} + \left[\frac{i-p}{\alpha-\phi p} - \frac{i-r}{\alpha-\phi r}\right]e^{(\phi r-\alpha)Q-\alpha A} \tag{25}$$

Although it is not possible to obtain a closed form solution to this equation, such solutions can be obtained in a variety of interesting special cases. First, consider the case in which there is no overdraft limit. (In this case we need the regularity conditions: $r > i$ and $\alpha > \phi r$. As a slight variation on this we might suppose that the first of these interest-rate inequalities hold, in which case the numerical results obtained by Miller and Sprenkle suggest that overdraft limits are not likely to be very relevant.) This case can be handled by setting Q to infinity so that the third term in (25) vanishes and we have:

$$A^* = \frac{-1}{\phi r+\alpha}\left[\log\left(\frac{\alpha^2-\phi^2 r^2}{2\alpha}\right) + \log\left(\frac{i-c}{r-i}\left(\frac{1}{\phi c+\alpha}\right) - \frac{1}{\phi r+\alpha}\right)\right] \tag{26}$$

Alternatively, in order to investigate the role which the overdraft limit plays in an interest arbitrage situation, we may set $r = i$, in which case (assuming Q is sufficiently large to make A negative and that $\alpha > \phi r$) we have:

$$A^* = \frac{1}{2\alpha}\left[\log\left(\frac{p-i}{i-c}\right) + \log\left(\frac{\phi c+\alpha}{\alpha-\phi p}\right)\right] - \left(\frac{1}{2} - \frac{\phi r}{2\alpha}\right)Q \tag{27}$$

where $\dfrac{1}{2} \geqslant \left[\dfrac{1}{2} - \dfrac{\phi r}{2\alpha}\right] \geqslant 0$

This shows that the initial overdraft is linear in the limit and that an increase in the limit increases the overdraft by something less than one half as much. In the Miller and Sprenkle linear utility case the effect is exactly one half. (Their result is true for any symmetric distribution.) A solution to their model can be obtained under (23) by setting ϕ to zero, in which case we have:

$$A^* = (1/\alpha)\{\log[(r-i) + ((r-i)^2 + (r-c)(p-r)e^{-\alpha Q})^{1/2}] - \log(r-c)\} \tag{28}$$

This relationship is potentially the most interesting from an empirical point of view since it covers both hard and soft arbitrage situations. Some experiments using this formula to explain the arbitrage component of company bank borrowing are reported in Section IV.5.

Finally, I would note that on this analysis the precautionary demands are not affected by financial wealth. This only affects holdings of time deposits and perhaps long-term assets. However, this analysis assumes an internal optimum which may not obtain. Moreover, both financial and real transactions will affect the demand for precautionary balances and may well be related to the overall level of financial wealth. It is important to make some allowance for these effects in empirical work.

3 The demand for speculative assets

Again assuming an internal optimum, the optimal demand for risky assets (G) follows from conditions (8) and (9) independently of (10) and (11) and is therefore not affected by the precautionary or transactional factors discussed in the previous section:

$$(r_G + \mu_g - i) = \phi[G\sigma_g{}^2 - W\sigma_{gl}] \tag{29}$$

This yields a simple linear solution:

$$G = \frac{\sigma_{gl}}{\sigma_g{}^2} W + \frac{r_G + \mu_g - i}{\phi\sigma_g{}^2} \tag{30}$$

This representation is similar to that of Buse (1975) who notes that capital gains on gilts will generally be negatively associated with changes in the price level so that the first term should be negative. Such results suggest that an increase in net financial wealth, increasing the exposure to inflation, will reduce holdings of gilts. However, if wealth enters the model in other ways this particular hedging effect may be offset. For example, the degree of risk aversion (ϕ) might be inversely related to wealth, in which case the holding of long-term securities would be a constant fraction of wealth. However, we would expect this argument to apply to total wealth or permanent income which may not be very closely related to financial wealth. Indeed, broad measures of income such as GDP or TFE might act as better indicators of the propensity to undertake risk than financial wealth does.

There may also be hedging effects which are not captured by a simple single-period model such as that employed here. Although empirical work has almost exclusively been based upon such models due to the simple linear form of the implied demand function, these emphasize capital certainty and therefore cannot properly explain the demand for long-term securities which offer income certainty. This point has been developed by Stiglitz (1970) who has shown that if individuals have a two-period decision horizon the notion of a safe asset becomes ambiguous. His model shows that if the expected returns on one- and two-period bonds are equal then investors will optimally hold both. In this situation the holding of the longer-term security acts as a hedge against future changes in interest rates. The investor's actual holdings will differ from the hedged position according to differences in expected rates of return.

The Stiglitz model abstracts from the effect of inflation by assuming that bonds offer returns in terms of *real* consumption. Of course, in practice, coupons are fixed in nominal terms and uncertain in real terms. If there is uncertainty about the future course of inflation they are therefore unlikely to constitute a useful hedge against changes in real interest rates. Nevertheless, Merton (1973) has shown that under fairly general assumptions about the utility function and the distribution of asset returns the demand for a long-term asset may be represented additively: by a hedging component plus a term in the expected yield differential. The latter term is shown to be linear, resembling the kind of expression obtained from a single-period mean-variance model. The hedging component may, however, be non-linear, a function of such variables as asset prices, wealth, incomes, and life expectancy. (See Merton (1973), 887–8.) This more general model may be represented as:

$$G = H(S,\mathbf{Z}) + \frac{r_G + \mu_g - i}{\phi\sigma_g{}^2} \tag{31}$$

where $H(.)$ represents the hedging demand, S a scale variable such as wealth or permanent income, and the vector $\mathbf{Z}$ any other state variables.

Merton goes on to show that if the propensity to undertake risk (ϕ^{-1}) is homogeneous of degree one in the scale variable the problem can be greatly simplified since the hedging term will also have this property. So in this case we have:

$$G = h(\mathbf{Z}) + k(r_G + \mu_g - i) \tag{32}$$

where

$$h = H/S, k = (\phi S \sigma_g^2)^{-1}$$

Despite its simple additive form, this model is general enough to accommodate most of the existing theories of the term structure as special cases. The 'Expectations Hypothesis' results if it is assumed that the market is dominated by short-term investors who are either indifferent to risk (so that ϕ approaches zero) or do not perceive it (σ^2 approaches zero). In either case portfolio equilibrium is only satisfied when the expected holding period yield gap ($r_G + g - i$) is zero. (This may be seen for example from (30).) At the other extreme the 'Market Segmentation Hypothesis' results if the propensity to undertake risk is very low or the perception of risk is extremely high, so that the demand reduces to the hedging component. As intermediate cases we have the Buse ($H < 0$) and Stiglitz ($H > 0$) models.

4 The broad demand for money

Given these independent precautionary and speculative asset-demand functions, the demand for time deposits follows immediately from the budget constraint, condition (11). In this sense we may consider it as a kind of residual or slack variable. In order to determine this we must use all of the optimality conditions (7) to (11), so the demand for time deposits will therefore reflect both speculative and precautionary or transactional influences as well as net financial wealth. For example, an investor who was in overdraft (but not subject to an overdraft limit) and who did not regard gilts as a good hedge against adverse changes in real interest rates would have a demand for time deposits represented by the conditional demand function:

$$
\begin{aligned}
I &= W - A - G \\
&= W\left(1 - \frac{\sigma_{gt}}{\sigma_g^2}\right) - \frac{r_G + \mu_g - i}{\phi\sigma_g^2} + \frac{1}{\phi r + \alpha}\left[\log\left(\frac{\alpha^2 - \phi^2 r^2}{2\alpha}\right)\right. \\
&\quad \left. + \log\left(\frac{i - c}{r - i}\left(\frac{1}{\phi c + \alpha}\right) + \frac{1}{\phi r + \alpha}\right)\right] \quad \text{(using (26) and (30))}
\end{aligned} \tag{33}
$$

Since he holds no sight deposits (at least at the beginning of his planning period) this determines his demand for broad money. On the other hand the broad demand for money of an investor who held sight deposits rather than being in overdraft is given by:

$$
\begin{aligned}
M &= I + A \\
&= W - G \\
&= W\left(1 - \frac{\sigma_{gt}}{\sigma_g^2}\right) - \frac{r_G + \mu_g - i}{\phi\sigma_g^2}
\end{aligned} \tag{34}
$$

In this case the broad demand for money is only affected by speculative effects since the precautionary and transactional effects balance out within the overall definition, simply determining its composition. Note that in either case a rise in the time-deposit rate lowers the overall demand for money, a property which is employed in Appendix II.

5   Some implications for empirical models of the demand for money

Several implications follow immediately from this analysis. The first and most obvious is that even under the relatively simple assumptions about uncertainty made here, the demand for the wider aggregates will be complex, involving speculative influences and the precautionary or transactional influences associated with overdraft borrowing. To the extent that non-banks act as liability managers it will be nonlinear in the differential between money market and overdraft interest rates.

However, the demand for narrow-money balances should be independent of speculative influences—being dominated by time deposits in this respect—and are unlikely to be seriously affected by nonlinear arbitrage effects.

Under a reasonable range of assumptions, the demand for broad money can be broken down at the micro level into additive transactional, precautionary, and speculative components, and this property comes over immediately to the macro level. The only difference is that at the sectoral level both overdrafts and sight deposits are present in the balance sheet.

Given the budget constraint we must ensure that the separate demand functions exhaust the exogenous wealth variable exactly, no matter how the other explanatory variables behave; the easiest way to impose these constraints being to model one item indirectly as a portfolio residual. In view of this constraint and the likely complexity of the demand for money function, an obvious way to proceed is to model the speculative and precautionary components indirectly through the demand for gilts and bank lending, determining the demand for broad money as a residual. The latter can then be broken down into cash, sight, and time deposits at a second stage using a model which is largely transactional or precautionary in nature. This has been the broad strategy pursued by the Treasury's financial modellers and followed in this book.

Such a strategy is not without its pitfalls however. It is obviously important to test whether the gilts and lending functions really are as separable as the basic assumptions imply.[6] So, having developed the gilt and bank-lending specifications on a single-equation basis it is then important to move to the more time-consuming systemwide methods, in order to check the separability restrictions and provide more efficient final estimates.

Lastly, it should be stressed that this appendix deals with the demand for money and not its supply, and its counterparts in the balance sheet of the non-bank private sector and *not* the so-called money-supply identity used in the text books and official statistics (e.g. CSO: *Financial Statistics*, July 1982, T7.3).

[6]One way of testing this is to run a Hausman (1978) *m*-test based on the difference between ordinary and generalized least squares estimates. A suitable test may be constructed given that if the advances and gilts equations really are 'seemingly unrelated' OLS estimates will be consistent but GLS (or ML) estimates, which take into account possible correlations between their errors, will be consistent but more efficient, as demonstrated by Zellner (1962).

The latter is identical given that it is derived from the market-clearing identities and balance-sheet equations of the other sectors of the system. It would therefore be meaningless to try to distinguish these demand and supply identities *ex post* when markets are in equilibrium. However, it is most important to distinguish them *ex ante* when money demand and supply may not be equal.[7]

[7]The technical relationships between the demand and supply identities are discussed in Spencer and Mowl (1978), Annex 4.

APPENDIX II

An Analysis of the Stability and Comparative-Static Properties of the Money-Market System

Introduction

This appendix develops a simple mathematical model of the UK financial system, reflecting the salient features of the system and incorporating some of the assumptions discussed in the previous appendix. It is a simplified version of the model developed in Spencer (1982). This study focuses on differential movements in reserve asset and other market rates and the implications these have for base rates and MLR. The first part of this annex looks at the stability properties of the model. The second looks at its comparative static properties, and in particular at the implications of the payment of market rates of interest on reserve assets.

1 Non-bank behavioural assumptions

In order to streamline the analysis the following assumptions are made about non-bank behaviour:

(i)   Given the short-term time-frame of the analysis the rate of substitution between real and financial assets is sufficiently small to allow feedbacks from the real sector to be neglected.

(ii) Non-banks do not hold reserve assets. By the same token their demands for other assets do not depend upon reserve asset interest rates (r_R).

(iii) Bank loans are all of the overdraft or non-bank demand determined variety.

(iv) The rate of substitution between wholesale deposit items and the longer-term assets in non-bank portfolios is sufficiently high to allow them to be considered to have the same expected rate of return (r_M), and be traded in a single unified market. These assets will be represented by the aggregate $(Z = M + L + G)$.

(v)   These items are gross substitutes: a rise in the own rate on any asset (liability) increases (decreases) the demand for that item without increasing the demand for any other asset or decreasing the demand for any other liability. Time and sight deposits are aggregated and, following the analysis of Appendix I, it is assumed that the retail time-deposit rate acts as an own rate on this aggregate, having a positive overall effect.

The first of these assumptions focuses attention upon the short-run behaviour of the financial markets, at the cost of leaving the model with little to say about the effect of monetary policy on the real economy. It could be relaxed by adding a market for physical capital to the system, along the lines of the Tobin–Brainard (1963) model.

Assumption (ii) clearly reflects the structure of the UK system in which resident non-banks typically hold negligible amounts of reserve assets, and non-resident holdings, though significant, do not seem to be very sensitive to relative UK interest rates. Since the banks in this treatment are just those subject to the $12\frac{1}{2}$ per cent rule, the discount houses are implicitly treated as non-banks, subject to a binding undefined-assets rule. This assumption can be relaxed without changing the qualitative nature of the results providing that gross substitutability is maintained.

Somewhat surprisingly, (iii) can also be relaxed without upsetting the analysis. This is demonstrated in my (1982) paper which develops a model in which the loan markets do not clear, and in which there are both demand- and supply-determined loans.

The remaining assumptions may also be defended either as simplifications, or in terms of empirical regularities. A unified parallel money market approach is justified on empirical grounds as shown in Section V 5 and although the results presented in Section VIII 5 are less clear-cut, there is evidence to suggest that the rate of substitution between these and longer-term financial assets is high. No prior assumptions are made about the degree of substitution between overdrafts and wholesale deposits in view of the results of Appendix I and Chapter IV which suggest that this is highly variable. Again, my 1982 paper shows that these assumptions can be weakened without changing the nature of the results, providing that (v) is maintained.

2 Bank behavioural assumptions

The following simplifying assumptions are made about bank behaviour:

(i)   Bank holdings of cash are negligible.

(ii) Holdings of excess reserve assets are separable, depending simply upon the differential between r_R and r_M.

(iii) Banks act as perfect competitors in the wholesale deposit and related asset markets.

The specification of banks administered rate decisions and the retail deposit and credit market allows for several alternative possibilities. The first is the competitive case, represented by equation (3) of Chapter IV. An empirical case based on the behaviour of banks under the two versions of the MLR system, 'the formula' and the 'administered rate', will also be investigated. In the first case the base rate tends to be positively related to both money-market and (through the MLR) reserve-asset rates, the weights being less than unity in sum. In the second case they follow MLR very closely but it is unclear whether the authorities set this in line with reserve or money-market rates since these behave in a similar way. Adopting the general formula:

$$r_B = f(r_M, r_R, \tau) \tag{1}$$

these three cases may be characterized in terms of the restrictions:

$$\text{Perfect Competition } f_{r_M} \geqslant 1, \ f_{r_R} \leqslant 0, \ f_{r_M} + f_{r_R} \geqslant 1 \text{ and } f_\tau \geqslant 0 \tag{2}$$

$$\text{MLR Formula: } \quad f_{r_M}, f_{r_R} \geqslant 0, \ f_{r_M} + f_{r_R} < 1 \text{ and } f_\tau = 0 \tag{3}$$

$$\text{Administered MLR: } \quad f_{r_M}, f_{r_R} \geqslant 0, \ f_{r_M} + f_{r_R} = 1 \text{ and } f_\tau = 0 \tag{4}$$

(where subscripts denote partial derivatives). Since there is no evidence to suggest that the cost of holding reserve assets is passed on to borrowers, the case of a 'naïve' banking system which simply sets base lending rates in line with money-market rates will also be considered, as a special case of (2).

$$f_{r_M} = 1; \; f_{r_R}, f_\tau = 0 \tag{5}$$

Reserve-asset requirements apply to both wholesale and retail deposits alike so they would be expected to drive a variable wedge between retail deposit and advances rates in a profit-maximizing system, this wedge varying endogenously with the difference between reserve-asset and other market rates. However, in order to keep the model simple it is convenient to work with just one administered bank rate. So in the various MLR cases this will be regarded as a 'base rate', to which all retail deposit and loan rates are linked, with fixed premiums or discounts. Given assumption 1.(v) this rate can then be treated as the own rate on both of these items (implying conditions (7) and (9) below. In the competitive case it is appropriate to assume that the retail-deposit rate equals the wholesale-deposit rate (allowing for differential costs additively if these are important) and to treat the latter as the own rate on retail deposits. The base rate (linked to the *net* cost of wholesale deposits) may then be treated as a lending rate (giving conditions (7) and (8)).

3 The algebraic model

Given these assumptions the model may be set out as follows. First there is the non-bank demand for marketable financial assets ($Z = M + L + G$), bank loans and retail deposits:

$$Z = Z(r_M, r_B) \quad Z_{r_M} > 0, Z_{r_B} \leqslant 0, (Z_{r_M} + Z_{r_B}) \geqslant 0 \tag{6}$$

$$A = A(r_M, r_B) \quad A_{r_M} \geqslant 0, A_{r_B} < 0, (A_{r_M} + A_{r_B}) \leqslant 0 \tag{7}$$

$$D = D(r_M, r_B) \quad \text{where:}$$

$$D_{r_M} \geqslant 0, D_{r_B} \leqslant 0 \quad \text{if} \quad r_D = r_M - k \text{ (competitive case)} \tag{8}$$

$$D_{r_M} \leqslant 0, D_{r_B} \geqslant 0 \quad \text{if} \quad r_D = r_B - k \text{ (MLR cases)} \tag{9}$$

These demand functions imply a demand for the remaining securities: those which either do not pay interest or have their interest rates fixed by the authorities or by some legal or other device. These may be thought of simply as notes and coin (C), simplifying the non-bank budget constraint to:

$$A = C + D + Z \tag{10}$$

Gross substitutability then implies:

$$C_{r_M} = A_{r_M} - D_{r_M} - Z_{r_M} \leqslant 0; \quad C_{r_B} = A_{r_B} - D_{r_B} - Z_{r_B} \leqslant 0 \tag{11}$$

In order to distinguish bank from non-bank demands the former will be indicated by a 'B' suffix. The banks' demand for reserves may be represented by:

$$RB = \tau(D - \alpha ZB) + X(r_M - r_R) \tag{12}$$

$$\text{where:} \quad 1 \geqslant \alpha \geqslant 0 \quad ZB = MB + LB + GB$$

It is also convenient to use the notation:

$$X' = \frac{\partial X}{\partial r_M} = -\frac{\partial X}{\partial r_R} \leqslant 0 \tag{13}$$

Equation (12) splits reserves into those required against retail (τD) and wholesale

$(-\tau\alpha Z)$ deposits together with excess reserves (X). The parameter α is a 'liability management' indicator showing the fraction of any change in ZB which is financed in the wholesale market.[1] It varies between zero (in which case banks rely exclusively on the asset-side liquidity) and unity (when they rely on liability-side liquidity). This parameter might also be used to model differential reserve-asset requirements, but these have not been employed in the UK.

Given the demand for reserves and the non-bank demand for advances and retail deposits, the banks' demand for market finance follows from the balance-sheet identity. This may be simplified to:

$$ZB = D - A - RB \tag{14}$$

The solution to equations (12) and (14) is then:

$$RB = \beta(X + \alpha\tau A + \tau(1 - \alpha)D) \tag{15}$$

where $\beta = (1 - \alpha\tau)^{-1}$

Now employ the market clearing identities:

$$0 = RB - R \tag{17}$$
$$0 = ZB + Z - G \tag{18}$$

(where R and G represent the authorities supply of reserves and long-term assets respectively) together with (1), (15), and (16) to give:

$$0 = \beta(X + \alpha\tau A + \tau(1 - \alpha)D) - R \tag{19}$$
$$0 = -\beta(X + \alpha\tau A + \tau(1 - \alpha)D) - C - G \tag{20}$$

Substituting (1), (6)–(9), and (12) and differentiating this system totally with respect to the endogenous interest rates and policy variables (τ, G, and R) then gives a differential system governing the behaviour of interest rates:

$$\begin{bmatrix} a_{RR} a_{RM} \\ a_{MR} a_{MM} \end{bmatrix} \begin{bmatrix} dr_R \\ dr_M \end{bmatrix} = \begin{bmatrix} dR \\ dG \end{bmatrix} + \begin{bmatrix} -a_{R\tau} \\ -a_{M\tau} \end{bmatrix} d\tau \tag{21}$$

where:

$$a_{RR} = \beta\{X' + f_{r_R}\tau[\alpha A_{r_B} + (1 + \alpha)D_{r_B}]\} \tag{22}$$
$$a_{RM} = \beta\{\tau\alpha(A_{r_M} + A_{r_B}f_{r_M}) + \tau(1 - \alpha)(D_{r_M} + D_{r_B}f_{r_M}) - X'\} \tag{23}$$
$$a_{MR} = -\{f_{r_R}[\tau\beta(\alpha A_{r_B} + (1 - \alpha)D_{r_B}) + C_{r_B}] + \beta X'\} \tag{24}$$
$$a_{MM} = -\{\tau\beta[\alpha(A_{r_M} + A_{r_B}f_{r_M}) + (1 - \alpha)(D_{r_M} + D_{r_B}f_{r_M})] + C_{r_M} + C_{r_B}f_{r_M} + \beta X'\} \tag{25}$$
$$a_{R\tau} = \beta^2[\alpha(X + A) + (1 - \alpha)D] + \beta f_\tau\tau(\alpha A_{r_B} + (1 - \alpha)D_{r_B}) \tag{26}$$
$$a_{M\tau} = -(a_{R\tau} + f_\tau C_{r_B}) \tag{27}$$

In the competitive case the sign of the first three of these terms follows immediately from (2), (6), (7) and (8):

$$a_{RR} \geqslant 0 \qquad a_{RM}, a_{MR} \leqslant 0 \tag{28}$$

The sign of the fourth is not immediately obvious but may be seen by rewriting it (using (10)) as:

$$a_{MM} = -\beta\{\tau[\alpha(A_{r_M}(1 - f_{r_M})^- + (A_{r_B} + A_{r_M})^- f_{r_M}^+] + X'^- +$$

$$\tau(1 - \alpha)[(A_{r_M} - Z_{r_M})^- + (A_{r_M} - Z_{r_B})^- f_{r_M}^+] + (1 - \tau)^+(C_{r_M} + C_{r_B}f_{r_M})^-]\} \geqslant 0 \tag{29}$$

[1] For simplicity it is assumed that changed in X, A, and D have the same effect on MB.

(where superscripts indicate qualitative restrictions on these terms). We are now in a position to look at the stability and comparative static properties of the system.

4(a) Conditions for stability under fixed reserve-asset rates

First consider a policy regime in which the authorities vary the supply of reserves (R) in order to fix r_R. The behaviour of this system is dictated by (20), and for stability it is necessary that a_{MM} defined in (25) be positive (i.e. an increase in the own interest rate increases excess demand in this market). The stability of a competitive system under this regime follows immediately from (29).

The sign of (25) is in general ambiguous, however, depending upon the term in square brackets and hence the reserve-asset ratio (τ) and the extent of bank-liability management (α). If either of these parameters is negligible[2] then conditions (8), (9), (11), and (13) ensure stability under all of the base-rate specifications considered above.[3] This is true for all of the policy regimes analysed here, highlighting the role which reserve assets and liability management play in the instability process. The only real difference between these regimes is that issues of wholesale deposits must be backed by reserve assets which involve a leakage from the system under specification (a) but which may have adverse effects on T-bill and base rates under alternatives (b) and (c) considered below.

Now suppose that the initial situation is such that interest-rate differentials make overdraft borrowing relatively cheap. Appendix I shows that this will also make it extremely interest sensitive. Moreover, if interest rates are such that bank reserves and non-bank holdings of cash have been run down to the effective minimum these will be interest inelastic.

If α and τ are positive, (25) will be dominated in this situation by the advances terms:

$$-\tau\alpha\beta(A_{r_M} + A_{r_B}f_{r_M}) = -\tau\alpha\beta[A_{r_M}(1 - f_{r_M}) + (A_{r_B} + A_{r_M})f_{r_M}]$$

Given (7), a *sufficient* condition for stability in a liability managed system with this policy regime is:

$$f_{r_M} \geq 1 \tag{30}$$

Moreover, the effect of interest rate differentials (A_{r_M}) will be much larger than that of the overall level $(A_{r_B} + A_{r_M})$ in this round-tripping situation, so we may consider this a *necessary* condition for global stability in a liability managed system with reserve requirements and fixed reserve-asset rates. This condition is shown as the vertically hatched area in Figure A.1, which shows the conditions which are necessary and sufficient for global stability under the various policy regimes.

---

[2] It might be argued that this is the case under the August 1981 arrangements, though prudential reserves might play the same role as required reserves under this system.

[3] This may be seen by rearranging (25) as:

$$-\beta\{\tau\alpha[Z_{r_M} + f_{r_M}Z_{r_B}] + \tau[(A_{r_M} - Z_{r_M})^- + f_{r_M}(A_{r_M} - Z_{r_M})^-]$$
$$+ (1 - \tau)(C_{r_M} + C_{r_B}f_{r_M})^- + X^-\}$$

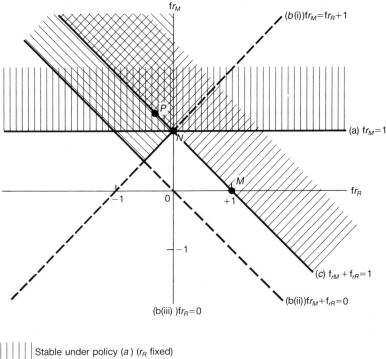

Fig. A.1. The administered rate formula—necessary and sufficient conditions for global stability of a liability-managed financial system

4(b) Fixed reserve-asset supply

If the reserve-asset supply is fixed, with both interest rates endogenous, stability requires that the matrix on the left-hand side of (21) has non-negative real roots. In this case this is satisfied as long as the determinant and trace of the matrix are both non-negative. Consider the former:

$$\text{Det} = a_{RR}a_{MM} - a_{RM}a_{MR}$$
$$= \beta \tau f_{r_R}[C_{r_B}(\alpha A_{r_M} + (1-\alpha)D_{r_M}) + C_{r_M}(\alpha A_{r_B} + (1-\alpha)D_{r_B})]$$
$$- \beta X'(C_{r_M} + C_{r_B}(f_M + f_R)) \tag{31}$$

This is clearly non-negative in the competitive case, as is the trace $a_{RR} + a_{RM}$ given (28) and (29). These may take on negative values in the other cases, however, leading to instability.

The second of the terms in the determinant is fairly harmless and will certainly be non-negative if:

$$f_{r_M} + f_{r_R} \geq 0 \tag{32}$$

This condition holds under all of the base-rate specifications considered above. The second term in (31) will however, be dominated by the first if bank excess reserves or private cash balances have been run down to the minimum. If in addition interest-rate differentials make company borrowing from banks relatively cheap, then (assuming τ and α are positive) the term in square brackets will be dominated by the advances terms and become negative. So to ensure stability in this situation it is necessary that:

$$f_{r_B} \leq 0 \tag{33}$$

In this situation the trace:

$$a_{RR} + a_{MM} = 2\beta X' + \beta\tau[(\alpha A_{r_B} + (1-\alpha)D_{r_B})(f_{r_R} - f_{r_M})$$
$$- (\alpha A_{r_M} + (1-\alpha)D_{r_M})] - C_{r_M} - C_{r_B}f_M \tag{34}$$

will also be dominated by the advances terms so repeating the arguments used to obtain (30); it is also necessary (and, in a liability managed system sufficient) that:

$$f_M \geq f_{r_R} + 1 \tag{35}$$

The boundaries of conditions (32), (33) and (35) are shown in the diagram and give the cross-hatched region which is stable under this regime. As in the previous regime, the MLR formula (3) violates these inequalities. If the retail-deposit terms were ever to dominate, conditions (33) and (35) might destabilize the system, but in this case both naïve and competitive models guarantee stability.

4(c)   Reserve-asset rates varies in line with other rates

Finally consider a regime in which the authorities vary reserve-asset rates in line with the rest of the market, meeting the banks' demand at this rate. Attention may again be confined to the money market in this case. The behaviour of this regime depends upon the effect of a rise in both interest rates upon excess demand in this market:

$$a_{MR} + a_{MM} = -\{C_{r_M} + \tau\beta(\alpha A_{r_M} + (1-\alpha)D_{r_M})$$
$$+ (f_{r_M} + f_{r_R})[C_{r_B} + \tau\beta(\alpha A_{r_B} + (1-\alpha)D_{r_B})]\} \tag{36}$$

which must be non-negative for stability. This condition can be shown to hold in the competitive case using a similar argument to that used to obtain (29). In order to avoid instability in the other cases when liability responses are dominant, it is necessary that:

$$f_{r_M} + f_{r_R} \geq 1 \tag{37}$$

The boundary of this condition is shown in the diagram as the line labelled (c). If the authorities vary the reserve ratio (or special deposit call) in order to preserve this interest differential the same condition is relevant.

Most obvious base-rate setting procedures are consistent with stability given this kind of policy specification as may be seen from the diagram. For example, the point marked p represents the base-rate response of a competitive banking system (2) which is unambiguously stable. The point marked N represents 'naïve' base-rate setting behaviour (5), the limiting case of (2), which is stable in all three regimes. Point M represents an extreme form of the MLR formula effect in which base rates are linked to MLR which is in turn linked to bill rate. The diagram shows that this kind of response (3), given by a point lying between N and M, is potentially unstable in regimes (*a*) and (*b*) but not (*c*). It also suggests that if base rates are simply sticky, characterized by a point lying within ONM in the diagram, there is very little that the authorities can do about this when deciding their MLR or reserve-asset supply policies. But there is little evidence to suggest that this case has ever been very relevant empirically.

5   The comparative-static properties of the model

Assuming that the system is stable, the comparative static properties follow trivially in policy regimes (*a*) and (*c*): any factor which increases excess demand in the money market will raise the associated interest rates given that (25) or (36) are positive.

As we have seen, the competitive and (considered as a special case) the naïve banking models are the only ones which guarantee global stability in regime (*b*). Given this, conditions (5) and (9), or (3) and (8), are sufficient to ensure that:

$$\frac{\mathrm{d}r_M}{\mathrm{d}R} = \frac{-a_{MR}}{\mathrm{Det}} \geqslant 0 \qquad \frac{\mathrm{d}r_M}{\mathrm{d}G} = \frac{a_{RR}}{\mathrm{Det}} \geqslant 0 \qquad (38)$$

$$\frac{\mathrm{d}r_R}{\mathrm{d}R} = \frac{a_{MM}}{\mathrm{Det}} \geqslant 0 \qquad \frac{\mathrm{d}r_R}{\mathrm{d}G} = \frac{-a_{RM}}{\mathrm{Det}} \geqslant 0 \qquad (39)$$

In words, a sale of any interest-bearing asset *for cash* increases both interest rates. This follows from the fact that reserves and other interest-bearing assets are substitutes under these assumptions so that their rates move in the same direction in response to this kind of shock.

The effect of a reserve-asset squeeze, induced either by an open-market operation $(\mathrm{d}R = -\mathrm{d}G)$ or a special-deposit call, follow in a straightforward manner.[4] In the latter case, for example:

$$\frac{\mathrm{d}r_R}{\mathrm{d}\tau} = \frac{a_{R\tau}(C_{rM} + C_{rB}f_{rM}) - a_{rM}f_{\tau}C_{rB}}{\mathrm{Det}} \leqslant 0 \qquad (40)$$

$$\frac{\mathrm{d}r_M}{\mathrm{d}\tau} = \frac{C_{rB}(f_{\tau}a_{RR} - f_{rR}a_{R\tau})}{\mathrm{Det}} \leqslant 0 \qquad (41)$$

It may seem curious at first sight that a reserve-asset squeeze reduces money-market and related interest rates. However, this follows quite naturally in a competitive system from the role of reserve assets as an input to the process of intermediation. A reserve-asset squeeze increases the cost of intermediation, reducing reserve-asset and deposit rates and tending to increase base-lending rates.

If the competitive (or naïve) banking assumptions are relaxed, the system may still be locally stable given a wide range of initial conditions. It is therefore interesting to

---

[4]The expression for $a_{R\tau}$ given by (26) assumes for simplicity that X and α are not affected by changes in τ. The model developed in Spencer (1984) suggests that these will be affected but in a way which ensures that $a_{R\tau}$ remains positive, preserving the qualitative nature of these results.

ask whether it is possible to obtain determinate comparative static results under alternative, arguably more factual, assumptions. In general this is not the case, the results depend upon the degree of liability management as well as the specific base-rate formula. However, there is one important case in which it is possible to obtain determinate results: the case of a policy which switches demand or supply from one market to the other, leaving the demand for cash unaffected. This includes open-market operations between reserve and long-term assets and also changes in the required reserve ratio (given $f_\tau = 0$). For example, the effect of an increase in the reserve ratio is unambiguously to reduce reserve-asset rates:

$$\frac{\mathrm{d}r_R}{\mathrm{d}\tau} = -a_{R\tau}(a_{RM} + a_{MM})/\mathrm{Det}$$

$$= a_{R\tau}(C_{r_M} + C_{r_B}f_{r_M})/\mathrm{Det} \leqslant 0 \tag{42}$$

The effect on other market rates and administered rates depends upon the effect of reserve-asset rates on base rates (f_{r_R}). If this is positive as in the case of the MLR formula this effect is to increase the former and depress the latter:

$$\frac{\mathrm{d}r_M}{\mathrm{d}\tau} = a_{R\tau}(a_{RR} + a_{MR})/\mathrm{Det} \tag{43}$$

$$= -a_{R\tau}C_{r_B}f_{r_R}/\mathrm{Det} \geqslant 0$$

$$\frac{\mathrm{d}r_B}{\tau} = a_{R\tau}f_{r_R}C_{r_M}/\mathrm{Det} \leqslant 0 \tag{44}$$

An open-market operation designed to reduce the supply of reserves by selling long-term assets $(\mathrm{d}R = -\mathrm{d}G)$ will, suitably scaled, have identical effects.

APPENDIX III

Financial Policy and the Determination of Prices in an Open Economy

This appendix examines the long-run effect of fiscal and financial policy in an open economy using a relatively simple static steady-state model of an open economy. I will be particularly interested in demonstrating the effect of such borrowing on nominal variables such as the price level and exchange rate and showing the difference which the financing arrangements and the degree of international capital mobility can make. The model is of a portfolio equilibrium variety in which both interest rates and the price level adjust to bring about the long-run solution. Closed-economy versions of this kind of model have been developed for example by Tobin and Buiter (1976) and Niehans (1975, 1978).

1 The relevance of financial policy

It is important to begin by looking in fairly general terms at some of the characteristics of public-sector debt and the issues which these raise. Perhaps the most important feature of such debt is that it is ultimately backed by the government's ability to levy taxes. For this reason, as Ricardo originally noted (Buchanan (1960)), it would make no difference in a world of fully rational individuals and perfect capital and insurance markets whether public expenditure were financed by taxation or by issuing government debt. Such individuals would be indifferent between paying the future taxes needed to meet the financing costs of such expenditure or paying an initial once and for all tax with the same present value. Financial policy, by which is meant the choice between debt finance and taxes (including the inflation taxes implicit in monetary finance), would be entirely irrelevant.[1] Moreover, government bonds which were backed by future taxes (rather than public-sector assets) would not be considered net wealth in aggregate since they would be matched by the capitalized value of future taxes.

Of course, the assumptions upon which the Ricardian equivalance theorem hold are rather stringent, and have been the subject of extensive debate. For the argument to hold in the case of perpetuities, for example, there must either be a single generation which lives for ever, or, as Barro (1974) has pointed out, the utility of the current generation must depend upon that of later generations, these utilities being linked by an unbroken chain of bequests. Otherwise, as the Diamond (1965) and Stiglitz (1983) models demonstrate, financial policy will have real effects on the economy since it causes a redistribution between generations.

---

[1]The Ricardian analysis assumes the use of lump-sum or other non-distortionary taxes. If this assumption is relaxed this leads to a theory of optimal defficits in which taxes are varied over time in order to equate the marginal cost of distortion in each period (see Barro (1979)).

Moreover if it is the case that some taxpayers are unable to borrow or face premium interest rates, the government can act as a kind of financial intermediary, reducing current taxes at the expense of future taxes, thus easing the effect of such constraints and increasing the general level of expenditure. The discount rates used by such individuals to capitalize these future tax liabilities will be greater than the rate used by bond holders to value the future interest stream, so to this extent government debt does represent net wealth, even at an aggregate level.

2   The sustainability of financial policy

The second characteristic of public-sector debt is that it is almost invariably denominated in money terms. This means that the real supply of these liabilities depends inversely upon the general price level, so that the system will tend to respond to an increase in supply by increasing the price level. Indeed, if the composition of public-sector liabilities remains unchanged in nominal terms, this is the only adjustment which is necessary. In this case financial policy simply determines whether public expenditure is financed by conventional taxes or by inflation taxes upon holders of government debt. Providing the lags are short enough there is no question of intergenerational effects in this case.[2]

For this reason it is important to distinguish between financial policies which simply switch between taxes and debt—keeping the overall composition unchanged—and those which change its composition. This is particularly important when considering the stability or sustainability of different policies. The first type of policy is sustainable since it simply implies inflationary finance which might in principle be continued forever. The second type of policy may not be sustainable. This is clear from the literature on the 'government budget constraint' which began with the papers by Blinder and Solow (1973) and Tobin and Buiter (1976) and is reviewed by Christ (1979).

This literature is concerned with the stability of different policy options, and in particular debt-financed fiscal policy, in a world in which bonds are considerd to be net wealth by the aggregate private sector. In this case bond issues imply future interest payments which must be financed by further bond issues, making for instability. Yet if the rate of economic growth exceeds the real interest rate, such policies can be sustained. Alternatively, if government spending is defined to include interest payments, and is taken as given, then a bond-finance rule is again stable.

Similar problems arise in a Ricardian world if the real interest rate exceeds the growth rate and public expenditure is fixed exclusive of debt interest payments. Barro (1976) notes that Ricardian equivalence does not hold in this case since it leads eventually to a situation in which the value of the national debt exceeds the present value of future tax capacity. This point also emerges from more recent papers by McCallum (1982) and Begg and Haque (1982).

The practical implication of these results is that unless the growth rate exceeds the real interest rate, changes in public-sector borrowing requirements must eventually force either a change in the rate of monetary growth and hence the inflation tax or a future fiscal contraction sufficient to meet the real coupon or redemption payments on

---

[2]To the extent that conventional and inflationary taxation is distortionary, financial policy is not entirely trivial but should again be aimed at minimizing the overall burden of taxation.

such borrowing. This point is brought out very clearly by the Sargent and Wallace (1981) model, developed by Buiter (1982).[3]

3 An open-economy model

It is obviously important to keep these points in mind when looking at the issues raised by financial policy in an open economy. However, in order to keep things simple I will confine the analysis to that of sustainable policy options—i.e. those in which a constant debt structure is maintained following any initial change. I will also assume a zero growth rate in output and velocity. This means that in any steady-state equilibrium the nominal stocks of money (M) and bonds (B) will be increasing at the same proportionate rate as the general price deflator (D). Using lower case letters to denote logarithms and dots to denote rates of change we have:

$$\dot{m} = \dot{b} = \dot{d} \qquad (1)$$

For simplicity I will also assume that these assets are only held by domestic residents and will consolidate the bank and non-bank sectors so that (M) actually represents the monetary base. Bonds are assumed to be conventional short-term stocks so that their real value depends inversely upon the general level of prices (D) but is not affected by interest rates.[4] The government budget constraint may therefore be represented as:

$$G + Bi/D - T = \dot{M}/D + \dot{B}/D \qquad (2)$$

where G and T represent government expenditure and conventional taxes in real terms and i the nominal bond rate.

In addition I suppose that residents hold overseas assets and physical capital and that the domestic economy produces just one good (Y), subject to the production function:

$$Y = Y(K) \qquad Y_K \geq 0 \qquad Y_{KK} \leq 0 \qquad (3)$$

where K is the physical capital stock. The supply of labour is assumed to be fixed and fully employed and is subsumed into this function. In equilibrium we may use the marginal productivity condition:

$$Y_K(K) = r \qquad (4)$$

where r is the real rate of return to physical capital in the domestic economy.

If the stock of overseas assets held by residents is represented in real foreign currency terms as F, r^* represents the real return on these assets and R denotes the terms of trade (or the price of overseas (EP^*) relative to domestic output (P)) then real private disposable income may be represented as:

$$Z = YR^{-\omega} + r^*FR^{1-\omega} + B(i - \dot{d})/D - M\dot{d}/D - T \qquad (5)$$

---

[3]This model assumes that the real interest rate exceeds the growth rate and that there is a strict limit to the bond-income ratio that the economy can sustain. This means that the adjustment following a fiscal expansion can be divided into two distinct phases. In the first phase there is residual bond finance, increasing the bond-income ratio to the limit. This must then remain constant during the final phase, forcing the authorities to issue money as well as bonds.

[4]The value of long-term bonds will depend inversely upon nominal bond rates. But since such revaluation effects reinforce the effect of changes in the bond rate on the excess demand for bonds, this makes no qualitative difference to our analysis and may for this reason be ignored.

where ω represents the weight of overseas goods in the general price index D. Using this together with the equilibrium condition (1) and the government budget constraint (2), allows real disposable income to be rewritten as:

$$Z = YR^{-\omega} + Fr^*R^{1-\omega} - G \qquad (6)$$

In words, this equation states that in equilibrium, private disposable income equals GNP less government expenditure, since the latter reduces disposable incomes either by conventional or 'inflation' taxes on financial assets.

I also assume that real private expenditure (E) depends upon real disposable income, real wealth (W) and interest rates:

$$E = E(W, Z, r, r^*, i, \dot{d})$$

which gives the obvious asset accumulation identity

$$\dot{W} = Z - E(W, Z, r, r^*, i, \dot{d})$$

Setting this expression to zero serves to determine the equilibrium value of wealth (say $\bar{W}$) as a function of income and interest rates:

$$\bar{W} = W(Z, r, r^*, i, \dot{d}) \qquad (7)$$

The conditions under which savings optimally behave in this way have been extensively explored (see for example, Merton (1971)). In the short run, wealth will tend to differ from this value and will appear as an independent argument in the short-run asset-demand functions, together with incomes and interest rates. For example, the demand for money function might be written in the form:

$$m = d + 1(W, Z, r, r^*, i, \dot{d}) \qquad 1_z, 1_w \geq 0 \qquad 1_r, 1_{r^*}, 1_i, 1_{\dot{d}} \leq 0 \qquad (8)$$

However, in equilibrium wealth will not be independent of these other influences and maybe substituted out of such a specification using (7). This equilibrium portfolio specification may reasonably be represented as:[5]

$$m = d + 1(Z, r, r^*, i, \dot{d}) \qquad 1_z \geq 0 \qquad 1_r, 1_{r^*}, 1_i, 1_{\dot{d}} \leq 0 \qquad (8)'$$

$$b = d + c(Z, r, r^*, i, \dot{d}) \qquad c_z, c_i, \geq 0 \qquad c_r, c_{r^*}, c_{\dot{d}} \leq 0 \qquad (9)'$$

$$K R^{-\omega} = k(Z, r, r^*, i, \dot{d}) \qquad k_z, k_r \geq 0 \qquad k_{r^*}, k_i \leq 0 \qquad (10)'$$

$$F R^{1-\omega} = f(Z, r, r^*, i, \dot{d}) \qquad f_z, f_{r^*} \geq 0 \qquad f_r, f_i \leq 0 \qquad (11)'$$

The equilibrium terms of trade or real exchange rate may be determined by setting the current account of the balance of payments to zero, or equivalently, equating the demand (H) and supply (Y) of home output:

$$Y(K) = H(Z, G, R) \qquad H_Z, H_G, H_R \geq 0 \qquad (12)$$

which I can assume can be inverted to give:

$$R = R(Z, G, K) \qquad R_K \geq 0, \qquad R_Z, R_G \leq 0 \qquad (13)$$

---

[5]The logarithmic bond-market specification is used for convenience and presumes that the supply of bonds is positive. Other cases can be handled using an equivalent linear formulation such as:

$$B/D = D(Z, r, r^*, i, \dot{d}) \qquad D_z, D_i \geq 0 \qquad D_{r^*}, D_r, D_{\dot{d}} \leq 0 \qquad (11)'$$

4 The comparative static properties of the system

Given a small country assumption, r^* may be taken as exogenous so that $(11)'$ simply dictates the equilibrium stock of overseas assets. Substituting out Z using (4), (6), and (13), this system may be represented in differential form as:

$$\begin{bmatrix} dm \\ db \\ 0 \end{bmatrix} = \begin{bmatrix} 1 & a_{12} & a_{13} \\ 1 & a_{22} & a_{23} \\ 0 & a_{32} & a_{33} \end{bmatrix} \begin{bmatrix} dd \\ di \\ dr \end{bmatrix} + \begin{bmatrix} b_{11} & b_{12} \\ b_{21} & b_{22} \\ b_{31} & b_{32} \end{bmatrix} \begin{bmatrix} dr^* \\ dG \end{bmatrix} \qquad (14)$$

where, adopting the normalization $R = 1$:

$a_{12} = r^* 1_z f_i A + 1_i \leqslant 0; \qquad a_{13} = 1_z AJ + 1_r \leqslant 0$

$a_{22} = r^* d_z f_i A + c_i \geqslant 0; \qquad a_{23} = d_z AJ + c_r \leqslant 0$

$a_{32} = r^* Q f_i A + k_i; \qquad a_{33} = k_z AJ + \omega k R_K / Y_{KK} + k_r - Y_{KK}^{-1} \geqslant 0$

$b_{11} = 1_{r^*} + 1_z A[f + r^* f_{r^*}]; \qquad b_{12} = -1_z A[1 + \omega YR_G] \leqslant 0$

$b_{21} = c_{r^*} + d_z A[f + r^* f_{r^*}]; \qquad b_{22} = -1_z A[1 + \omega YR_G] \leqslant 0$

$b_{31} = k_{r^*} + QA[f + r^* f_{r^*}]; \qquad b_{32} = -QA[1 + \omega YR_G] + \omega k R_G$

and where:

$$A = [1 - r^* f_z + \omega YR_z]^{-1}; J = (Y_K - \omega YR_K)/Y_{KK} + r^* f_r; Q = (k_z + \omega k R_z)$$

Most of the qualitative restrictions on these expressions follow directly from those of $(8)'-(11)'$ given the regularity conditions:

$$A \geqslant 0; \qquad J \leqslant 0 \qquad (15)$$

The only exceptions are for a_{22} and a_{33}, where it is necessary to employ stability conditions. These also dictate that the determinant of the system is (and that of the principal minor $(a_{22} a_{33} - a_{23} a_{32})$) is positive definite:

$$\text{Det} = a_{22} a_{33} + a_{13} a_{32} - a_{23} a_{32} - a_{12} a_{33} \geqslant 0 \qquad (16)$$

The differential coefficients associated with r^* cannot be signed directly since the more obvious substitution effects are offset by income effects. However, there is perhaps some presumption that the former will outweigh the latter, so that these terms are on balance negative.

Reflecting this ambiguity, the effect of overseas interest rates on domestic rates and prices cannot be determined unequivocally. However, the effect of changes in m and b follow a straightforward manner:

$$\frac{di}{dm} = \frac{-a_{33}}{\text{Det}} \leqslant 0 \qquad\qquad \frac{di}{db} = \frac{a_{33}}{\text{Det}} \geqslant 0$$

$$\frac{dd}{dm} = \frac{a_{22} a_{33} - a_{23} a_{32}}{\text{Det}} \geqslant 0 \qquad\qquad \frac{dd}{db} = \frac{a_{13} a_{32} - a_{12} a_{33}}{\text{Det}} \qquad (17)$$

The structure of these differentials is clearly such that equiproportionate changes in the supply of money and bonds (i.e. $dm = db$) exert an equiproportionate effect on

Appendix III

prices and do not affect rates of return or real variables. Since the real exchange rate is unaffected in this case there will be an equiproportionate effect on the nominal exchange rate. Increases in the supply of bonds will tend to increase the price level. By the same token, increases in the money supply, given a fixed supply of bonds, will have a less than proportionate effect on prices. In the limiting case of a perfectly interest-elastic demand for money function$(a_{22}, -a_{12} \to \infty)$, bonds and money will have identical effects and the composition of the debt will be irrelevant. On the other hand the pure monetarist result obtains in a variety of special cases:

(a) When $(a_{13}a_{32} - a_{12}a_{33}) = 0$. It is interesting that the usual interest inelasticity of the demand for money argument $(1_r = 1_i = 0)$ is insufficient to guarantee neutrality in this case due to the income effects of changes in the stock of overseas assets and physical capital. Indeed, the only plausible case in which this condition holds is one in which the demand for neither money nor physical capital depends upon the bond rate—a case examined by Niehans (1974) for the closed economy. In this model we also require that the demand for overseas assets is independent of the bond rate, in which case $a_{32} = a_{12} = 0$.

(b) When bonds, physical and overseas assets are perfect substitutes so that the overall demand for these assets is met through the current account of the balance of payments and $di = dr = dr^*$. In this case (14) degenerates to:

$$dm = dd + (b_{11} + a_{12} + a_{13})dr^* + b_{12}dG \qquad (14)''$$

(c) Bonds are not net wealth. In this case (14) degenerates to:

$$\begin{bmatrix} dm \\ 0 \end{bmatrix} = \begin{bmatrix} 1 & a_{13} \\ 0 & a_{33} \end{bmatrix} \begin{bmatrix} dd \\ dr \end{bmatrix} + \begin{bmatrix} b_{11} & b_{12} \\ b_{31} & b_{32} \end{bmatrix} \begin{bmatrix} dr^* \\ dG \end{bmatrix} \qquad (14)'''$$

APPENDIX IV

Index of Algebraic Symbols Employed

Table A.IV shows a simplified balance sheet and market-matrix representation of the Treasury financial model using the symbols employed in this book. For the purposes of this presentation several items, notably bank-reserve assets, have been consolidated. The other symbols are listed in alphabetical order below. This listing also gives a fuller description of the non-bank resident items appearing in the table, a full description being found in Spencer and Mowl (1978). The mnemonics in square brackets are those used in this reference and in various editions of the Treasury macroeconomic model manual.

A Bank advances to non-bank residents. Note that in Appendix I (which follows the notation of Miller and Sprenkle (1981)) this represents the bank balance, positive values indicating deposits and negative values overdrafts, [LENDPR].

B Miscellaneous liabilities of non-bank residents (mainly equity issues and local authority mortgages), [MISCPR].

C Non-bank resident holdings of notes and coin, [CASHPR].

D Either: non-bank resident holdings of retail time deposits, [BDEPPR]; or general cost of living index, depending upon context.

E Nominal exchange rate, represented as cost of overseas currency. This symbol is also used in places, notably Chapter VIII, to denote the expectations operator.

F Foreign-currency borrowing from UK banks (net of f.c. deposits) by UK residents, [SWIPPR].

G Stock of UK public-sector debt held by non-bank residents, [GILTPR].

g *Ex-post* quarterly capital gain on gilt-edged stocks. A precise definition is to be found in Spencer (1981) Annex I, [GILTREV].

K Either physical capital stock, or a constant, depending upon context.

L Non-bank resident holdings of Local Authority temporary debt, [LATDPR].

M non-bank resident holdings of certificates of bank deposit, [CDEPPR].

M_s General representation of the money supply.

M_s^* The overseas money supply.

N Money-market position of banking sector, net of required reserves and special deposits, (equation V(4)).

P Domestic currency price of domestic output.

P^* Price of overseas (or world) output in foreign currency.

P_T Domestic currency price of traded goods.

P_T^* Foreign currency price of traded goods.

P_{NT} Domestic currency price of non-traded goods.

Q Overdraft limit.

R Real exchange rate or terms of trade, (equation IX(1)$'$).

r Domestic nominal interest rate, with subscript denoting instrument where

Table A.IV. Simplified balance sheet of the model (minus sign indicates liability, rows and columns each sum to zero)

Instrument	Public sector (G)	Commercial banks (B)	Discount houses (D)	B of E banking dept.	Non-bank private sector	Overseas sector (F)	Associated interest rates Symbol	Description
1. Notes and Coin[a]	-CG	CB		-BE[c]	C			
2. Reserve assets[a]	-RG	RB	-RD[d]			RF	r_R	3-month T-bill
3. Long-term public-sector debt[b]	-GG	GB	GD		G	GF	r_G^i	20-year gilt
4. Bank advances		AB			-A[h]	-AF	r_B	base lending rate
5. £ retail deposits		-DB	DD		D	DF	r_D	7-day deposit
6. Wholesale bank deposits		MB	MD		M	MF	r_M^g	3-month interbank
7. LA temporary deposits	-LG	LB	LD		L	LF	r_L^g	3-month LA deposit
8. Net foreign-currency borrowing[c]		FB	FD		-F	FF	r_F	3-month covered Eurodollar
9. Miscellaneous	BG	-BB	-BD	BE[e]	-B	-XF[f]		
10. Net financial worth	WG	WB	WD		W	WF		

Notes:

[a] Including Special Deposits and Bankers' Balances at the Bank of England.

[b] Including national savings media.

[c] F.c. borrowing from UK banks less f.c. deposits.

[d] Call-money liabilities net of holdings of Treasury and commercial bills.

[e] Government indebtedness to Bank of England, banking department. (Equals net B of E, BD supply of reserve assets and special deposits).

[f] Official exchange reserves—a liability of the overseas sector.

[g] In model simulations the LA and wholesale bank-deposit markets are consolidated into a unified parallel money market, as explained in Section V.5, with the 3-month LA deposit rate (r_L) representing the rate of return on both items and a market clearing identity, given by equation V(9).

[h] For the purposes of Appendix I, A represents the value of the bank balance, positive values representing credit balances and negative values representing overdrafts.

[i] A 5 year rate was used in the work reported in Chapter V.

	this is specific (see Table A.1.).
r^*	Overseas nominal interest rate.
s	Interest rate equivalent cost of SSD scheme to banks (equation $V(7)$).
T	Bank reserve assets required against retail deposits, (i.e. τDB).
t	Interest-rate equivalent cost of reserve-asset and special-deposit schemes to banks, (equation $V(6)$).
T_r	Quarterly purchase of gilt-edged stocks by non-bank residents, [GILTRAN].
t_r	Above, as a fraction of existing holdings.
u, v, w	Typically represent stochastic error terms.
W	Net financial wealth of non-bank private sector at current market prices [NETWPR]
X	Bank holdings of excess reserves (equation $V(3)$).
x	Expected rate of appreciation of exchange rate.
Y	Gross domestic product.
μ_g	Expected capital gains on gilt-edged stocks (EG).
τ	Required reserve ratio ($12\frac{1}{2}$ per cent) plus special-deposit call, represented as a fraction.
σ	Additional fraction of liabilities effectively required under SSD scheme, represented by average fraction in empirical work (equation $V(8)$).

BIBLIOGRAPHY

ANDERSON, G. J. and HENDRY, D. F. (1984) 'An Econometric Model of United Kingdom Building Societies', *Oxford Bulletin of Economics and Statistics* (August)

ANDO, A. and SHELL, K. (1975) Annex to Ando, A and Modigiliani, F. 'Some Reflections on describing Structures of Financial Sectors', in Fromm, G. and Klein, L. (eds) *The Brookings Model: Perspectives and recent developments* (Amsterdam)

ARCHIBALD, G. C. and LIPSEY, R. G. (1958) 'Monetary and Value Theory: A Critique of Lange and Patinkin', *Review of Economic Studies* (October)

ARROW, K. J. (1965) *Aspects of the Theory of Risk Bearing* (Helsinki)

ARTIS, M. J. (1978) 'Monetary Policy—part II' in Blackaby (ed.) *British Economic Policy 1960–74* (Cambridge)

—— and CURRIE, D. A. (1981) 'Exchange Rate and Monetary Targets', in Eltis and Sinclair (1981)

—— and LEWIS, M. K. (1976) 'The Demand for Money in the UK 1963–1973', *Manchester School* (June)

——, —— (1981) *Monetary Control in the United Kingdom* (Oxford)

—— and MILLER, M. H. (1981) *Essays in Fiscal and Monetary Policy* (Oxford)

BALASSA, B. (1964) 'The Purchasing Power Parity, Doctrine: A Reappraisal', *Journal of Political Economy* (December)

BALL, R. J., BURNS, T. and WARBURTON P. J. (1979) 'The London Business School Macroeconomic Model of the UK Economy: An Exercise in International Monetarism', in Ormerod (1979)

BANK of ENGLAND (1971a) 'Key Issues in Monetary and Credit Policy', *Bulletin* (June)

—— (1971b) 'Reserve Ratios and Special Deposits', *Bulletin* (September)

—— (1971c) 'Reserve Ratios: Further Definitions', *Bulletin* (December)

—— (1973) 'Competition and Credit Control: Modified Arrangements for the Discount Market', *Bulletin* (September)

—— (1982) 'The Supplementary Special Deposit Scheme', *Bulletin* (March)

BARBER, J. M. (ed.) (1984) 'HM Treasury Macroeconomic Model: Supplement to the 1982 Manual', Government Economic Service Working Paper No. 71 (June)

BARGE, J. and WISE P. J. (1977) 'Competition and Credit Control—Six Years on', *Journal of the Institute of Bankers* (April)

BARRO, R. J. (1974) 'Are Government Bonds net Wealth?', *Journal of Political Economy*, 82 (Supplement)

—— (1976) 'Reply to Buchanan and Feldstein', *Journal of Political Economy* (April)

—— (1979) 'On the Determination of the Public Debt', *Journal of Political Economy* (October)

BEAN, C. R. (1978) 'The Determination of Consumer's Expenditure in the UK', GES Working Paper No. 48 (July)

BEENSTOCK, M. and BELL, S. R. (1979) 'A Quarterly Econometric Model of the Capital Account of the UK Balance of Payments', *Manchester School* (March)

—— and LONGBOTTOM, J. A. (1982) 'Money Debt and Prices in the United Kingdom', *Economica* (November)

BEGG, D. K. H. (1982), *The Rational Expectations Revolution in Economics* (London)

—— and HAQUE, M. B. (1982) 'Financing Government Expenditure: Monetary and Fiscal Policy and Open Market Operations', London Business School EFU Discussion Paper 104 (December)

BELL, S. R. (1978) 'Bank Lending to Industrial and Commercial Companies, mimeo, HM Treasury

BENNETT, A. (1986) 'Expenditure, Wealth and the Rate of Interest', *Economic Modelling* (January)

—— and GRICE, J. (1984) 'The Demand for Sterling M3 and other Aggregates in the UK', *Manchester School* (September)

BILSON, J. F. (1980) 'Recent Developments in Monetary Models of Exchange Rate Determination', *IMF Staff Papers* (December)

BLACKABY, F. T. (1978) *British Economic Policy, 1960–1974* (Cambridge)

BLANCHARD, O. J. and WATSON, M. W. (1982) 'Bubbles, Rational Expectations and Financial Markets', Harvard Institute of Economic Research Discussion Paper No. 877

BLINDER, A. S. and SOLOW, R. M. (1973) 'Does Fiscal Policy Matter?', *Journal of Public Economics* (April)

BRAINARD, W. C. (1964) 'Financial Intermediaries and a Theory of Monetary Control', *Yale Economic Essays* Vol. 4, No. 1

BRITTAN, S. W. (1982) 'How to end the Monetarist Controversy', Hobart Paper No. 90 (London)

BRITTON, A. J. C. (ed.) (1983) *Employment, Output and Inflation: The National Institute Model of the British Economy* (London)

BUCHANAN, J. M. (1960) *Fiscal Theory and Political Economy* (London)

BUITER, W. H. (1982) 'Deficits, Crowding Out and Inflation', *LSE Centre for Labour Economic Discussion Paper No. 143*

—— and MILLER, M. H. (1981) 'Monetary Policy and International Competitiveness, The Problem of Adjustment', in W. A. Eltis and P. J. N. Sinclair (1981)

BURGER, A. E. (1971) *The Money Supply Process* (Belmont)

BURNS, T., LOBBAN, P. W. M. and WARBURTON, P. J. (1977) 'Forecasting the Real Exchange Rate'. *LBS Economic Outlook* (January)

BUSE, A. (1975) 'Testing a simple Portfolio Model of Interest Rates', *Oxford Economic Papers* (March)

BYATT, I. C., LOMAX, R., POWELL, S. and SPENCER, P. D. (1982) 'North Sea Oil and Structural Adjustment', Government Economic Service Working Paper No. 54

CHICK, V. (1973) *The Theory of Monetary Policy* (London)

CHRIST, C. F. (1979) 'On Fiscal and Monetary Policies and the Government Budget Restraint', *American Economic Review* (September)

COGHLAN, R. (1981) 'Money, Credit and the Economy' (Oxford)

CORDEN, W. M. and NEARY, J. P. (1982) 'Booming Sector and de-Industrialisation in a Small Open Economy', *Economic Journal* (December)

COURAKIS, A. S. (1974) 'Clearing Bank Asset Choice Behaviour' *Oxford Bulletin of Economics and Statistics* (August)

CURRIE, D. A. (1981) 'Fiscal and Monetary Policy and the Crowding Out Issue', in Artis and Miller (1981)

CUTHBERTSON, K. (1983) 'The Monetary Sector', in Britton (1983)

—— and FOSTER, N. (1982) 'Bank Lending to Industrial and Commercial Companies in Three Models of the UK Economy', *NIER Review* (November)

DAVIDSON, J., HENDRY, D., SRBA, F. and YEO, S. (1978) 'Econometric Modelling of the Aggregate Time Series Relationship between Consumers Expenditure and Income in the UK' *Economic Journal* (June)

DEATON, A. S. (1977) 'Involuntary Saving through Unanticipated Inflation', *American Economic Review* (January)

DENNIS, G. E. J. (1982) 'Monetary Policy and Debt Management', in Llewellyn *et al.* (1982)

DIAMOND, P. A. (1965) 'National Debt in a Neoclassical Growth Model', *American Economic Review* (December)

DIXIT, A. K. (1978) 'The Balance of Trade in a model of Temporary Equilibrium with Rationing', *Review of Economic Studies* (October)

DORNBUSCH, R. (1974) 'Real and Monetary Aspects of the Effects of Exchange Rate Changes' in Aliber (ed.) *National Monetary Policies and the International Financial System* (Chicago)

—— (1976a) 'Monetary Policy under Exchange Rate Flexibility, NBER Working Paper No. 311 (January)

—— (1976b) 'Exchange Rate Expectations and Monetary Policy', *Journal of International Economics* (March)

—— (1976c) 'Expectations and Exchange Rate Dynamics', *Journal of Political Economy* (December)

—— (1980) 'Exchange Rate Economics: Where Do We Stand?' *Brookings Papers on Economic Activity*, 1

—— and FISCHER, S. (1980) 'Exchange Rates and the Current Account', *The American Economic Review* (December)

EASTWOOD, R. K. and VENABLES, A. J. (1982) 'The Macroeconomic Implications of a Resource Discovery in an Open Economy', *Economic Journal* (June)

EDGEWORTH, F. Y. (1888) 'The Mathematical Theory of Banking', *Journal of the Royal Statistical Society* (March)

ELTIS, W. A. and SINCLAIR, P. J. N. (eds) (1981) *The Money Supply and the Exchange Rate* (Oxford)

FFORD, J. S. (1983a) 'Setting Monetary Objectives', *Bank of England Quarterly Bulletin* (June)

—— (1983b) 'Competition, Innovation and Regulation in British Banking' *Bank of England Quarterly Bulletin* (September)

FLEMING (1962) 'Domestic Financial Policies Fixed and Under Floating Exchange Rates' *IMF Staff Papers* (November)

FORSYTH, J. (1980) 'Public Sector Borrowing and the Exchange Rate', *Morgan Grenfell Economic Review* (March)

—— and KAY, J. A. (1980) 'The Economic Implications of North Sea Oil Revenues', *Fiscal Studies* (March)

FRENKEL, J. (1976) 'A Monetary Approach to the Exchange Rate: Doctrinal Aspects and Empirical Evidence', Ch. 1 in Frenkel and Johnson (1976) *The Economics of Exchange Rates*

—— (1981) 'Flexible Exchange Rates, Prices and the Role of News: Lessons from the 1970s', *Journal of Political Economy* (August)

—— and JOHNSON, H. G. (1976) *The Monetary Approach to the Balance of Payments* (London)

FRIEDMAN, B. M. (1977) 'Financial Flow Variables and the Short Run Determination of Long Term Interest Rates', *Journal of Political Economy* (August)

GIRTON, L. and ROPER, D. (1976) 'Theory and Implications of Currency Substitution', Federal Reserve Board International Finance Discussion Papers No. 56

GOLDBERGER, A. S. (1964) *Econometric Theory* (London)

GOODHART, C. A. E. (1984) *Monetary Theory and Practice* (London)

GOWLAND, D (1978) *Monetary Policy and Credit Control* (London)

GREEN, C. J. (1982) 'Money Market Arbitrage and Commercial Banks' Base Rate Adjustments in the UK', mimeo, University of Manchester (May)

GREY, M. R. and PARKIN, J. M. (1973) 'Portfolio Diversification as Optimal Precautionary Behaviour', in Morishma (ed.) *The Theory of Demand* (Oxford)

GRICE, J. W. (1981) 'Wealth Effects and Expenditure Functions: A Survey of the Evidence', in Artis and Miller (1981)

GRIFFITHS, B., BATCHELOR, R. A., BENDLE, E. and WOOD, G. E. (1980) 'Reforming Monetary Control in the United Kingdon', *The Banker* (May)

GROSSMAN, H. I. (1965) 'A Stochastic Model of Commercial Bank Behaviour', *American Economist* (July)

GURLEY, J. and SHAW, E. S. (1960) *Money in a Theory of Finance* (Washington)

HACCHE, G. and TOWNEND, J. (1981) 'Exchange Rates and Monetary Policy: Modelling Sterling's Effective Exchange Rate 1972–1980', in Eltis and Sinclair (1981)

HALL, M. J. B. (1983) *Monetary Policy since 1971: Conduct and Performance* (London)

HAUSMAN, J. A. (1978) 'Specification Tests in Econometrics', *Econometrica* (November)

HENDRY, D. F. and SRBA, F. (1980) 'Autoreg: A Computer Program for Dynamic Econometric Models with Autoregressive Errors', *Journal of Econometrics* (January)

HICKS, J. R. (1937) 'Mr Keynes and the Classics: A Suggested Interpretation', *Econometrica* (April)

—— (1935) 'A Suggestion for Simplifying the Theory of Money', *Econometrica* (January)

—— (1982) 'The Cost of Inflation', Ch. 20 in *Collected Essays on Economic Theory* (Oxford)

HUTTON, J. (1977) 'A Model of Short Term Capital Movements, the Foreign Exchange Market and Official Intervention in the UK', *Review of Economic Studies* (January)

HM TREASURY (1979), (1980), (1981) 'Macroeconomic Model Technical Manual'

—— (1980b) 'Monetary Policy and the Economy', *Economic Progress Report* (July)

ISARD, P. (1977) 'How far can we push the Law of One Price?', *American Economic Review* (December)

JAFFEE, D. W. and RUSSELL, T. (1976) 'Imperfect Information, Uncertainty and Credit Rationing', *Quarterly Journal of Economics* (November)

JOHNSON, H. G. (1976). 'The Monetary Approach to Balance of Payments Theory', in Frenkel and Johnson (1976)

JOHNSTON, R. B. (1983a) *The Economics of the Euro-Market, History Theory and Policy* (London)

—— (1983b) 'The Demand for Non Interest Bearing Money in the UK' Government Economic Service Working Paper No. 66 HM Treasury

JONSON, P. D., MOSES, E. R. and WYMER, C. R. (1976) 'A Minimal Model of the Australian Economy', Reserve Bank of Australia Discussion Paper 7601.

JUDD, J. P. and SCADDING, J. L. (1982) 'The Search for a Stable Demand for Money Function', *Journal of Economic Literature* (September)

KALDOR, LORD, N. (1970) 'The "New" Monetarism', *Lloyds Bank Review* (July)

—— (1980) 'Memorandum of Evidence on Monetary Policy', in 'Memoranda on Monetary Policy', House of Commons Treasury and Civil Service Select Committee HMSO (Cmnd. 7202)

KEATING, G. (1984) 'The Financial Sector of the LBS Model', *Financial Outlook*, No. 1, Vol. I (London)

KINGSTON, G. H. and TURNOVSKY, S. J. (1977) 'Monetary and Fiscal Policies under Flexible Exchange Rates and Perfect Myopic Foresight', *Scandinavian Journal of Economics* (September)

KRAVIS, I. and LIPSEY, R. E. (1978) 'Price Behaviour in the Light of Balance of Payments Theories', *Journal of International Economics* (March)

LAFFONT, J. J. and GARCIA, R. (1977) 'Disequilibrium econometrics for business loans', *Econometrica* (November)

LIPTON, A., POTERBA, J., SACHS, J. and SUMMERS, L. (1982) 'Multiple Shooting in Rational Expectations Models', *Econometrica* (September)

LOMAX, R. and MOWL, C. J. (1978) 'Balance of Payments Flows and the Monetary Aggregates in the United Kingdom', Government Economic Working Paper No. 5.

LLEWYLLYN, D., DENNIS, G. E. J., HALL, M. J. B. and NELLIS, J. G. (1982) *The Framework of UK Monetary Policy* (London)

—— (1982) 'The Money Supply in the UK, in Llewellyn *et al.* (1982)

LUCAS, R. E. (1976) 'Econometric Policy Evaluation: A Critique', in 'The Phillips' Curve and Labour Markets', Carnegie Rochester Conference Series on Public Policy (1976)

MCCALLUM, B. J. (1975) 'Rational Expectations and the Natural Rate Hypothesis', *Manchester School* (March)

—— (1982) 'Are Bond Financed Deficits Inflationary?: A Ricardian Analysis', National Bureau of Economic Research Working Paper No. 905

MCKINNON, R. I. (1982) 'Currency Substitution and Instability in the World Dollar Standard' *American Economic Review* (June)

MADDALA, G. S. and NELSON, F. D. (1974) 'Maximum Likelihood Methods for Markets in Disequilibrium', *Econometrica* (November)

MALKIEL, B. G. (1966) *The Term Structure of Interest Rates: Expectations and Behaviour Patterns* (Princeton)

MARKOVITZ, H. (1859) *Portfolio Selection: Efficient Diversification of Investments* (New York)

MEADE, J. E. (1978) 'The Meaning of Internal Balance', *Economic Journal* (September)

——, VINES, D. and MACIEKOWSKI, J. E. (1983) *Demand Management* (London)

MERTON, D. C. (1971) 'Optimum Consumption and Portfolio Rules in a Continuous Time Model', *Journal of Economic Theory* (July)

—— (1973) 'An Intertemporal Asset Pricing Model', *Econometrica* (September)

MELLON, W. G. and ORR, D. (1961) 'Stochastic Reserve Losses and Expansion of Bank Credit', *American Economic Review* (September)

MIDDLETON, P. E., MOWL, C. J., ODLING-SMEE, J. C. and RILEY, C. J. (1981) 'Monetary Targets and the PSBR', in Batchelor and Wood (eds.) *Monetary Targets* (London)

MILLER, M. J. and SPRENKLE, C. (1981) 'The Precautionary Demand for Money', *Economica* (July)

MILLS, T. C. (1982) 'The Information Content of the UK Monetary Aggregates', Bank of England Discussion Paper

MINFORD, A. P. L. (1981) 'The Exchange Rate and Monetary Policy', in Eltis and Sinclair (1981)

——, MARWAHA, S., MATTHEWS, K. and SPRAGUE, A. (1984) 'The Liverpool Macro-economic Model of the United Kingdom', *Economic Modelling* (January)

——, MATTHEWS, K. and MARWAHA, S. (1979) 'Terminal Conditions as a Means of Ensuring Unique Solutions for Rational Expectations Models with Forward Expectations', *Economic Letters* (November)

—— and PEEL, D. A. (1984) *Rational Expectations and the New Macroeconomics* (Oxford)

MOORE, B. J. and THREADGOLD, A. R. (1985) 'Bank Lending and the Money Supply', *Economica* (March)

MORGAN, B. (1978) *Monetarists and Keynesians: Their Contribution to Monetary Theory* (London)

MUELLBAUER, J. and PORTES R. (1978) 'Macroeconomic Models with Quantity Rationing', *Economic Journal* (December)

MUNDELL, R. A. (1963) 'Capital Mobility and Stabilisation Policy under Fixed and Flexible Exchange rates', *Canadian Journal of Economics and Political Science* (November)

MUSSA, M. (1976) 'The Exchange Rate, the Balance of Payments, and Monetary and Fiscal Policy under a Regime of Controlled Floating', *Scandinavian Journal of Economics* (March)

—— (1979) 'Empirical Regularities in the Behaviour of Exchange Rates and Theories of the Foreign Exchange Market', in 'Policies for Employment, Prices and Exchange Rates', Brunner and Meltzer (eds.) Carnegie Rochester Conference Series on Public Policy (1979)

NEARY, J. P. (1983) 'Real and Monetary Aspects of the Dutch Disease', AUTE, Oxford Conference Paper (March)

—— and PURVIS, D. D. (1981) 'Sectoral Shocks in a Dependent Economy: Long Run Adjustment and Short Run Accommodation', seminar paper no. 188, Institute for International Economic Studies (Stockholm)

NIEHANS, J. (1975) 'Some Doubts about the Efficacy of Monetary Policy under Flexible Exchange Rates', *Journal of International Economics*, Vol. 5 (August)

—— (1978) *The Theory of Money* (Baltimore)

—— (1981) 'The Appreciation of Sterling: Causes, Effects and Policies', Centre for Policy Studies (London)

NORTON, W. E. (1969) 'Debt Management and Monetary Policy in the UK', *Economic Journal* (September)

ODLING-SMEE, J. and HARTLEY, N. (1978) 'Some Effects of Exchange Rate Changes', GES Working Paper No. 2 (March)

OKUN, A. (1975) 'Inflation, its Mechanics and Welfare Costs', *Brookings Papers on Economic Activity*, 2

ORMEROD, P. (1979) *Economic Modelling: Current Issues and Problems in Macro-Economic Modelling in the UK and the US* (London)

PARKIN, M. J., GRAY, M. R. and BARRETT, R. J. (1970) 'The Portfolio Behaviour of Commercial Banks', in Hilton and Heathfield (eds.) *The Econometric Study of the UK* (London)

PHILLIPS, C. A. (1924) *Bank Credit* (New York)

PIERCE, D. G. and SHAW, D. M. (1979) *Monetary Economics: Theories, Evidence and Policy* (London)

PORTER, R. C. (1961) 'A Model of Bank Portfolio Selection', *Yale Economic Essays* No. 1

PRATT, J. (1964) 'Risk Aversion in the Small and in the Large', *Econometrica* (January)

REID, M. (1982) *The Secondary Banking Crisis, 1973–1975* (London)

REVELL, J. R. S. (1973) *The British Financial System* (London)

RICHARDSON, P. E. (1981) 'Money and Prices: A Simulation Study using the Treasury Model' GES Working Paper No 41, H, Treasury (March)

RILEY, C. J. (1976) 'A Model of Building Society Behaviour', in Artis and Nobay (eds.) 'Macroeconomics', Proceedings of the 1974 AUTE Conference (London)

—— (1982) 'Non-traded Goods and the Long Run Effects of Macroeconomic Policy', *Manchester School* (September)

SALTER, W. E. G. (1959) 'Internal and External Balance: The Role of Price and Expenditure Effects', *Economic Record* (August)

SARGENT, T. J. and WALLACE, N. (1973) 'Rational Expectations and the Dynamics of Hyperinflation', *International Economic Review* (June)

—— and WALLACE, N. (1981) 'Some Unpleasant Monetarist Arithmetic' *Federal Reserve Bank of Minneapolis Quarterly Review* (December)

SAVAGE, D. (1978) 'The Monetary Sector of the NIESR Model', NIESR Discussion Paper No. 23

SPENCER, P. D. (1976) 'A Disequilibrium Model of Personal Sector Bank Advances', paper presented to the Oxford Conference of the Money Study Group, (September).

—— (1981) 'A Model of the Demand for British Government Stocks, 1967–1977', *Economic Journal* (December)

—— (1982) 'Bank Regulation, Credit Rationing and the Determination of Interest Rates', *Manchester School* (March)

—— (1984) 'Speculative and Precautionary Aspects of Bank Behaviour in the United Kingdom under Competition and Credit Control, 1972–1980', *Economic Journal* (September)

—— (1985a) 'Bounded Shooting: A Method for Solving Large Non-linear Econometric Models under the Consistent Expectations Assumption', *Bulletin of the Oxford Institute of Economics and Statistics* (February)

—— (1985b) 'Speculative and Precautionary Aspects of Bank Behaviour: Some Further Results', mimeo, HM Treasury

—— and MOWL, C. J. (1978) 'A Financial Sector for the Treasury Model, Part One', GES Working Paper No. 17, HM Treasury (December)

STIGLITZ, J. E. (1970) 'A Consumption-Oriented Theory of the Demand for

Financial Assets and the Term Structure of Interest Rates', *Review of Economic Studies* (July)

—— (1983) 'On the Relevance or Irrelevance of Public Financial Policy', National Bureau of Economic Research Working Paper No. 1106

—— and WEISS, A. (1981) 'Credit Rationing in Markets with Imperfect Information', *American Economic Review* (June)

TOBIN, J. (1963) 'Commercial Banks as Creators of Money', in Carson (ed) *Banking and Monetary Studies* (Homewood)

—— (1965) 'The Theory of Portfolio Selection', in Hahn and Brechling (eds.) *The Theory of Interest Rates* (London)

—— (1969) 'A General Equilibrium Approach to Monetary Theory', *Journal of Money, Credit and Banking* (January)

—— and BRAINARD, W. C. (1963) 'Financial Intermediaries and the Effectiveness of Monetary Controls', *American Economic Review* (May)

—— and BUITER, W. (1976) 'Long Run Effects of Fiscal and Monetary Policy on Aggregate Demand', in Stein (ed.) *Monetarism* (Amsterdam)

VEENDORP, E. C. H. (1975) 'Stable Spillovers amongst Substitutes', *Review of Economic Studies* (September)

WALLIS, K. F. (1980) 'The Econometric Implications of the Rational Expectations Hypothesis', *Econometrica* (January)

WILSON, C. A. (1979) 'Anticipated Shocks and Exchange Rate Dynamics', *Journal of Political Economy* (June)

WILSON, H. (1978) 'Evidence on the Financing of Industry and Trade', Committee to Review the Functioning of Financial Institions, Vol. V (March)

WILLS, H. R. (1981) 'The Simple Economics of Bank Regulation', *Economica* (August)

WREN-LEWIS, S. (1985) 'A Model of Private Sector Earnings Behaviour', *Bulletin of the Oxford Institute of Economics and Statistics* (February)

WYMER, C. R. (1978) 'AISMUL Manual', IMF mimeo (March)

ZAWADSKI, K. K. F. (1981) *Competition and Credit Control* (Oxford)

ZELLNER, A. (1962) 'An Efficient Method for Estimating Seemingly Unrelated Regressions', *Journal of the American Statistical Association* (June)

INDEX